KJV BIBLE ANSWERS SERIES:

The Forgotten Commandment
& The Mark of the Beast CRISIS

By *O. Cary Rodgers, Jr.*

The Forgotten Commandment &
The Mark of the Beast Crisis

Inspiration & Thanks: God the Father, Jesus the Son, and the Holy Spirit
Written by: O. Cary Rodgers, Jr.
Edited by: Elene, Carlene, & Elijah Rodgers
Cover by: Carlene Rodgers
Graphics by: Carlene, Elijah, & Nehemiah Rodgers
Special Thanks: Eliyah Rodgers
Published by: Eliyah's Tidings Publications
                        Pathway to Peace Ministries
                        11775 NC 109 South
                        Peachland, NC 28133 USA

All Bible Scriptures are from the King James Version (KJV)

"How beautiful upon the mountains are the feet of him that bringeth **good tidings, that publisheth peace**; that bringeth good tidings of good, that publisheth salvation; that saith unto Zion, Thy God reigneth!"

\- Isaiah 52:7

"Sharing the Gospel & Equipping the Workers"

Share to ALL the World!
Books are available at a low cost by the boxful.
Phone: 704-695-1441
Web: PathwaytoPeace.net
E-mail: info@PathwaytoPeace.net

ISBN# 978-0-9981055-6-7

CONTENTS

PREFACE

IN LOVING MEMORY OF
ELIYAH MICHAELA RODGERS

This Bible study book is written in loving memory of our 2 ½ year old daughter, Eliyah Michaela Rodgers. She was nicknamed "Juniorita" because she looked just like her mother. She loved to give and receive lots of hugs and kisses. She was graceful as a flower and as playful as a bird. She had a spark in her eyes that revealed the love in her heart. Eliyah loved God and her family and joined them in the effort of sharing the everlasting gospel of Jesus Christ. Her life and the events that led up to her death have inspired us as a family and ministry to greatly increase our efforts and boldness in sharing and teaching God's Bible Truth to the world. We have hope in the promise of the resurrection at the second coming of Jesus Christ (**1 Thessalonians 4:13-18**). We will see Eliyah again. She is just sleeping in Jesus. Those who conspired and are responsible for her death will see that God's Bible Truth will NEVER be stopped. It will only get bolder and louder as we get closer to the end of time. In the meantime, we must go forward in faith and share the contents of this book far and wide.

Bible Truth is absolute. It cannot be changed. Just like in math 1 + 1 will always be 2 throughout eternity. It is absolute. 1 + 1 will never be any other number besides two - period. There are no philosophies or theories that can change that. How many ways can someone dial your phone number right? One, of course. How many ways can someone dial your phone number wrong? Many! God's Bible Truth helps you dial the right "number" to connect to Jesus, holiness, and eternal life. Satan's many lies lead you to dial the wrong "number." There is only one Truth that is absolute and eternal, the Word of God. Jesus Christ says in **John 14:6**, "I am the way, the TRUTH, and the life: no man cometh unto the Father, but by me." It does not matter if you believe it or not, God's Truth is truth. God's Bible Truth will never fade, get old, or pass away. **1 Peter 1:23–25** says, [23]"Being born again, not of corruptible seed, but of incorruptible, by the **word of God, which liveth and abideth for ever**. [24]For all flesh *is* as grass, and all the glory of man as the flower of grass. The grass withereth, and the flower thereof falleth away: [25]But the **word of the Lord endureth for ever**. And this is the word which by the gospel is preached unto you." **Psalm 119:89** settles it. It says, "For ever, O LORD, **thy word is settled in heaven**." Don't let anyone fool you,

God's Word is more prophetically alive and relevant today then ever before in Earth's history. Nevertheless, it only becomes relevant and alive in your life if you study it and apply its Truth in your life.

This book presents God's Bible Truth about the "forgotten" commandment and the fulfillment of Bible prophecies that will lead to the mark of the beast crisis. These are Bible Truths that are very relevant for today. Many people have been led astray by the many lies and distractions of Satan that have kept them in bondage.

This Bible study book is designed to "set the captives free!" Jesus says in **John 8:32**, "And ye shall know the truth, and the truth shall make you free." Bible Truth sets you free. Lies keep you in bondage. This book is written in a Bible study format that is simple to understand yet a very in-depth Bible study that allows the Bible to be its own interpreter by comparing scripture with other Bible scripture to confirm the Truth. Originally, the Old Testament was written in Hebrew and the New Testament in Greek. In this study Hebrew and Greek dictionaries will be used to understand certain words in its original language. **To get a full and complete understanding of the contents of this book, start from the beginning of the book and study chapter by chapter in order.** As you study, you will notice many Bible scriptures are used to clearly reveal Truth. **2 Peter 1:20, 21** says, [20]"Knowing this first, that **no prophecy of the scripture is of any private interpretation**. [21]For the prophecy came not in old time by the will of man: but holy men of God spake *as they were* moved by the Holy Ghost." No one has the right to alter or to tamper with God's Word. It stands alone and has proven itself as the Truth over the years. **2 Timothy 3:16** says, "**All scripture *is* given by inspiration of God**, and *is* profitable for doctrine, for reproof, for correction, for instruction in righteousness." ALL means ALL! From Genesis to Revelation, the Bible is God's book, His Truth. Bible Truth is from God Himself. He owns it.

The question is do you believe that God's Word is Truth? The contents of this book will convict and inspire you if you are sincerely seeking God's Truth for the last days. It is only designed to lead you to Truth. It does not seek popularity, fame, praise, or rewards. All those things will fade and pass away, but God's TRUTH, His WORD, stands and endures forever. Our prayer is that you are not only convicted by the Truth, but that you are encouraged, converted, and transformed by the Truth when you believe it and live by it through Jesus Christ. Study carefully and prayerfully. We are living in the last days and prophecy is fast fulfilling. We hope you are blessed by reading and studying the contents of this book.

OCR, family, and Pathway to Peace Ministries

WORDS OF INSPIRATION

GOD DID NOT WANT IT TO BE SO

Death was not a part of God's original plan.
To live forever was His endowment to man
He placed in the Garden of Eden the tree of life
For Adam and Eve to enjoy without strife
But they chose to eat from the forbidden tree
And failed the test of loyalty
God warned them of the results of sin
It would surely cause suffering and even death at the end
Now, because of sin there is misery and woe
But from the beginning, God did not want it to be so

God even made a way to regain what was lost
By offering His own Son to die on the cross
His love for us is greater than words can express
So with His actions, He shows us and with His tender caress
Jesus says, "My child, I have given my all to redeem your life
Please accept my gift, for *with my life, I have paid the price.*"
With a heart full of compassion, He stretches out His arms of love
And in our sorrow as He holds us, He says to us, "Look above!
Remember the promise that I gave as I left
I will come again and receive you to myself."

Though in this life we will experience tribulation
If we patiently endure, it will be turned to jubilation
We have to look beyond our present situation
Beyond the chaos witnessed in every nation
To the time when there will be no more sickness, death, or strife
When we will receive the reward of eternal life
Though Satan comes to steal, kill, and destroy,
Jesus came to give us abundant life, peace, and joy.
So when you see death, misery, and woe
Remember God did not want it to be so

Poem by *Elene Rodgers*

THE GREATEST TRAGEDY

The greatest tragedy is not if I loose all of my wealth
The greatest tragedy is not if I loose my good health
The greatest tragedy is not if I loose mother, father, sister, brother, son, daughter, husband, or wife
The greatest tragedy is not if I loose even my own life
The greatest tragedy of them ALL
Is if I loose my faith in God and FALL
Oh what intense sorrow and pain!!!
For eternal life I would never gain
My precious Savior and those bereaved of
I would not see again in the Promise Land above
So I must press on in faith for now
And keep my hands on the gospel plow
For the greatest joy I do see
In what God has promised for you and me
To live forever with Him in glory
Throughout the ceaseless time of eternity
The gift of salvation is offered to all
So take heed to the pleading call
It cost the life of God's dear Son
To offer salvation to everyone
So today, choose to serve God with your whole heart
And from His law and testimonies never depart
Serve God and Him only in sincerity and in truth
And from ungodliness remain aloof
For there is a crown that awaits every soul
That keeps his eyes on the eternal goal!!!

Poem by *Elene Rodgers*

SECTION ONE:

The Forgotten Commandment

CHAPTER 1
ALL TEN

Friend, did you know that there is a commandment in the Ten Commandments that God wants us never to forget? Do you know what commandment this is? Have you forgotten it yourself? If you have, you are not alone. There are millions of sincere Christians who have also forgotten it or simply ignore it.

As you begin this study understand that the only way to worship God and truly keep ALL of His commandments is to open your heart to Him and allow His Spirit to dwell within you. Jesus says, "Behold, I stand at the door, and knock: if any man hear my voice, and open the door, I will come in to him, and will sup with him, and he with me." - **Revelation 3:20**. God does <u>not</u> force us to worship Him. It is an invitation. He invites us to come to Him and learn who He is and what He has done for us. We respond by inviting Him to come and dwell within us. When He dwells within us, we delight to do His will, and His law will be in our hearts according to **Psalm 40:8**. **Philippians 2:13** explains this process, "For it is God which worketh in you both **to will** and **to do** of his good pleasure."

So before you study, PRAY and INVITE the Spirit of God to dwell within you so that you may love God and His law and see the wonderful things in His Law. **Psalms 119:18** says, "Open thou mine eyes, that I may behold wondrous things out of thy law." Ask God to give you clear understanding of His Word.

In the first section of this book, we will study about a seemingly "forgotten commandment." This study will take you on a Biblical journey to Truth that will bless your life and give you a deeper understanding of Jesus Christ and His love for you. Let's allow the Bible to speak for itself on this very important topic.

<u>Are we to keep ALL of God's commandments?</u>

John 14:15 (Jesus says) - "If ye love me, keep my commandments."

Ecclesiastes 12:13 - "Fear God, and keep his commandments: for this *is* the whole *duty* of man."

<u>What are the three main purposes of the Ten Commandments of God</u>

<u>also known as His Law?</u>

1 – Define and reveal sin clearly
1 John 3:4 - "Whosoever committeth sin transgresseth also the law: for sin is the transgression of the law."

Romans 3:20 - "Therefore by the deeds of the law there shall no flesh be justified in his sight: for by the law *is* the knowledge of sin."

Romans 7:7 - "What shall we say then? *Is* the law sin? God forbid. Nay, I had not known sin, but by the law: for I had not known lust, except the law had said, Thou shalt not covet."

Like a Mirror
A mirror is used to examine yourself, whether you have food or dirt on your face. It cannot clean your face, it only reveals the dirt. You need a wash cloth to clean your face. The Ten Commandments reveal your condition, whether you have the dirt of sin in your life, but it cannot clean it.

2 – Standard of Righteousness in which we are judged
Psalm 119:172 - "My tongue shall speak of thy word: for **all thy commandments are righteousness**."

Ecclesiastes 12:13, 14
13 "Let us hear the conclusion of the whole matter: Fear God, and keep his commandments: for this *is* the whole *duty* of man.
14 For God shall bring every work into judgment, with every secret thing, whether *it be* good, or whether *it be* evil."

James 2:11, 12
11 "For he that said, Do not commit adultery, said also, Do not kill. Now if thou commit no adultery, yet if thou kill, thou art become a transgressor of the law.
12 So speak ye, and so do, as they that shall be **judged by the law of liberty**."

Bible Definition: **Righteous (Hebrew) = just, lawful**

Speed Limit Sign
A speed limit sign reveals the law in order to keep you safe, but the sign cannot make you obey the law. The sign only displays the law. Without the sign you would be unaware of the law or that you have broken the law. Similarly, the Ten Commandments cannot make you righteous or lawful. The commandments are only the standard of righteousness that reveal the

law.

3 – Conversion Tool that points us to Jesus

Psalms 19:7 - "The law of the LORD *is* perfect, converting the soul: the testimony of the LORD *is* sure, making wise the simple."

Galatians 3:24 - "Wherefore the law was our schoolmaster *to bring us* unto Christ, that we might be justified by faith."

Bible Definition: **Convert = Turn to, to return, to turn back**

Points You to Jesus
Even though God's law cannot cleanse you from sin, it points you to Jesus Christ who can clean you and save you from sin. When Christ dwells within you He will work in you to do His good pleasure (**Philippians 2:13**). He will forgive you and cleanse you from all unrighteousness (**1 John 1:9**) and cover you with His righteousness (**Philippians 3:9**).

Is obeying God and His Ten Commandments "legalism"?

John 14:21 - "He that hath my commandments, and keepeth them, he it is that loveth me: and he that loveth me shall be loved of my Father, and I will love him, and will manifest myself to him."

Obedience to the truth motivated by God's love is NEVER legalism. Would it make sense to mock God's obedient children by calling them "legalists"? Of course not. Are you a child of God?

Is it enough to know about the commandments of God without obeying ALL of them?

James 1:23-25
23 "For if any be a hearer of the word, and not a doer, he is like unto a man beholding his natural face in a glass:
24 For he beholdeth himself, and goeth his way, and straightway forgetteth what manner of man he was.
25 But whoso looketh into the perfect law of liberty, and continueth *therein,* he being not a forgetful hearer, but a doer of the work, this man shall be blessed in his deed."

What did God write His Law on and what did He call them?

Exodus 31:18 - "And he gave unto Moses, when he had made an end of communing with him upon mount Sinai, **two tables of testimony, tables of**

stone, written with the finger of God."

Deuteronomy 4:13 - "And he declared unto you **HIS COVENANT**, which he commanded you to perform, even **TEN COMMANDMENTS**; and he wrote them upon **two tables of stone**."

God makes it clear that our part of the covenant or contract with Him is to obey His Ten Commandments. This is a sacred contract between God and His people written in stone by His own finger.

What are God's Ten Commandments?

Exodus 20:1, 2
1 "And God spake all these words, saying,
2 I am the LORD thy God, which have brought thee out of the land of Egypt, out of the house of bondage."

Exodus 20:3 - 17
TEN COMMANDMENTS
1. "Thou shalt have no other gods before me.
2. Thou shalt not make unto thee any graven image, or any likeness of any thing that is in heaven above, or that is in the earth beneath, or that is in the water under the earth: Thou shalt not bow down thyself to them, nor serve them: for I the LORD thy God am a jealous God, visiting the iniquity of the fathers upon the children unto the third and fourth generation of them that hate me and showing mercy unto thousands of them that love me, and keep my commandments.
3. Thou shalt not take the name of the LORD thy God in vain; for the LORD will not hold him guiltless that taketh his name in vain.
4. Remember the Sabbath day, to keep it holy. Six days shalt thou labour, and do all thy work: But the seventh day is the Sabbath of the LORD thy God: in it thou shalt not do any work, thou, nor thy son, nor thy daughter, thy manservant, nor thy maidservant, nor thy cattle, nor thy stranger that is within thy gates: For in six days the LORD made heaven and earth, the sea, and all that in them is and rested the seventh day: wherefore the LORD blessed the Sabbath day, and hallowed it.
5. Honour thy father and thy mother: that thy days may be long upon the land which the LORD thy God giveth thee.
6. Thou shalt not kill.
7. Thou shalt not commit adultery.

8. Thou shalt not steal.
9. Thou shalt not bear false witness against thy neighbour.
10. Thou shalt not covet thy neighbour's house, thou shalt not covet thy neighbour's wife, nor his manservant, nor his maidservant, nor his ox, nor his ass, nor any thing that is thy neighbour's."

All of the Ten Commandments are equally important, still valid, and remain unchanged. According to Exodus 31:18, the Ten Commandments were written on stone by the finger of God which represents the permanence and eternal origin of God's Commandments. They have always existed, even before man sinned. **Psalm 111:7, 8** says, "...all his commandments *are* sure. They stand fast for ever and ever, *and are* done in truth and uprightness." God still wants to write His commandments on the hearts and minds of all people. **Hebrews 10:16** says, "This *is* the covenant that I will make with them after those days, saith the Lord, I will put my laws into their hearts, and in their minds will I write them."

What do the Ten Commandments teach us about love?

Matthew 22:37-40

37 "Jesus said unto him, Thou shalt love the Lord thy God with all thy heart, and with all thy soul, and with all thy mind.
38 This is the first and great commandment.
39 And the second *is* like unto it, Thou shalt love thy neighbour as thyself.
40 On these two commandments hang all the law and the prophets."

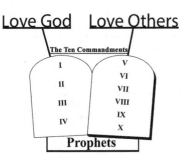

1 John 4:8 - "He that loveth not knoweth not God; for God is love."

Romans 13:10 - "Love worketh no ill to his neighbour: therefore love *is* the fulfilling of the law."

The Ten Commandments teach us about practical love. Matthew 22:40 reveals that the Ten Commandments hang on loving God and others. Loving God and others is not a substitute of the Ten Commandments, but a summary. The Ten Commandments teach us the details how to love God and others. The first four commandments teach how to love God and the last six commandments teach us how to love others.

<u>How does God's Ten Commandment Law directly reflect His character?</u>

Look at the following table of examples of how the character of the Ten Commandments perfectly reflect and match the character of God.

Characteristic	God is...	God's Law is...
Love	1 John 4:8 - "...God is love."	**Romans 13:10** - "...love is the fulfilling of the law."
Holy	**Psalm 99:9** - "...the LORD our God is holy."	**Romans 7:12** - "...the law is holy, and the commandment holy, and just, and good."
Perfect	**Psalm 18:30** - "As for God, his way is perfect..."	**Psalm 19:7** - "The law of the LORD is perfect..."
True	John 3:33 - "...God is true."	**Psalm 119:142** - "...thy law is the truth."
Pure	1 John 3:3 - "...He[God] is pure."	**Psalm 19:8** - "...the commandment of the LORD is pure."
Righteousness	**Psalm 145:17** - "The LORD is righteous in all his ways..."	**Psalm 119:172** - "...for all thy commandments are righteousness."
Faithful	1 Corinthians 1:9 - "God is faithful..."	**Psalm 119:86** - "All thy commandments are faithful..."
Unchangeable	Malachi 3:6 - "For I am the LORD, I change not."	**Matthew 5:18** - "...Till heaven and earth pass, one jot or one tittle shall in no wise pass from the law, till all be fulfilled."
Eternal	Deuteronomy 33:27 - "The eternal God is thy refuge..."	**Psalm 119:7, 8** - "...all His commandments are sure. They stand fast for ever and ever."

Isn't this beautiful and enlightening? The Bible is very clear, God's Law is a perfect reflection of God. When you truly accept God you will also obey His commandments. If anyone attacks the commandments of God they are directly attacking the character of God!

CHAPTER 2
REMEMBER THE SABBATH DAY

Most people acknowledge the Ten Commandments, but there is one commandment within the Ten Commandments in which God knew many people would forget or ignore.

<u>Which commandment of God's Ten Commandments has been forgotten, ignored, or rejected?</u>

Upon further review of the Ten Commandments, which commandment begins with the word "remember"? The Fourth Commandment in **Exodus 20:8-11**, "<u>Remember</u> the sabbath day, to keep it holy. Six days shalt thou labour, and do all thy work: But the seventh day *is* the sabbath of the LORD thy God: *in it* thou shalt not do any work, thou, nor thy son, nor thy daughter, thy manservant, nor thy maidservant, nor thy cattle, nor thy stranger that *is* within thy gates: For *in* six days the LORD made heaven and earth, the sea, and all that in them *is*, and rested the seventh day: wherefore the LORD blessed the sabbath day, and hallowed it."

The fourth commandment is the only commandment that begins with "REMEMBER." It is apparent that God never wanted us to forget the fourth commandment which is a Divine command to remember the seventh-day Sabbath and keep it holy.

Bible Definition: **Sabbath (Hebrew) = Rest**

<u>Weekly Special Rest Day</u>
God has given us a special holy day or special rest day on the seventh day each week! Let's learn more!

Even before the Ten Commandments were given in Exodus chapter 20, God set apart from each other day of the week the special importance of the Sabbath in Exodus 16:29 and 30.

Exodus 16:29, 30
29 "See, for that the LORD hath given you the sabbath, therefore he giveth you on the sixth day the bread of two days; abide ye every man in his place, let no man go out of his place on the seventh day.
30 So the people rested on the seventh day."

When was the seventh-day Sabbath (Rest) established?

Genesis 2:1-3
1 "Thus the heavens and the earth were finished, and all the host of them.
2 And on the seventh day God ended his work which he had made; and he rested on the seventh day from all his work which he had made.
3 And God blessed the seventh day, and sanctified it: because that in it he had rested from all his work which God created and made."

Bible Definition: **Rest (Hebrew) = Sabbath**

The seventh day of rest or Sabbath was established at the creation of this world after God ended His work of Creation.

Based on Genesis 2:1-3, what are the three main things that God did on the seventh day of Creation?

1. **Rested** - Sabbath
2. **Blessed it** - Special seventh-day Sabbath benefits that only God can give
3. **Sanctified it** - Dedicated for a holy and sacred purpose

What does the Sabbath specifically commemorate?

Exodus 31:16, 17
16 "Wherefore the children of Israel shall keep the sabbath, to observe the sabbath throughout their generations, *for* a perpetual covenant.
17 It *is* a sign between me and the children of Israel for ever: for *in* six days the LORD made heaven and earth, and on the seventh day he rested, and was refreshed."

The seventh-day Sabbath is a sacred time to commemorate God as the Creator and Savior. Jesus Christ our Creator and Redeemer at the beginning established His Sabbath as a special day to commemorate His relationship to us and our relationship to Him. Like the anniversary celebration of a married couple is a special day to commemorate their relationship and commitment to each other, the Sabbath is a special day to commemorate our Creator and renew our commitment to Him. Even though we worship God and serve God throughout the week, there is no other day like the seventh-day Sabbath, it is special.

If all people around the world truly kept God's seventh-day Sabbath holy, there would be no atheist or anybody who did not believe in God. Every seventh-day Sabbath would be a reminder of the reality of our wonderful and powerful Creator. **Since the Sabbath points to Creation and the Creator, God, it is tangible proof that God exist!** We have no excuse. **Romans 1:20** says, "For the invisible things of him from the creation of the world are clearly seen, being understood by the things that are made, *even* his eternal power and Godhead; so that they are without excuse."

What does the Bible say about Jesus as our Creator and Savior?

John 1:1-3, 14
1 "In the beginning was the Word, and the Word was with God, and the Word was God.
2 The same was in the beginning with God.
3 All things were made by him; and without him was not any thing made that was made.
14 And the Word was made flesh, and dwelt among us, (and we beheld his glory, the glory as of the only begotten of the Father,) full of grace and truth."

Colossians 1:14-17
14 "In whom we have redemption through his blood, even the forgiveness of sins:
15 Who is the image of the invisible God, the firstborn of every creature:
16 For by him were all things created, that are in heaven, and that are in earth, visible and invisible, whether they be thrones, or dominions, or principalities, or powers: all things were created by him, and for him:
17 And he is before all things, and by him all things consist."

Ephesians 3:9 - "And to make all *men* see what *is* the fellowship of the mystery, which from the beginning of the world hath been hid in God, who created all things by Jesus Christ."

The Bible reveals that Jesus, the second person of the Godhead, is not only our Savior but also our Creator. Jesus is the Creator of the seventh-day Sabbath in which He rested, blessed, and made holy. The seventh-day Sabbath is the only day of the week that Jesus sets apart as holy. **Even though the other six days are good, the seventh day is the only day that is holy unto God.**

Which day is the seventh day of the week?

Saturday is the seventh day of the week according to any standard calendar. Also, a standard dictionary such as the Webster's dictionary clearly defines Saturday as the seventh day of the week.

When we go back to Creation in Genesis chapters 1 and 2, God only named the days by its number 1 through 7. The names of each day that we have today were actually added by pagan (worshipers of false gods) cultures and empires, such as the Romans. They worshiped the stars and planets. For example, they named the first day of the week, "Sunday", in honor of their most worshiped and popular god, known as the Sun god. Monday was named in honor of their god, Moon - in summary: Tuesday, Mars; Wednesday, Mercury; Thursday, Jupiter; Friday, Venus; and Saturday, Saturn.

How does the New Testament confirm that the Holy Sabbath is the seventh day of the week, Saturday?

Let's explore some texts at the time of Christ's death on the cross and resurrection from the tomb.

Jesus died on the sixth day of the week, Friday preparation day, before the seventh-day Sabbath began.

John 19:31-33

31 "The Jews therefore, because it was **the preparation**, that the bodies should not remain upon the cross on the sabbath day, (for that sabbath day was an high day,) besought Pilate that their legs might be broken, and *that* they might be taken away.

32 Then came the soldiers, and brake the legs of the first, and of the other which was crucified with him.

33 But when they came to Jesus, and saw that he was dead already, they brake not his legs."

The women who prepared the body of Jesus rested on the seventh-day Sabbath.

Luke 23:53-56

53 "And he took it down, and wrapped it in linen, and laid it in a sepulchre that was hewn in stone, wherein never man before was laid.

54 And that **day was the preparation**, and the sabbath drew on.

55 And the women also, which came with him from Galilee, followed after,

and beheld the sepulchre, and how his body was laid.

56 And they returned, and prepared spices and ointments; and **rested the sabbath day according to the commandment.**"

The sixth day, Friday, before Sabbath is known as the preparation day, a day to prepare for God's holy Sabbath.

Jesus rose early on the first day of the week - Sunday

Mark 16:2 - "And very early in the morning the **first day of the week**, they came unto the sepulchre at the rising of the sun."

Mark 16:9 - "Now when Jesus was risen **early the first day of the week**, he appeared first to Mary Magdalene, out of whom he had cast seven devils."

The first day of the week is Sunday. This is confirmed by dictionaries and any standard calendar.

In summary, Jesus died on the sixth day, Friday. He rested in His tomb during the seventh-day Sabbath, Saturday. Then rose from the tomb early the first day of the week, Sunday.

Is there other proof that the seventh day of the week is the Bible Sabbath of God?

•   The descendants of Abraham, the Jews, who have been around for almost 4000 years never lost track of the seven-day weekly cycle. Many still recognize the seventh-day Sabbath beginning on sunset Friday until sunset Saturday.

•   The Sabbath is found in the names of over one hundred languages to represent the seventh day of the week, Saturday.

For example, the word for the seventh day of the week, Saturday, in Spanish is "Sabado" which means Sabbath. In Spanish **Exodus 20:8** says, "Acuérdate del **sábado** para santificarlo." (Reina-Valera 1995) All Spanish speaking people plus others should not be confused.

In French the word for seventh day or Saturday is "Samedi" which means Sabbath. In Italian it's "Sabbato" which means Sabbath. And in Russian Saturday is "Subbota" which also means Sabbath.

The following table are more examples of proof that the seventh day is the Sabbath.

Language	Word for Saturday/7th Day	Meaning
Greek	Sabbaton	Sabbath
Latin (Italy)	Sabbatum	Sabbath
Spanish (Spain)	Sábado	Sabbath
Portuguese (Portugal)	Sabbado	Sabbath
Italian (Italy)	Sabbato	Sabbath
French (France)	Samedi	Sabbath day
High German (Germany)	Samstag	Sabbath
Prussian (Prussia)	Sabatico	Sabbath
Russian (Russia)	Subbota	Sabbath
Polish	Sobota	Sabbath
Hebrew	Shabbath	Sabbath
Afaghan	Shamba	Sabbath
Hindustani	Shamba	Sabbath
Persian	Shambin	Sabbath
Arabic	Assabt	The Sabbath
Turkish	Yomessabt	Day Sabbath
Malay	Ari-Sabtu	Day Sabbath
Abyssinian	Sanbat	Sabbath
Lusatian (Saxony)	Sobota	Sabbath
Bohemian	Sobota	Sabbath
Bulgarian (Bulgaria)	Subbota	Sabbath
New Slovenian (Illyria, in Austria)	Sobota	Sabbath
Illyrian (Dalmatia, Servia)	Subota	Sabbath
Wallachian (Roumania or Wallachia)	Sambata	Sabbath
Roman (Sapin, Catalonia)	Dissapte	Day Sabbath
Ecclesiastical Roman (Italy)	Sabbatum	Sabbath
D'oc. French (ancient and modern)	Dissata	Day Sabbath

Norman French (10th -11th Centuries)	Sabbedi	Sabbath Day
Wolof (Senegambia, West Africa)	Alere-Asser	Last Day Sabbath
Congo (West Equatorial Africa)	Sabbado or Kiansbula	Sabbath
Orma (South of Abyssiania)	Zam-ba-da	Sabbath
Kazani - TARTAR (East Russia)	Subbota	Sabbath
Osmanlian (Turkey)	Yome-es-sabt	day of the Sabbath
Arabic (Very old names)	Shi-yar	Chief or rejoicing day
Ancient Syriac	Shab-ba-tho	Sabbath
Chaldee Syriac (Kurdistan,Urumia,Persia)	Shaptu	Sabbath
Babylonian Syriac (A Very Old Language)	Sa-Ba-tu	Sabbath
Maltese (Malta)	Is-sibt	the Sabbath
Ethiopic (Abyssinia)	San-bat	Sabbath
Coptic (Egypt)	Pi sabbaton	the Sabbath
Tamashek (Atlas mountains, Africa)	A-hal es-sabt	the Sabbath
Kabyle (North Africa, Ancient Numidan)	Ghas assebt	the Sabbath day
Hausa (Central Africa)	Assebatu	the Sabbath
Pasto (Afghanistan)	Shamba	Sabbath (pleasantest day of the week)
Pahlivi (ancient Persian)	Shambid	Sabbath
Persian (Persia)	Shambah	Sabbath
Armenian (Armenia)	Shapat	Sabbath
Kurdish (Kurdistan)	Shamba	Sabbath
Ndebele (Zimbabwe)	Sabatha	Sabbath
Shona (Zimbabwe)	Sabata	Sabbath

- See more at: www.sabbathtruth.com/free-resources/article-library/id/912/ which-day-of-the-week#sthash.fWM1aZjH.dpuf

This is proof that at one time the seventh-day Sabbath truth was honored around the world, but it is apparent that most of the world has forgotten it.

When does the seventh-day Sabbath officially begin?

To answer this question we must go back to the origin of the seven-day weekly cycle which was established at Creation. Think about it, the complete revolution of the moon around the earth determines a month. The complete revolution of the earth around the sun determines a year. But who or what determines our seven-day weekly cycle? Why not have a 10 day week or a 15 day week cycle? **Our seven-day weekly cycle is not determined by the moon nor the sun, it was created by God and God alone according to the Bible.** Exodus 20:11 says, "For *in* six days the LORD made heaven and earth, the sea, and all that in them *is,* and rested the seventh day: wherefore the LORD blessed the sabbath day, and hallowed it."

In Genesis chapter 1, God clearly defines a 24 hour literal day at Creation. He also reveals when a new day actually begins. Notice what God says at the end of each day of Creation:

Genesis 1:5 - "And God called the light Day, and the darkness he called Night. And the **evening and the morning were the first day.**"
Genesis 1:8 - "And God called the firmament Heaven. And the **evening and the morning were the second day.**"
Genesis 1:13 - "And the **evening and the morning were the third day.**"
Genesis 1:19 - "And the **evening and the morning were the fourth day.**"
Genesis 1:23 - "And the **evening and the morning were the fifth day.**"
Genesis 1:31 - "And God saw every thing that he had made, and, behold, *it was* very good. And the **evening and the morning were the sixth day.**"

Evening is defined as dusk, night, or sunset. According to the Bible a new day actually begins at dusk or when the sun sets. There are 24 literal hours from evening to evening. The origin of a day beginning at 12 o'clock midnight is a man-made concept.

Seventh-day Sabbath = Sunset Friday to Sunset Saturday

Since the Bible reveals that each day officially begins when the sun sets in the evening, the official beginning of the seventh-day Sabbath begins when the sun sets on Friday evening and ends when the sun sets on Saturday evening.

Sabbath Day

Sunday	Monday	Tuesday	Wed.	Thurs.	Friday	Saturday
1	2	3	4	5	6	7

Have there been calendar changes that changed the seven-day weekly cycle?

Gregorian Calendar, October 1582

No. There have been minor changes to the calendar over the centuries, but these changes did not alter the seven-day weekly cycle. For example, in October 1582 AD, ten days were removed from the calendar that month in order to keep up with the solar cycle. But this **change did not alter the seven-day weekly cycle** in which the first day of the week is Sunday and the seventh day of the week is Saturday because the week is not based on the earth revolving around the sun or the moon revolving around the earth.

Thought question: Do you think that God would allow a special and important blessing such as the holy seventh-day Sabbath to be lost by man?

What did Jesus do on the seventh-day Sabbath?

Luke 4:16 - "And he [Jesus] came to Nazareth, where he had been brought up: and, as his custom was, he went into the synagogue on the sabbath day, and stood up for to read."

Luke 4:31 - "And came down to Capernaum, a city of Galilee, and taught them on the sabbath days."

Whose example should we follow?

1 Peter 2:21 - "For even hereunto were ye called: because Christ also suffered for us, leaving us an example, that ye should follow his steps:"

1 John 2:6 - "He that saith he abideth in him ought himself also so to walk, even as he walked."

What day did the apostles and the early church worship on after the death and resurrection of Jesus Christ?

Acts 13:14, 15, 42-44
14 "But when they departed from Perga, they came to Antioch in Pisidia, and went into the synagogue on the sabbath day, and sat down.
15 And after the reading of the law and the prophets the rulers of the synagogue sent unto them, saying, Ye men and brethren, if ye have any word of exhortation for the people, say on.
42 And when the Jews were gone out of the synagogue, the Gentiles besought that these words might be preached to them the next sabbath.
43 Now when the congregation was broken up, many of the Jews and religious proselytes followed Paul and Barnabas: who, speaking to them, persuaded them to continue in the grace of God.
44 And the next sabbath day came almost the whole city together to hear the word of God."

Who was the Sabbath made for and whose day is it?

Mark 2:27, 28
27 "And he said unto them, The sabbath was made for man, and not man for the sabbath:
28 Therefore the Son of man is Lord also of the sabbath."

Exodus 20:10 - "But the seventh day *is* the sabbath of the LORD thy God: *in it* thou shalt not do any work, thou, nor thy son, nor thy daughter, thy manservant, nor thy maidservant, nor thy cattle, nor thy stranger that *is* within thy gates."

Revelation 1:10 - "I was in the Spirit on the Lord's day, and heard behind me a great voice, as of a trumpet."

The seventh day weekly holy Sabbath is the Lord's day that was created by Him for our benefit. The Sabbath was not made just for the Jews and the people in the Old Testament, it was made as a blessing for ALL of us. The Sabbath was established at Creation before sin and many years before the Jews. Abraham, the father of the Jews was not born until over 2000 years after Creation.

The seventh-day Sabbath was made to bless us with benefits that come directly from God with true prosperity mentally, physically, spiritually, and financially. The only way to experience these special blessings is to honor God on His holy day and keep it holy as the fourth commandment reveals.

The Sabbath was not made for the animals of Creation, they go about doing their normal tasks instinctively the way God designed them seven days a week. Bees, seven days a week, go and pollinate and get nectar. But those made in the image of God, to reflect the character of God, are given something special that nothing else in Creation has the benefit of, the Holy Sabbath Rest DAY!

What does God command us to do on His Holy seventh-day Sabbath?

1) Remember - Don't forget

Exodus 20:8 - "Remember the sabbath day, to keep it holy."

2) Rest - Cease from your regular work or employment

Exodus 20:9-11
9 "Six days shalt thou labour, and do all thy work:
10 But the seventh day *is* the sabbath of the LORD thy God: *in it* thou shalt not do any work, thou, nor thy son, nor thy daughter, thy manservant, nor thy maidservant, nor thy cattle, nor thy stranger that *is* within thy gates:
11 For *in* six days the LORD made heaven and earth, the sea, and all that in them *is,* and rested the seventh day: wherefore the LORD blessed the sabbath day, and hallowed it."

Leviticus 19:30 - "Ye shall keep my sabbaths, and reverence my sanctuary: I *am* the LORD."

God values work greatly. **2 Thessalonians 3:10** says "...if any would not work, neither should he eat." We should work hard and value work six days a week. However, God has a very special day like no other, the seventh-day Sabbath. This is a special "holiday" that God gives us Divine permission to take off! God is the boss of all bosses. Who would you rather obey? This also includes common chores or household labor such as cutting the lawn, washing the car, or getting groceries. These things can wait until after the Sabbath hours. Those who obey God's fourth commandment not only have a spiritual revival each week, but they will experience less stress, longevity, and quality time with family and believers in Christ. Try it and experience it for yourself!

3) Call the Sabbath a delight - not doing your own pleasure nor having secular activities or conversions

Isaiah 58:13 - "If thou turn away thy foot from the sabbath, from doing thy pleasure on my holy day; and call the sabbath a delight, the holy of the LORD, honourable; and shalt honour him, not doing thine own ways, nor finding thine own pleasure, nor speaking thine own words."

Bible Definition: **Delight (Hebrew) = Luxury**

The seventh-day Sabbath is truly a luxury that is available to ALL of us. It does not matter if you are rich or poor, you can enjoy the benefits and blessings of this luxurious day. This is a day that comes at the end of a hectic and busy week. This is a day to look forward to and get excited about. This is why God says that we should "call the Sabbath a delight!"

Remember, the seventh-day Sabbath is sacred and blessed by our Creator and Savior, Jesus Christ. It is a day to commune with God and fulfill His commission to bless others. The Lord is holy, His seventh-day Sabbath is holy and He and His day should be totally respected by those who benefit from it. The Sabbath is the Lord's Day not ours, God is the honorable King of kings. On God's holy day we should refrain from doing things just for our pleasure such as playing secular games, watching secular TV programming or news, going shopping, or having secular conversations. We must remember that on the Sabbath day God wants 100% of our attention without any worldly distractions. Secular activities and conversations on God's holy day will distract your attention away from God and mess up your blessing that God has for you if you keep His holy day holy.

During the time of Christ, the Jewish leaders misrepresented the Sabbath by making it a burden. Jesus taught that is was not a day that is a burden, but a delight. He taught that we should minister, heal, and do good on the Sabbath as He did.

4) No buying or selling

The following scriptures are a lesson of no buying and selling on God's holy day from Nehemiah to a people who forgot about God's seventh-day Sabbath. Nehemiah reminded them of the forgotten commandment.

Nehemiah 10:31 - "And *if* the people of the land bring ware or any victuals on the sabbath day to sell, *that* we would not buy it of them on the sabbath, or on the holy day..."

Nehemiah 13:15-22

15 "In those days saw I in Judah *some* treading wine presses on the sabbath, and bringing in sheaves, and lading asses; as also wine, grapes, and figs, and all *manner of* burdens, which they brought into Jerusalem on the sabbath day: and I testified *against them* in the day wherein they sold victuals.

16 There dwelt men of Tyre also therein, which brought fish, and all manner of ware, and sold on the sabbath unto the children of Judah, and in Jerusalem.

17 Then I contended with the nobles of Judah, and said unto them, What evil thing *is* this that ye do, and profane the sabbath day?

18 Did not your fathers thus, and did not our God bring all this evil upon us, and upon this city? yet ye bring more wrath upon Israel by profaning the sabbath.

19 And it came to pass, that when the gates of Jerusalem began to be dark before the sabbath, I commanded that the gates should be shut, and charged that they should not be opened till after the sabbath: and *some* of my servants set I at the gates, *that* there should no burden be brought in on the sabbath day.

20 So the merchants and sellers of all kind of ware lodged without Jerusalem once or twice.

21 Then I testified against them, and said unto them, Why lodge ye about the wall? if ye do *so* again, I will lay hands on you. From that time forth came they no *more* on the sabbath.

22 And I commanded the Levites that they should cleanse themselves, and *that* they should come *and* keep the gates, to sanctify the sabbath day. Remember me, O my God, *concerning* this also, and spare me according to the greatness of thy mercy."

The Sabbath is holy. It is not a day to buy and sell. If someone owns a business that sells products or services, it should be closed on God's holy day. There are many examples of business owners who closed their business on the Sabbath and kept it holy as the Bible reveals. Though their faith was tested, they were blessed by God because of their faithfulness to Him and His Word.

5) Main cooking and food preparations should be done before the Sabbath – No baking or boiling

The following scriptures are a lesson of food preparation before the Sabbath from the Israelites who were given manna from heaven. God gave them specific instructions on what they were to do with the manna on the day before the Sabbath.

Exodus 16:15-28

15 "And when the children of Israel saw *it,* they said one to another, It *is* manna: for they wist not what it *was.* And Moses said unto them, This *is* the bread which the LORD hath given you to eat.

16 This *is* the thing which the LORD hath commanded, Gather of it every man according to his eating, an omer for every man, *according to* the number of your persons; take ye every man for *them* which *are* in his tents.

17 And the children of Israel did so, and gathered, some more, some less.

18 And when they did mete *it* with an omer, he that gathered much had nothing over, and he that gathered little had no lack; they gathered every man according to his eating.

19 And Moses said, Let no man leave of it till the morning.

20 Notwithstanding they hearkened not unto Moses; but some of them left of it until the morning, and it bred worms, and stank: and Moses was wroth with them.

21 And they gathered it every morning, every man according to his eating: and when the sun waxed hot, it melted.

22 And it came to pass, *that* on the sixth day they gathered twice as much bread, two omers for one *man:* and all the rulers of the congregation came and told Moses.

23 And he said unto them, This *is that* which the LORD hath said, To morrow *is* the rest of the holy sabbath unto the LORD: **bake *that* which ye will bake *to day,*** and **seethe [boil] that ye will seethe**; and that which remaineth over lay up for you to be kept until the morning.

24 And they laid it up till the morning, as Moses bade: and it did not stink, neither was there any worm therein.

25 And Moses said, Eat that to day; for to day *is* a sabbath unto the LORD: to day ye shall not find it in the field.

26 Six days ye shall gather it; but on the seventh day, *which is* the sabbath, in it there shall be none.

27 And it came to pass, *that* there went out *some* of the people on the seventh day for to gather, and they found none.

28 And the LORD said unto Moses, How long refuse ye to keep my commandments and my laws?"

The lesson we learn from the sixteenth chapter of Exodus, is that we should have our main cooking, baking and boiling, done before the Sabbath. When we enter into the holy Sabbath hours God does not want us "sweating" in the kitchen getting a meal together from "scratch." The Sabbath meal should already be prepared the day before. On the Sabbath day, all you should have to do is warm your Sabbath meal and enjoy the fellowship with your family and friends. Because you prepared your meal before the Sabbath, your clean up should be light.

6) Weekly Holy Assembly & Worship with God's people

Leviticus 23:3 - "Six days shall work be done: but the seventh day *is* the sabbath of rest, an **holy convocation [assembly]**; ye shall do no work *therein: it is* the sabbath of the LORD in all your dwellings."

Bible Definition: Holy Convocation = Holy assembly or worship service

Hebrews 10:24, 25
24 "And let us consider one another to provoke unto love and to good works:
25 Not forsaking the assembling of ourselves together, as the manner of some *is;* but exhorting *one another:* and so much the more, as ye see the day approaching."

Matthew 18:20 - "For where two or three are gathered together in my name, there am I in the midst of them."

The seventh-day Sabbath, as the scriptures reveal, is a holy day in which the believers of Jesus Christ assembly together to worship our Creator and Savior. It is a day to go to church and learn more about God's truth, to spiritually grow, and fellowship with like believers.

In summary: What does God command us to do on the holy seventh-day Sabbath Rest Day?

1. Remember - Don't forget
2. Rest - Cease from your regular work or employment
3. Call the Sabbath a delight - not doing your own pleasure nor having secular activities or conversions
4. No buying or selling
5. Main cooking and food preparations should be done before the Sabbath
6. Weekly Holy assembly & worship with God's people

<u>**Is Jesus delighted when we minister to others on His holy Sabbath day?**</u>
Let's look at what Jesus taught in Mark 3:1-4.

Mark 3:1-4
1 "And he entered again into the synagogue; and there was a man there which had a withered hand.
2 And they watched him, whether he would heal him on the sabbath day; that they might accuse him.
3 And he saith unto the man which had the withered hand, Stand forth.
4 And he saith unto them, Is it lawful to do good on the sabbath days, or to do evil? to save life, or to kill? But they held their peace."

The Pharisees, the Jewish leaders at the time of Jesus, made the Sabbath a burden to all people. They added their own rules of what could and could not be done on the Sabbath. Their rules were not approved by God. They were against the principles and purpose of the Sabbath. For example, they made rules that a person was in violation of the Sabbath if they walked so many steps, or physically carried something that weighed a certain amount. They added so many "rules" to the Sabbath that the people had a complete misconception of the true meaning of the Sabbath. Jesus reveals to us the true meaning of the Sabbath. The Sabbath of course is a special day to honor God, but it is also a day in which we should reach out to others. For example, it is good on the Sabbath to visit the sick and shut in. It is good to relieve those suffering from pain and despair on the Sabbath day. The Sabbath is also a time to reach out to your community and share the gospel of Jesus Christ.

<u>**Are nature walks a great activity to do on the Sabbath?**</u>

Genesis 1:1 - "In the beginning God created the heaven and the earth."

Psalm 33:6 - "By the word of the LORD were the heavens made; and all the host of them by the breath of his mouth."

Psalm 19:1 - "The heavens declare the glory of God; and the firmament sheweth his handywork."

Psalm 8:3, 4
3 "When I consider thy heavens, the work of thy fingers, the moon and the stars, which thou hast ordained."
4 What is man, that thou art mindful of him? and the son of man, that thou

visitest him?"

Psalm 111:4 - "He hath made his wonderful works to be remembered: the LORD *is* gracious and full of compassion."

Romans 1:20 - "For the invisible things of him from the creation of the world are clearly seen, being understood by the things that are made, *even* his eternal power and Godhead; so that they are without excuse."

Remember the Sabbath connects us back to Creation and our Creator. Besides going to church, the seventh-day Sabbath is also a delightful time to get out in nature and reflect upon the wonderful Creation of God. It is a great day to take your family on a nature walk and talk about the goodness of God and the wonderful things in His Creation. You will find this to be a great time to commune with God in nature. It is also relaxing and refreshing after a busy work week.

What is the best way to bring in the Sabbath each week?

Psalm 100:4 - "Enter into his gates with thanksgiving, *and* into his courts with praise: be thankful unto him, *and* bless his name."

Psalm 96:2 - "Sing unto the LORD, bless his name; shew forth his salvation from day to day."

Colossians 3:16, 17
16 "Let the word of Christ dwell in you richly in all wisdom; teaching and admonishing one another in psalms and hymns and spiritual songs, singing with grace in your hearts to the Lord.
17 And whatsoever ye do in word or deed, *do* all in the name of the Lord Jesus, giving thanks to God and the Father by him."

The Sabbath is a holy "temple of time." This time is sacred. We should enter the Sabbath with thanksgiving, singing, praise, and worship to our Creator and Savior, every Friday evening at sunset, when Sabbath begins. Also, it is appropriate to end each Sabbath with singing and praises. If you are not keeping the Sabbath and worshiping God on His holy day, you are truly missing a blessing. After every Sabbath you will feel rejuvenated mentally, physically, and spiritually. You will be recharged to take on another busy week. Jesus invites you to remember His holy day and experience the rest, blessings, and a closer relationship with Him.

What special promise does God give to those who keep the seventh-day Sabbath holy?

Isaiah 58:13, 14
13 "If thou turn away thy foot from the sabbath, *from* doing thy pleasure on my holy day; and call the sabbath a delight, the holy of the LORD, honourable; and shalt honour him, not doing thine own ways, nor finding thine own pleasure, nor speaking *thine own* words:
14 Then shalt thou delight thyself in the LORD; and I will cause thee to ride upon the high places of the earth, and feed thee with the heritage of Jacob thy father: for the mouth of the LORD hath spoken *it*."

Remember, the seventh-day Sabbath was made to benefit us and glorify God. Those who are sincerely obedient and keep the Lord's Sabbath holy as the scriptures reveal, will be greatly blessed by God and prosper. Is that you, friend? Are you ready to ride upon the high places of the earth? Remember the seventh-day Sabbath and keep it holy. God wants to make us the head and not the tail, but we must be obedient to ALL of God's commandments in order to have His great blessings for us.

Deuteronomy 28:13 - "And the LORD shall make thee the head, and not the tail; and thou shalt be above only, and thou shalt not be beneath; if that thou hearken unto the commandments of the LORD thy God, which I command thee this day, to observe and to do *them*."

What is a sign that you are truly loyal to the God of Heaven?

Ezekiel 20:12 - "Moreover also I gave them my sabbaths, to be a **sign** between me and them, that they might know that I *am* the LORD that sanctify them."

Ezekiel 20:20 - "And hallow my sabbaths; and they shall be a **sign** between me and you, that ye may know that I *am* the LORD your God."

Exodus 31:13 - "Speak thou also unto the children of Israel, saying, Verily my sabbaths ye shall keep: for it *is* a **sign** between me and you throughout your generations; that *ye* may know that I *am* the LORD that doth sanctify you."

Bible Definition: Sign = **monument, mark, or evidence**

John 14:15 - "If ye love me, keep my commandments."

Keeping the seventh-day Sabbath holy is a sign or proof of your loyalty and love toward Jesus our Creator and Savior God. Remember, Mark 2:28 reveals that Jesus Christ is the Lord of the Sabbath. It is His holy day that He established for His glory on the seventh day. All Christians who are loyal to God will prove their allegiance to God by keeping holy His seventh-day Sabbath. Like a flag is a symbol of our allegiance to our country, the Sabbath is a symbol of our allegiance to our Creator. Jesus has already shown us proof of how much He loves us by dying for our sins. The keeping of the Sabbath and all of His commandments are practical and tangible evidence of your faith in Him and love for Him. Talk is worthless without action.

What are more promises and blessings that God gives to those who keep ALL of His commandments including the seventh-day Sabbath?

Deuteronomy 6:2 - "That thou mightest fear the LORD thy God, to keep all his statutes and his commandments, which I command thee, thou, and thy son, and thy son's son, all the days of thy life; and that thy **days may be prolonged**."

Exodus 15:26 - "And said, If thou wilt diligently hearken to the voice of the LORD thy God, and wilt do that which is right in his sight, and wilt give ear to his commandments, and keep all his statutes, **I will put none of these diseases upon thee, which I have brought upon the Egyptians:** for I *am* the LORD that healeth thee."

Psalms 119:165 - "**Great peace** have they which love thy law: and nothing shall offend them."

Deuteronomy 28:1-13
1 "And it shall come to pass, if thou shalt hearken diligently unto the voice of the LORD thy God, **to observe *and* to do all his commandments** which I command thee this day, that the LORD thy God will **set thee on high above all nations of the earth**:
2 And all these **blessings** shall come on thee, and overtake thee, if thou shalt hearken unto the voice of the LORD thy God.
3 **Blessed** *shalt* thou *be* in the city, and **blessed** *shalt* thou *be* in the field.
4 **Blessed** *shall be* the fruit of thy body, and the fruit of thy ground, and the fruit of thy cattle, the increase of thy kine, and the flocks of thy sheep.
5 **Blessed** *shall be* thy basket and thy store.

6 **Blessed** *shalt* thou *be* when thou comest in, and **blessed** *shalt* thou *be* when thou goest out.

7 The LORD shall cause thine enemies that rise up against thee to be smitten before thy face: they shall come out against thee one way, and flee before thee seven ways.

8 The LORD shall command the **blessing upon thee in thy storehouses,** and in all that thou settest thine hand unto; and he shall **bless thee in the land** which the LORD thy God giveth thee.

9 The LORD shall **establish thee an holy people** unto himself, as he hath sworn unto thee, **if thou shalt keep the commandments of the LORD thy God, and walk in his ways.**

10 And all people of the earth shall see that thou art called by the name of the LORD; and they shall be afraid of thee.

11 And the LORD shall make thee plenteous in goods, in the fruit of thy body, and in the fruit of thy cattle, and in the fruit of thy ground, in the land which the LORD sware unto thy fathers to give thee.

12 The LORD shall open unto thee his good treasure, the heaven to give the rain unto thy land in his season, and to bless all the work of thine hand: and thou shalt lend unto many nations, and thou shalt not borrow.

13 And the LORD shall **make thee the head, and not the tail; and thou shalt be above only,** and thou shalt not be beneath; **if that thou hearken unto the commandments of the LORD thy God, which I command thee this day, to observe and to do** *them.*"

John 15:10, 11

10 "If ye keep my commandments, ye shall **abide in my love;** even as I have kept my Father's commandments, and abide in his love.

11 These things have I spoken unto you, that my joy might remain in you, and *that* **your joy might be full**."

Wow, what awesome blessings from the Lord found in both the Old and New Testaments of the Bible! Jesus wants us to clearly understand the blessings of obedience. He explains it again in **John 14:23**, "Jesus answered and said unto him, If a man love me, he will keep my words: and my Father will love him, and we will come unto him, and make our abode with him." What a blessing! When the Spirit of God dwells in us we will love Him and His law. **Psalm 119:97** says, "O how love I thy law! it is my meditation all the day." The last book and chapter of the Bible in **Revelation 22:14** reveals that the blessing of entering into the Heavenly kingdom are given to those who "**do** His commandments", ALL of them.

<u>Can you "naturally" in your sinful "flesh" keep God's Ten</u>
<u>Commandments including the seventh-day Sabbath without Divine help?</u>

Romans 7:14 - "For we know that the **law is spiritual**: but I am carnal, sold under sin."

Romans 8:1-9
1 "There is therefore now no condemnation to them which are in Christ Jesus, who walk not after the flesh, but after the Spirit.
2 For the law of the Spirit of life in Christ Jesus hath made me free from the law of sin and death.
3 For what the law could not do, in that it was weak through the flesh, God sending his own Son in the likeness of sinful flesh, and for sin, condemned sin in the flesh:
4 That the righteousness of the law might be fulfilled in us, who walk not after the flesh, but after the Spirit.
5 For they that are after the flesh do mind the things of the flesh; but they that are after the Spirit the things of the Spirit.
6 For to be carnally minded is death; but to be spiritually minded is life and peace.
7 Because the carnal mind is enmity against God: for it is not subject to the law of God, neither indeed can be.
8 So then they that are in the flesh cannot please God.
9 But ye are not in the flesh, but in the Spirit, if so be that the Spirit of God dwell in you. Now if any man have not the Spirit of Christ, he is none of his."

Bible Definition: **Flesh / Carnal = Sinful nature**

The law of God is Spiritual, but we are naturally sinful. Our sinful nature, the flesh, is naturally against the law of God, including the seventh-day Sabbath. Remember, according to 1 John 3:4, sin is the disobedience of God's law. The commandments of God reveal sin. So how can we be in sin and keep the commandments of God? The scriptures reveal that it is literally impossible to keep the Sabbath commandment in your sinful flesh. The commandments of God are not the works of the flesh but the works of the Spirit. In other words, we must be converted through the power and grace of Jesus. Remember, the commandments of God reflect the character of God. We must have the character of God in order to keep the law of God. When we stay connected to Jesus daily, and allow the spirit of God to work in us, He give us the power and desire to reflect the character of God and keep ALL of His Ten Commandments. **Philippians 2:13** says, "For it is God which **worketh in you both to will and to do** of his good pleasure." **Hebrews 13:20, 21** says, [20]"Now the God of peace, that brought again from the dead our Lord Jesus, that great shepherd of the sheep, through the blood of the everlasting covenant, [21]Make you perfect in every good work to do his will, **working in you that which is wellpleasing in his sight**, through Jesus Christ; to whom be glory for ever and ever. Amen." The reason why so many people ignore or reject the seventh-day Sabbath truth is because they are operating in their "flesh," not allowing the power of God to convert them in the ways of God.

Can we have true spiritual rest in Jesus and reject the seventh-day Sabbath commandment?

Hebrews 4:1-11
1 "Let us therefore fear, lest, a promise being left *us* of entering into his rest, any of you should seem to come short of it.
2 For unto us was the gospel preached, as well as unto them: but the word preached did not profit them, not being mixed with faith in them that heard *it.*
3 For we which have believed do enter into rest, as he said, As I have sworn in my wrath, if they shall enter into my rest: although the works were finished from the foundation of the world.
4 For he spake in a certain place of the seventh *day* on this wise, And God did rest the seventh day from all his works.
5 And in this *place* again, If they shall enter into my rest.
6 Seeing therefore it remaineth that some must enter therein, and they to whom it was first preached entered not in because of unbelief:
7 Again, he limiteth a certain day, saying in David, To day, after so long a time; as it is said, To day if ye will hear his voice, harden not your hearts.
8 For if Jesus had given them rest, then would he not afterward have spoken of another day.
9 There remaineth therefore a rest to the people of God.
10 For he that is entered into his rest, he also hath ceased from his own works, as God *did* from his.
11 Let us labour therefore to enter into that rest, lest any man fall after the same example of unbelief."

The seventh-day Sabbath is a reminder of how God works in us. It takes the power of the Creator to "recreate us" to make us holy again. **Psalms 51:10** says, "Create in me a clean heart, O God; and renew a right spirit within me." It is not by our own works that we are saved but it is the grace of God. [8]"For by grace are ye saved through faith; and that not of yourselves: it is the gift of God: [9]Not of works, lest any man should boast. [10]For we are his workmanship, created in Christ Jesus unto good works, which God hath before ordained that we should walk in them." - **Ephesians 2:8-10**. Our man made works cannot cleanse us from sin, only Jesus. Grace is not a license to sin, it reveals sin through the law and the points us to Jesus. Grace is manifested through the ministry of Jesus to cleanse us from sin and give us victory over sin. When we open our heart to Jesus His life will permeate the soul. His life of perfect obedience will shine out of our hearts "unto good works." **1 John 3:24** says, "And he that keepeth his commandments dwelleth in him, and he in him. And hereby we know that he abideth in us, by the Spirit which he hath given us." Grace is a gift that we can only receive by faith in Jesus.

"But thanks be to God, which giveth us the victory through our Lord Jesus Christ." - **1 Corinthians 15:57**. Why would anyone choose to perish when the provision has been made for them to be saved? Those who reject God's grace cannot obey God's law. They will be unworthy to enter His kingdom. When others reject or ignore God's holy Sabbath, it is impossible for them to enter into God's true spiritual rest. **Hebrews 4:6 and 11 reveal that the reason why many people do not enter the seventh-day Sabbath rest is because of unbelief.**

The Sabbath reminds us of the power and love of God who is our Creator and Savior. He invites all "Come unto Me, all ye that labor and are heavy-laden, and I will give you rest." - **Matthew 11:28**. In order to have God's rest we must submit to His Divine authority and allow God to work in us to do all He commands.

Will those who are saved continue to keep the seventh-day Sabbath holy and worship God in Heaven and the new earth on His holy day throughout eternity?

Isaiah 66:22, 23
22 "For as the new heavens and the new earth, which I will make, shall remain before me, saith the LORD, so shall your seed and your name remain.
23 And it shall come to pass, *that* from one new moon [new month] to

another, and from one sabbath to another, shall all flesh come to worship before me, saith the LORD."

Remember, the seventh-day Sabbath is eternal. It will be kept holy by all of those saved in the Heavenly kingdom and the new Earth. Can you image coming before Jesus for worship each Sabbath in Heaven? It will be an awesome worship service. Howbeit all of God's people can worship before Jesus our Creator and Savior, each Sabbath now. You don't have to wait until you get to Heaven, now is the time to experience the glory and blessings of God's holy day.

Is it okay to disregard or ignore the seventh-day Sabbath commandment as written in the fourth commandment? Is it really important?

1 John 3:4 - "Whosoever committeth sin transgresseth also the law: for sin is the transgression of the law."

Sin is the disobedience of God's Law. Is the Sabbath command a part of God's law? Yes.

James 2:10, 11
10 "For whosoever shall keep the whole law, and yet offend in one *point,* he is guilty of all.
11 For he that said, Do not commit adultery, said also, Do not kill. Now if thou commit no adultery, yet if thou kill, thou art become a transgressor of the law."

Bible Definition: **Transgressor = lawbreaker, violator, or disobedient**

Even if only one link in a chain is broken, the entire chain is broken. Similarly, if a person breaks one of God's commandments, that person is guilty of breaking them ALL. Remember, the Sabbath commandment is not an option but a Divine command to be obeyed along with the other nine commandments.

What is the final payment or judgment for disobedience to God and His law, including breaking the seventh-day Sabbath commandment?

Romans 6:23 - "For the wages of sin *is* death; but the gift of God is eternal life through Jesus Christ our Lord."

The penalty for sin is eternal death, but God offers the gift of **eternal life** to ALL people. He does not want anyone to perish. You must make a decision. Choose life!

Exodus 31:14, 15
14 "Ye shall keep the sabbath therefore; for it *is* holy unto you: every one that defileth it shall surely be put to death: for whosoever doeth *any* work therein, that soul shall be cut off from among his people.
15 Six days may work be done; but in the seventh *is* the sabbath of rest, holy to the LORD: whosoever doeth *any* work in the sabbath day, he shall surely be put to death."

A true understanding of the Creator and obedience to Him would lead to a peaceful and lawful society. "Thy word have I hid in mine heart, that I might not sin against thee." - **Psalms 119:11.** Men created in the image of God, loving God and loving others was the Creator's intent at the beginning. But if men are led to forget their Creator the way is opened for unrestrained evil. That's why the penalty for breaking the Sabbath was so great.

The keeping of God's seventh-day Sabbath holy is truly important because it is a matter of eternal life or eternal death for those who have been presented and convicted by the Holy Spirit of this truth. When a person is not aware of a certain truth in the Bible and that person is living up to all the light that he or she knows, God winks at his or her ignorance according to **Acts 17:30.** It says, "And the times of this ignorance God winked at; but now commandeth all men every where to repent." However, when that person is given the knowledge of truth and ignores it or rejects it, to him or her it is sin. **James 4:17** says, "Therefore to him that knoweth to do good, and doeth *it* not, to him it is sin." Friend, pray that you follow the conviction of the Holy Spirit and obey this truth about God's seventh-day Sabbath.

What was one of the reasons why Judah, the Israelite people, were taken into captivity?

Nehemiah 13:17, 18
17 "Then I contended with the nobles of Judah, and said unto them, What evil thing *is* this that ye do, and profane the sabbath day?
18 Did not your fathers thus, and did not our God bring all this evil upon us, and upon this city? yet ye bring more wrath upon Israel by profaning the sabbath."

Bible Definition: **Profane = defile, violate**

One of the reasons why Judah went into Babylonian captivity was because they broke the seventh-day Sabbath.

Is just going to church on the seventh-day Sabbath an automatic ticket to Heaven?

Romans 1:18, 21,22, 29-32
18 "For the wrath of God is revealed from heaven against all ungodliness and unrighteousness of men, **who hold the truth in <u>unrighteousness</u>**;
21 Because that, when they knew God, they glorified him not as God, neither were thankful; but became vain in their imaginations, and their foolish heart was darkened.
22 Professing themselves to be wise, they became fools,
29 Being filled with all unrighteousness, fornication, wickedness, covetousness, maliciousness; full of envy, murder, debate, deceit, malignity; whisperers,
30 Backbiters, haters of God, despiteful, proud, boasters, inventors of evil things, disobedient to parents,
31 Without understanding, covenantbreakers, without natural affection, implacable, unmerciful:
32 Who knowing the judgment of God, that they which commit such things are worthy of death, not only do the same, but have pleasure in them that do them."

1 Corinthians 6:9-11
9 "Know ye not that the unrighteous shall not inherit the kingdom of God? Be not deceived: neither fornicators, nor idolaters, nor adulterers, nor effeminate, nor abusers of themselves with mankind,
10 Nor thieves, nor covetous, nor drunkards, nor revilers, nor extortioners, shall inherit the kingdom of God.
11 And such were some of you: but ye are washed, but ye are sanctified, but ye are justified in the name of the Lord Jesus, and by the Spirit of our God."

Just going to church on the seventh-day Sabbath does not give anyone an automatic ticket to Heaven. It must be made very clear, going to church every seventh-day Sabbath is important for all Christians, but we must make sure that we are clothed with the righteousness of Jesus Christ and filled with the Holy Spirit to do the will of the Father, seven days a week, twenty-four hours a day. Through the power of the Holy Spirit, we will with gladness keep ALL of God's Ten Commandments and NOT partake in sin and unrighteousness in ANY form. This is true worship. Remember, true worship requires truth but it also requires the Spirit of God dwelling in us and God will not dwell in unrighteousness. Romans chapter 1 makes this point clear by showing how some can hold the truth of the seventh-day Sabbath in unrighteousness.

God offers to cleanse the unrighteous from sin so He can save them from it. This is LOVE. **1 John 1:9** says, "If we confess our sins, he is faithful and just to forgive us our sins, and to cleanse us from all unrighteousness." **Isaiah 55:7** says, "Let the wicked forsake his way, and the unrighteous man his thoughts: and let him return unto the LORD, and he will have mercy upon him; and to our God, for he will abundantly pardon." In other words, if a person rejects God's offer to pardon them and continues in unrighteousness though he or she has the truth of the seventh-day Sabbath, the Bible is very clear, that person will not inherit the kingdom of God.

What does the last book of the Bible and the last chapter of the Bible say about the great blessing of keeping God's commandments?

Revelation 22:14 - "Blessed are they that **do his commandments**, that they may have right to the tree of life, and may enter in through the gates into the city."

Revelation 22:14 proves again that God's commandments are eternal and we must be obedient to ALL of them, including the seventh-day Sabbath, through the power of Jesus Christ. It also proves that Jesus never abolished His holy Ten Commandments. The blessing only comes through obedience to God's Commandments.

Friends, God's truth of His holy seventh-day Sabbath can no longer be forgotten, ignored, or rejected. God is appealing to your heart to be faithful to ALL of His Word. The Ten Commandments of God is not a buffet, we cannot pick and choose what we like or don't like. The Ten Commandments are a delicious meal all by itself which includes the most delightful dessert, the holy seventh-day Sabbath. Eat it. You will be greatly blessed by God.

Did Jesus come to change or abolish His commandments, especially the seventh-day Sabbath command?

Matthew 5:17, 18

17 "**Think not that I am come to destroy the law**, or the prophets: **I am not come to destroy**, but to fulfil.

18 For verily I say unto you, Till heaven and earth pass, one jot or one tittle shall in no wise pass from the law, till all be fulfilled."

Malachi 3:6 - "For I am the LORD, I change not."

Psalm 19:7 says, "The law of the LORD *is* perfect." Why would Jesus come to get rid of or abolish a perfect law? Do you think Jesus would want to destroy His perfect Ten Commandments which promotes a loving relationship between us and God, and a loving relationship with others? The Ten Commandments promote a healthy society. They promote a society to keep God first in all things. The commandments recognize God as our Creator and Lord of the seventh-day Sabbath. The Ten Commandments of God promote a crime free society. They promote an honest and truthful society. Jesus did not come to destroy His law and get rid of His holy Sabbath, but He came to give us a better understanding of it.

NO SABBATH CHANGE TO SUNDAY

Even though the majority of the Christian world goes to church on Sunday, Jesus did not change the seventh-day Sabbath to the first day of the week. Referring to the seventh-day Sabbath rest, **Hebrews 4:8, 9** makes it plain, [8]"For if Jesus had given them rest, then would he not afterward have spoken of another day. [9]There remaineth therefore a rest to the people of God."

Does the Bible teach to keep Sunday holy in honor of the resurrection?

No. God did not give us a day to commemorate His resurrection. He gave us the solemn service of baptism. According to Romans 6:3-5, baptism by immersion commemorates the death, burial, and resurrection of Jesus Christ.

Romans 6:3-5

3 "Know ye not, that so many of us as were baptized into Jesus Christ were baptized into his death?

4 Therefore we are buried with him by baptism into death: that like as Christ was raised up from the dead by the glory of the Father, even so we also should walk in newness of life.

5 For if we have been planted together in the likeness of his death, we shall be also in the likeness of his resurrection."

MISAPPLIED TEXTS

Even though the Bible reveals several texts from Genesis to Revelation concerning the seventh-day Sabbath, there are some people who ignore this evidence and misapply Bible scriptures to try to prove that the seventh-day Sabbath changed to Sunday. Let's briefly take a look at these misapplied texts and get a clear understanding of their context. The texts in question are **Acts 20:7**, **1 Corinthians 16:1, 2**, and **Revelation 1:10**. Let's first look at Acts 20:7.

Acts 20:7 - "And upon the first day of the week, when the disciples came together to break bread, Paul preached unto them, ready to depart on the morrow; and continued his speech until midnight."

Some people, based on Acts 20:7, assume that Paul and the disciples are having a Sunday "sabbath" church service, but the Sabbath is not mentioned at all in the text nor in passages before or after it. The passages of scriptures before and after Acts 20:7 put everything into context so we can get a clearer understanding. Read **Acts 20:1-13**. It is clear that Paul was on a missionary journey from city to city. He and those traveling with him stopped in Troas for seven days. It has been already established in this study that the apostles and the New Testament Christians kept the seventh-day Sabbath holy. It is clear that a day begins in the evening according to Genesis chapter 1. In Acts 20:7 the seventh-day Sabbath ended at sunset and the first day of the week began. From sunset that night Paul continued to preach "until midnight." Verse 8 confirms that it was evening because it says "there were many lights in the upper chamber, where they were gathered together." Paul planned to depart on the "morrow" or the day following. The "morrow" would be Sunday morning and it was on that day that Paul took his journey. This text actually refutes the first day as the Sabbath because Paul would not have taken such a long journey on the holy Sabbath.

The main reason why this meeting was recorded was not to show that there was a change of the Sabbath, but to tell us about the miracle that happened after a young man died and was brought back to life through the power of God after falling asleep and falling out of a third story window in the upper room where Paul was preaching.

Now let's briefly look at 1 Corinthians 16:1, 2

1 Corinthians 16:1, 2
1 "Now concerning the collection for the saints, as I have given order to the churches of Galatia, even so do ye.
2 Upon the first day of the week let every one of you lay by him in store, as God hath prospered him, that there be no gatherings when I come."

Again, in this text the word "Sabbath" is not used or implied. Paul was simply taking care of the business of the collection and distribution of goods and it was done on the first day of the week. It was not uncommon for the New Testament church to sell their possessions and collect their goods to distribute to others who had need. In **Acts 2:44, 45** it says, [44]"And all that believed were together, and had all things common; [45]And sold their possessions and goods, and parted them to all men, as every man had need." Also **Acts 4:37** says, "Having land, sold it, and brought the money, and laid it at the apostles' feet." This shows that there were organized times that they brought those things together to the apostles so they could be distributed.

Now let's briefly look at Revelation 1:10.

Revelation 1:10 - "I was in the Spirit on **the Lord's day**, and heard behind me a great voice, as of a trumpet."

This was the disciple John describing a vision he had on "the Lord's day" in Revelation chapter 1. The first day, Sunday, is not even mentioned in the text nor any of the texts around it. To understand which day is "the Lord's day" the Lord Himself makes it very clear in the Ten Commandments. In Exodus 20:10 He says, "But the **seventh day is the sabbath of the LORD** thy God..." That's very clear. The "Lord's day" is the seventh-day Sabbath. So God gave John a vision on the seventh-day Sabbath. Let's continue to study.

CHAPTER 3
WHAT WAS NAILED?

Did Jesus nail the law and the Sabbath to the cross when He died based on Colossians 2:14 & 16?

There are many who misapply this passage of scripture to try to prove that Jesus abolished or "nailed" His Ten Commandments to the cross including the seventh-day Sabbath. Let's look at this and get Biblical clarity.

Colossians 2:14, 16 - "¹⁴Blotting out the handwriting of ordinances that was against us, which was contrary to us, and took it out of the way, nailing it to his cross; ¹⁶Let no man therefore judge you in meat, or in drink, or in respect of an holyday, or of the new moon, or of the sabbath *days*."

It is clear that a law was "nailed to the cross" or abolished at the death of Jesus but it was not God's Ten Commandments. Think about it, if Jesus did not come to destroy the law, He also did not "nail" His holy Ten Commandments to the cross. So what law was "nailed"?

Colossians 2:14 says, "Blotting out the handwriting of ordinances that was against us." Do you think God's Ten Commandments are against us?

1 John 5:2, 3
2 "By this we know that we love the children of God, when we love God, and keep his commandments.
3 For this is the love of God, that we keep his commandments: and his commandments are not grievous."

God's Ten Commandments are not against us, they are for us. Remember they teach us how to practically love God and others. What is truly "against us" is sin! The payment for sin is eternal death!

What were the "handwriting of ordinances that was against us"?

Referring to the "handwriting of ordinances," **Colossians 2:17** says, "Which are a **shadow of things to come**; but the **body is of Christ**." "Ordinances" in Greek is "dogma" which means a civil, ceremonial, or ecclesiastical laws or degrees according to Strong's Greek Dictionary. The "handwriting of ordinances" in Colossians 2:17 is referring to the ceremonial laws of the Old Testament that pointed to the ministry of Jesus Christ in the New Testament.

In Exodus 25:8, God instructed Moses to build a sanctuary in the wilderness for the Israelites on their way to the Canaan land. God gave Moses specific instructions on how to build the sanctuary and what specific services and feast days that were to be associated with the sanctuary which is found in Exodus chapters 25-30 and the book of Leviticus. Because these instructions were written by the hand of Moses they were known as the law of Moses. They were also known as the ceremonial laws, or the law of ordinances.

In summary, the building, furniture, and many items in the sanctuary and its ceremonial services, including the feast days, were symbolic lessons of the plan of salvation that pointed to the ministry of Jesus Christ on earth and in Heaven. According to Hebrews 8:5, this earthly sanctuary that Moses built was a miniature model of the Heavenly sanctuary. **Hebrews 10:1** refers to these ceremonial laws as "a shadow of good things to come, and not the very image of the things, can never with those sacrifices which they offered year by year continually make the comers thereunto perfect." This is in perfect harmony with Colossians 2:17.

For example, the ceremonial laws instructed those who wanted forgiveness of sin to bring a sin offering to the sanctuary such as a lamb without blemish. Each time that sin offering was made on the altar in the sanctuary, it pointed to the prophecy and ministry of Jesus who would die for the sins of the world. John the Baptist revealed that Jesus is the fulfillment of the sin offering that was made in the sanctuary. He says in **John 1:29**, "The next day John seeth Jesus coming unto him, and saith, **Behold the Lamb of God**, which taketh away the sin of the world." Also, **1 Peter 1:18, 19** says, [18]"Forasmuch as ye know that ye were not redeemed with corruptible things, as silver and gold, from your vain conversation received by tradition from your fathers; [19]But with the precious blood of Christ, as of a lamb without blemish and without spot." Hebrews chapter 9 confirms that all the animal sacrifices that were associated with the earthly sanctuary were fulfilled through Jesus when he spilled His blood on the cross of Calvary. This is why we don't have to do animal sacrifices today. They were fulfilled, or "nailed to the cross."

But why were the handwriting of ordinances "against us"? Think about it. Every time an animal sin offering was killed it was a witness or evidence against the offender that it was his or her sins that killed an innocent animal. This was the "handwriting of ordinances that was against us, which was contrary to us" according to Colossians 2:14. But praise God,

these sacrificial ordinances were blotted out and "nailed to the cross" of
Jesus Christ. Hebrews chapters 9 and 10 make it clear that it was not the
animal sacrifices associated with the sanctuary that cleansed man from sin.
Hebrews 10:4 says, "For it is not possible that the blood of bulls and of goats
should take away sins." Think about it. If Jesus Christ did not die for our
sins, the killing of lambs in the sanctuary service would have been worthless.
The innocent blood of the animals would still be a witness against the
offender. They would still be in sin and would suffer the penalty of eternal
death as a result.

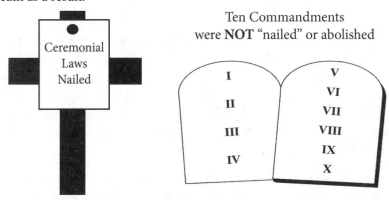

Now, let's briefly look at **Colossians 2:16**. It says, [16]"Let no man therefore
judge you in meat, or in drink, or in respect of an holyday, or of the new
moon, or of the sabbath *days*." Since this is within the same context of
Colossians 2:14, this is also referring to the law of ordinances "nailed to the
cross." The holy days and the sabbaths days mentioned in verse 16 are not
referring to the weekly holy seventh-day Sabbath that God established at
Creation. Remember, the Hebrew word "sabbath" simply means rest. The
"sabbath days" spoken of in Colossians 2:16, were ceremonial rest days or
sabbaths for the people to rest and not work on those days. The ceremonial
holy days or feast days did not necessarily fall on the seventh day of the week
for each ceremony or celebration. For example, the Day of Atonement was
on the seventh month and tenth-day every year. It was commemorated on
the same date each year which could fall on any day of the week, like your
birthday. That feast was a "holy day" or a sabbath rest day in which no
one worked. Referring to the Day of Atonement as a ceremonial sabbath,
Leviticus 16:30, 31 says, [30]"For on that day shall the priest make an
atonement for you, to cleanse you, that ye may be clean from all your sins
before the LORD. [31]It shall be a sabbath of rest unto you, and ye shall afflict
your souls, by a statute for ever."

The Jewish Christians believed that the converted Gentile Christians should keep the feast days, ceremonies, and holy days that were connected to the sanctuary. This caused some tension between the two. But Paul cleared up much confusion. Paul made it clear to the Jewish Christians not to judge the Gentile Christians who did not commemorate the feast days or holy days because these were fulfilled in the sacrifice and Heavenly ministry of Christ and that no one was obligated to keep them.

Again, the seventh-day Sabbath commandment is a part of the eternal Ten Commandments and NOT a ceremonial sabbath day. You will find throughout the Old Testament that when God is referring to His holy seventh-day Sabbath that is part of His law, He refers to it as "My Sabbaths". For example **Exodus 31:13** says, "Speak thou also unto the children of Israel, saying, Verily **my sabbaths** ye shall keep: for it *is* a sign between me and you throughout your generations; that *ye* may know that I *am* the LORD that doth sanctify you." And **Ezekiel 20:20** says, "And hallow **my sabbaths**; and they shall be a sign between me and you, that ye may know that I *am* the LORD your God."

Now let's look at an example in the Old Testament when God is referring to the ceremonial sabbaths and not the seventh-day Sabbath of the Ten Commandments. **Leviticus 23:32** says, "It *shall be* unto you a sabbath of rest, and ye shall afflict your souls: in the ninth *day* of the month at even, from even unto even, shall ye celebrate **your sabbath**." This text is only referring to the ceremonial sabbath. Notice at the end of verse 32 God referred to this special ceremonial rest day as "your sabbath." He did not call it "My Sabbath." Why? Because God is referring to the ceremonial sabbath.

What happened in the temple in Israel at the death of Christ that was a sign that the sacrificial ceremonial laws ended at the cross?
Mark 15:37, 38
37 "And Jesus cried with a loud voice, and gave up the ghost.
38 And the veil of the temple was rent in twain from the top to the bottom."

The heavy thick veil that separated the Holy from the Most Holy place in the temple was torn from top to the bottom. Unseen hands from heaven ripped the veil in the temple as a sign that Jesus was the literal fulfillment of the ceremonies and sacrifices that were made in the temple.

Misapplied Text: Romans 14:5
Another misapplied text that people try to use, including ministers, to refute God's seventh-day Sabbath is Romans 14:5. Let's briefly study it.

Romans 14:5 - "One man esteemeth one day above another: another esteemeth every day *alike*. Let every man be fully persuaded in his own mind."

The Greek word "esteemeth" means "distinguish." - Strong's Greek Dictionary. First of all, Romans 14:5 is not referring to God's holy seventh-day Sabbath because it was God that distinguished the Sabbath day for a holy purpose, not man. It is the Lord's day, not man's. God told us to "Remember the Sabbath day, to keep it holy." This is God's command, not a preacher, teacher, pastor, or denomination. Secondly, there is not one reference in Romans 14:5 to the seventh-day Sabbath. Sometimes people misquote the text by saying it says, "<u>Let no man</u> esteem one day above another..." However, that is not what the text says. "Let no man" was added. Thirdly, do you think that Paul who kept the seventh-day Sabbath and who wrote the book of Romans would tell everyone to stop keeping it? If Jesus didn't change it, why would Paul? Fourthly, the church in Rome had the same issue like the church in the book Colossians. In the book of Romans, Paul told the Jewish Christians in Rome that the ceremonial feast days were not necessary to be kept, but let every man be "fully persuaded in his own mind" to keep them or not. He revealed that no feast day after the death of Christ was greater than the other days and that Gentiles nor Jews were obligated to commemorate them.

What does the Bible call Christians who say they love God but do not obey ALL His commandments?

1 John 2:3, 4
3 "And hereby we do know that we know him, if we keep his commandments.
4 He that saith, I know him, and keepeth not his commandments, is a liar, and the truth is not in him."

What does Jesus say about those who teach that we do not have to keep God's seventh day holy?

Matthew 5:19 - "Whosoever therefore shall break one of these least commandments, and shall teach men so, he shall be called the least in the kingdom of heaven: but whosoever shall do and teach *them*, the same shall be called great in the kingdom of heaven."

The Bible does not teach that Jesus changed the seventh-day Sabbath to another day or abolished it. Those who teach that we do not have to keep God's holy Sabbath will be condemned by the law of God that they teach others to reject or ignore.

SECTION TWO:

The Mark of the Beast CRISIS

CHAPTER 4
BE PREPARED AND READY

Thought Questions: If Jesus did not abolish His Ten Commandments nor change His seventh-day Sabbath to another day, why do so many professed Christians worship on Sunday, the first day of the week, instead of the seventh day of the week Saturday? Does it really matter which day of the week we honor and worship God? Does Satan have a counterfeit Sabbath?

The Christian church of Jesus worshiped and kept holy the seventh-day Sabbath. There was no confusion of which day was the Sabbath among Christians. However, what did Satan do to cause confusion and who did he use? The Bible gives us the answers.

In this section of the study, entitled "The Mark of the Beast Crisis," you are going to get answers to the previous thought questions and learn more about why you must be loyal to God's true Sabbath in these last days of Earth's history. You will learn how the Sabbath relates to the "Mark of the Beast" that is revealed in Revelation chapter 14. You will learn the difference between the "Mark of God" and the "Mark of the Beast".

This section of the Bible study will be a very enlightening and powerful study straight from the Word of God. Make sure you sincerely pray and ask God for deeper understanding of His Word before you move on to the next section of the study.

In the mark of the beast crisis, Satan as a snake moves almost without notice to deceive billions of people to reject God's truth and embrace his destructive lies. In **John 10:10** Jesus says, "The thief cometh not, but for to steal, and to kill, and to destroy: I am come that they might have life, and that they might have *it* more abundantly." Jesus clearly exposes Satan's main purpose in life. Satan does not care what nationality you are, if you are rich or poor, young, or old. His main objective is to steal your peace and happiness, and to take your life. He wants you lost for eternity with no hope of living with Jesus in the Heavenly kingdom. Jesus Christ came not only to give you life, but to give you a more abundant life that you can get only through Him. This more abundant life is the wonderful gift of salvation that leads to eternal life! This is a promise that you must freely accept and hold on to. God is not a respecter of persons. All, including you, are offered this great gift. Jesus says in **John 3:16, 17**, ¹⁶"For God so loved the world, that he gave his only begotten Son, that whosoever believeth in him should not perish, but have everlasting life. [17] For God sent not his Son into the world to condemn the world; but that the world through him might be saved." Will you take this gift of eternal life? Hold on to it tightly! Don't let Satan steal this gift from you with his deceptions, lies, and threats. Time is extremely short. The mark of the beast crisis is upon us!

What amazing promise is given to those who believe and live by EVERY WORD of Jesus Christ?

1 Thessalonians 4:16, 17
16 "For the Lord himself shall descend from heaven with a shout, with the voice of the archangel, and with the trump of God: and the dead in Christ shall rise first:
17 Then we which are alive *and* remain shall be caught up together with them in the clouds, to meet the Lord in the air: and so shall we ever be with the Lord."

Hebrews 9:28 - "So Christ was once offered to bear the sins of many; and unto them that look for him shall he appear the second time without sin unto salvation."

John 14:1-3, 27
1 "Let not your heart be troubled: ye believe in God, believe also in me.
2 In my Father's house are many mansions: if *it were* not *so,* I would have told you. I go to prepare a place for you.
3 And if I go and prepare a place for you, I will come again, and receive you unto myself; that where I am, *there* ye may be also.
27 Peace I leave with you, my peace I give unto you: not as the world giveth, give I unto you. Let not your heart be troubled, neither let it be afraid."

James 5:7-8
7 "Be patient therefore, brethren, unto the coming of the Lord. Behold, the husbandman waiteth for the precious fruit of the earth, and hath long patience for it, until he receive the early and latter rain.
8 Be ye also patient; stablish your hearts: for the coming of the Lord draweth nigh."

Jesus will fulfill His promise. He is coming again soon to take His faithful ones to live with Him throughout the ceaseless time of eternity. Sin will be no more; "affliction shall not rise up the second time" according to Nahum 1:9. There will be no more pain, misery, or death! Please, don't let Satan steal this away from you! Hold on to God's truth and salvation. Hold on and don't let go! Even though the mark of the beast crisis is upon us and this world is about to experience a time of trouble such as never was since there was a nation, Jesus is telling His people, "Don't be troubled and stressed out, remember the promise, I am coming again to receive you unto Myself. Be prepared." **You must be prepared and ready.** You don't have to be caught off guard. **This study is designed to reveal the truth of the seventh-day Sabbath and its importance, and to prepare you for the mark of the beast crisis.**

<u>What does Jesus instruct you to do to be prepared for His second coming and not swept away by the mark of the beast crisis and the time of trouble?</u>

Luke 21:33-36
33 "Heaven and earth shall pass away: but my words shall not pass away.
34 And take heed to yourselves, lest at any time your hearts be overcharged with surfeiting, and drunkenness, and cares of this life, and *so* that day come upon you unawares.
35 For as a snare shall it come on all them that dwell on the face of the whole earth.
36 **Watch** ye therefore, and **pray always**, that ye may be accounted worthy to escape all these things that shall come to pass, and to stand before the Son of man."

Matthew 24:42-44
42 "**<u>Watch</u>** therefore: for ye know not what hour your Lord doth come.
43 But know this, that if the goodman of the house had known in what watch the thief would come, he would have watched, and would not have suffered his house to be broken up.
44 Therefore be ye also ready: for in such an hour as ye think not the Son of man cometh."

Matthew 25:13 - "**<u>Watch</u>** therefore, for ye know neither the day nor the hour wherein the Son of man cometh."

Mark 13:33 - "Take ye heed, **<u>watch</u>** and **<u>pray</u>**: for ye know not when the time is."

Mark 13:35-37
35 "**Watch** ye therefore: for ye know not when the master of the house cometh, at even, or at midnight, or at the cockcrowing, or in the morning:
36 Lest coming suddenly he find you sleeping.
37 And what I say unto you I say unto all, **Watch**."

Watch, watch, watch, pray, pray, pray, and be ready. This is Jesus' urgent plea to His people. The Greek word for "watch" means to "keep awake" according to the Strong's Greek Dictionary. We all must take heed to this urgent call from Jesus Himself. We cannot afford for one moment to be asleep spiritually. It is by continuing in Christ by prayer, studying of God's Word and Bible prophecies, and obeying and sharing His Word that keeps you awake. This is not the time to be drunk with the cares, worries, and deceptions of Satan in this life. Satan is serving a cocktail mixture of truth and error to the whole world that is designed to make all people drunk and sleepy. Are you sleep?

If you are sleep, spiritually, what is the Bible telling you to do now?

Romans 13:11-14
11 "And that, knowing the time, that now *it is* high time to **awake out of sleep**: for now *is* our salvation nearer than when we believed.
12 The night is far spent, the day is at hand: let us therefore cast off the works of darkness, and let us put on the armour of light.
13 Let us walk honestly, as in the day; not in rioting and drunkenness, not in chambering [cohabitation] and wantonness [out of control, lust], not in strife and envying.
14 But put ye on the Lord Jesus Christ, and make not provision for the flesh, to *fulfil* the lusts *thereof.*"

It's time to wake up, watch, pray, and study God's Word so you can be ready. This is not the time to waste in useless entertainment and activities. We must fight, fight, fight with the mighty arm of God. You cannot stay awake in this spiritual battle against Satan unless you have let go of every sin and sinful activities. You MUST cast off the works of darkness and put on the whole armor of Jesus Christ in order to fight and have total victory over sin. **Ephesians 6:11–13** says, [11]"Put on the whole armour of God, that ye may be able to stand against the wiles of the devil. [12] For we wrestle not against flesh and blood, but against principalities, against powers, against the rulers of the darkness of this world, against spiritual wickedness in high *places.* [13]

Wherefore take unto you the whole armor of God, that ye may be able to withstand in the evil day, and having done all, to stand." The "wiles of the devil" are Satan's deceptions that he will constantly throw at you. If you fail to have the whole armor on; the belt of truth, shield of faith, breastplate of righteousness, gospel shoes of peace, helmet of salvation, the sword of God's Word, and praying always according to **Ephesians 6:14-18**, it will literally be impossible for you to make it through the final crisis. You will be swept away by Satan's cunning devises. The Word of God and prayer are the only offensive weapons that you can use to aggressively fight against the Devil. It's study and prayer time. It's time to pray and study God's Word like you never studied it before. We are living in a time where you need to cancel all your worldly entertainments, cable, movies, and satellite dish channels and spend more time in prayer and God's Word.

As you continue in this study, continually pray that the Holy Spirit will lead you to all Bible truth and give you understanding of His Word and the mark of the beast crisis. The mark of the beast crisis is right upon us and many do not even know what it is even though the Bible speaks about it. Are you ready?

The true seventh-day Sabbath that was established by God at Creation points to the true Creator and Savior, Jesus Christ. It reveals true worship and exposes false worship. Satan hates all the truths of God's Word, especially the commandments of God and even more specifically the seventh-day Sabbath. Continue to study.

Are you prepared & ready?

CHAPTER 5
WARNING & DETECTOR OF TRUTH!

W**hat warning does Jesus give His faithful people in the last days concerning the Devil's hatred?**

Revelation 12:12 - "...Woe to the inhabiters of the earth and of the sea! for the devil is come down unto you, having great wrath, because he knoweth that he hath but a short time."

The Devil, also known as Satan, knows that his days are numbered and that his time will soon come to an end. His goal is to deceive the world away from the worship of the true God of heaven to himself. Satan wants the whole world to be in rebellion against God and be lost.

What will Satan do to the faithful people of God in the last days who keep ALL the commandments of God, including the seventh-day Sabbath?

Revelation 12:17 - "And the dragon was wroth with the woman, and went to **make war** with the remnant of her seed, which keep the commandments of God, and have the testimony of Jesus Christ."

According to **Revelation 12:9**, the dragon is Satan. The woman represents God's true church according to **Isaiah 54:5, 6**; **Ephesians 5:23-32**; and **2 Corinthians 11:2**. "Remnant" means the remaining ones. The remnant in the last days are the ones who are the faithful few who live by ALL the commandments of God and have the testimony of Jesus Christ. They are obedient to God's holy seventh-day Sabbath. Satan hates the remnant with a passion and attacks them with all out war with intense persecution. God's remnant people expose the lies of Satan with the truth of God's Word and their true Christian example.

Remember, truly keeping the seventh-day Sabbath holy reveals who you are loyal to, the God of Heaven by loving and obeying Him, or Satan through the keeping of man's traditions that directly conflict with God's Word. Satan greatly hates the true seventh-day Sabbath and he will intensify his attacks on it and those who keep it as we get closer to the end of time.

What warnings does the Bible give about how Satan will attack God's true worship?

2 Peter 2:1-3
1 "But there were false prophets also among the people, even as there shall be false teachers among you, who privily shall bring in damnable heresies, even denying the Lord that bought them, and bring upon themselves swift destruction.
2 And many shall follow their pernicious ways; by reason of whom the way of truth shall be evil spoken of.
3 And through covetousness shall they with feigned words make merchandise of you: whose judgment now of a long time lingereth not, and their damnation slumbereth not."

Acts 20:29, 30
29 "For I know this, that after my departing shall grievous wolves enter in among you, not sparing the flock.
30 Also of your own selves shall men arise, speaking perverse things, to draw away disciples after them."

Matthew 7:15 - "Beware of false prophets, which come to you in sheep's clothing, but inwardly they are ravening wolves."

Matthew 24:11 - "And many false prophets shall rise, and shall deceive many."

Matthew 24:24 - "For there shall arise false Christs, and false prophets, and shall shew great signs and wonders; insomuch that, if *it were* possible, they shall deceive the very elect."

2 Corinthians 11:13-15
13 "For such *are* false apostles, deceitful workers, transforming themselves into the apostles of Christ.
14 And no marvel; for Satan himself is transformed into an angel of light."
15 Therefore *it is* no great thing if his ministers also be transformed as the ministers of righteousness; whose end shall be according to their works."

Based on all the scriptures you just read, Satan uses professed Christians or religious organizations, claiming to be ministers of Bible truth, to directly attack God's truth including the seventh-day Sabbath. Many hide their true motives to get money, power, and influence, and feed their covetous lust. Many are deceived themselves and are deceiving others as revealed in **2 Timothy 3:13** - **"But evil men and seducers shall wax worse and worse, deceiving, and being deceived."** This has already happened in the past. It is happening now, and will only intensify as we get closer and closer to the end of time. This is the reason why it is critically important that you study the Word of God for yourself so you can distinguish truth from error. A false minister or preacher will not tell you he or she is false! Satan's false ministers are not that obvious. What makes them so deceptive is that they mix truth and error, but God gives us a tool that reveals who is true and who is false, the Holy Bible.

The Holy Bible is the detector of truth and error. 1 John 4:1 says, "Beloved, believe not every spirit, but try [test] the spirits whether they are of God: because many false prophets are gone out into the world." You should NEVER accept any religious doctrine or action unless you first test it based on the Word of God. You do not have to be ignorant in knowing the difference between Bible truth and error. **1 John 4:6** says, "We are of God: he that knoweth God heareth us; he that is not of God heareth not us. Hereby know we the spirit of truth, and the spirit of error." Don't be confused, let the Bible be your truth and error detector.

<u>**What clearly reveals that a minister, church, or ministry is true or false?**</u>

Isaiah 8:20 - "To the **law** and to the **testimony**: if they speak not according to this word, *it is* because *there is* no light in them."

All true ministers, churches, and ministries are obedient to ALL of God's Ten Commandments including the seventh-day Sabbath and have the testimonies of Jesus Christ from Genesis to Revelation. Isaiah 8:20 makes it clear if any minister, church, or ministry does not teach ALL the commandments of God and the testimonies of Jesus they are not true. If anyone claims the righteousness of Christ but rejects the seventh-day Sabbath and teach others to reject it also, the Bible says that there is NO LIGHT in them. The Bible has exposed them as false. As you can see, Isaiah 8:20 is a simple, powerful, and text that you want to commit to memory.

<u>**What should you do if you are supporting a minister, or part of a church that the Bible in Isaiah 8:20 exposes as false?**</u>

1 Timothy 6:5 - "Perverse disputings of men of corrupt minds, and **destitute of the truth**, supposing that gain is godliness: from such **withdraw** thyself."

2 Timothy 3:5 - "Having a form of godliness, but denying the power thereof: from such **turn away**."

2 Thessalonians 3:14 - "And if any man obey not our word by this epistle, note that man, and have **no company with him**, that he may be ashamed."

Revelation 18:4 - "And I heard another voice from heaven, saying, **Come out of her**, my people, that ye be not partakers of her sins, and that ye receive not of her plagues."

2 Corinthians 6:14 - "**Be ye not unequally yoked** together with unbelievers: for what fellowship hath righteousness with unrighteousness? and what communion hath light with darkness?"

Amos 3:3 - "Can two walk together, except they be agreed?"

The Bible is straight forward. There is no room for compromise. The Bible reveals that if you are supporting a minister or are a part of a church organization that is not following ALL of God's Word, ALL His commandments including the seventh-day Sabbath, withdraw yourself and support. Pray and find a minister or church group that is following ALL of God's Word, His Ten Commandments, and seventh-day Sabbath. Why is this critical? Your salvation depends on it. If you follow those who are blind with no light, what does that make you? Blind with no light. Jesus says in **Luke 6:39**, "And he spake a parable unto them, Can the blind lead the blind? shall they not both fall into the ditch?" The blind cannot lead the blind without falling.

If you truly are loyal to God, how must you worship Him?

John 4:23, 24
23 "But the hour cometh, and now is, when the true worshippers shall worship the Father in spirit and in truth: for the Father seeketh such to worship him.
24 God *is* a Spirit: and they that worship him must worship *him* in **spirit and in truth**."

Psalm 119:151 - "Thou *art* near, O LORD; and <u>**all thy commandments** *are* **truth**</u>."

John 16:13 - "Howbeit when he, the Spirit of truth, is come, **he will guide you into all truth**: for he shall not speak of himself; but whatsoever he shall hear, that shall he speak: and he will shew you things to come."

The Holy Spirit will guide us into ALL truth. He will guide us to God's commandments because they are true. Those who truly worship God must keep ALL the commandments of God, including the seventh-day Sabbath! If you are not, you are not worshiping God in truth. **1 John 3:18** says, "My little children, let us not love in word, neither in tongue; but in deed and in truth." Talk is cheap, but action is gold. **1 John 2:4** says, "He that saith, I know him, and keepeth not his commandments, is a liar, and the truth is not in him."

Remember what **Revelation 22:14** says, "Blessed are they that <u>**do**</u> his commandments, that they may have right to the tree of life, and may enter in through the gates into the city." All those who will enter in the kingdom of God are loyal to Christ and obedient to ALL of His commandments. God will not have disobedience in Heaven. We must learn to obey Him now.

<u>**Who are those who will not make it into the kingdom of God?**</u>

Revelation 22:15 - "For without are dogs [impure mind], and sorcerers, and whoremongers, and murderers, and idolaters, and <u>**whosoever loveth and maketh a lie**</u>."

It is critical that you know the truth for yourself. You need to know the difference between truth and lies, God's true church and Satan's counterfeit church; the true Sabbath and the false sabbath, and true worship and false worship. Let's continue to study.

CHAPTER 6
TRUE VS. FALSE CHURCH

Satan's main goal is to deceive the whole world and lead all to eternal death to be lost forever. Based on what has been studied so far, Satan will use ministers who are connected to a false Christian church organization to deceive many people. Satan has cleverly set up churches who have rejected Bible Truth to teach others to also rejected it. Satan's "religious" ministers claim to be ministers of light and righteousness, but do not keep ALL of God commandments including the seventh-day Sabbath. Nevertheless, God has true ministers in His true church that keep all His commandments. Remember, for everything that God has that is genuine, Satan has counterfeits that closely resemble the genuine. Christ only has one true church. Satan has multiple professors of truth with different opposing views, but all claiming to be a part of Christ's one true church. Again, the Bible is your only detector of who is a part of Christ's one and only true church or not in these last days - period.

You need to be aware of Satan's counterfeits, if you are not you will be a victim of his deceptions. In this study, his false church system and those who follow it will be exposed by the Bible. Also, the mark of the beast crisis will be revealed and what you need to do in order not to receive it. Before that is done let's first look at the one true church of Christ and its standards so you can know the difference between God's true church and Satan's counterfeits.

3 ANGELS' MESSAGE

How does the Bible clearly reveal true worship versus false worship, God's true church versus Satan's false church, the "mark" of God versus the mark of the beast?

This answer can be found in the prophetic book of Revelation. This is not a book to fear, but to embrace and study. **Amos 3:7** says, "Surely the Lord GOD will do nothing, but he revealeth his secret unto his servants the prophets." This is what Revelation is all about. The name "Revelation" means to "be revealed." It reveals the truth of Jesus Christ and exposes the lies and character of Satan. It reveals God's true church and exposes Satan's false church. **Revelation 1:1** begins with these powerful and comforting words, "The Revelation of Jesus Christ." The entire theme of the book centers around Jesus Christ. According to **2 Timothy 3:16**, all of God's prophecies from Genesis to Revelation are "given by inspiration of God, and *is* profitable for doctrine, for reproof, for correction, for instruction in righteousness." **2 Peter 1:20, 21** says, [20]"Knowing this first, that no prophecy of the scripture is of any private interpretation. [21]For the prophecy came not in old time by the will of man: but holy men of God spake *as they were moved* by the Holy Ghost."

In Revelation 14:6-13, God divinely inspired the prophet John, a disciple of Christ, to write down an urgent prophetic message known as the **Three Angels' Message** that clearly contrasts the difference between true worship and false worship, God's true church and Satan's false church, the mark of God and the mark of the beast. The three angels' message will be used as the foundation of this study as we explore and learn more about the mark of the beast crisis. The mark of the beast crisis is ONLY clearly understood by doing a complete study of these powerful messages. Please pray for clear understanding as you continue your study in God's prophetic Word. The Holy Spirit promises that He will lead you to ALL truth.

First Angel's Message

<u>**What is the message of the first angel and how is God's true church revealed?**</u>

Revelation 14:6, 7
6 "And I saw another angel fly in the midst of heaven, having the everlasting gospel to preach unto them that dwell on the earth, and to every nation, and kindred, and tongue, and people,
7 Saying with a loud voice, Fear God, and give glory to him; for the hour of his judgment is come: and worship him that made heaven, and earth, and the sea, and the fountains of waters."

<u>**The First Angel's Message in Revelation 14:6, 7**</u> **reveals true worship that is connected to God's true church.** In this context, "angel" in the Greek is referring to the messengers of God bringing tidings. In verse 6, the messengers of God preach the everlasting gospel of the purpose, work, ministry, example, and promises of Jesus Christ that must go to all the world. Then verse 7 clearly reveals that we must worship the Creator God, the One who made heaven and earth and the sea, in order to abide in God's truth. Remember that keeping God's holy seventh-day Sabbath, truly connects us to our Creator. It is a major part of true worship.

Also, verse 7 reveals that we are to fear God which means to reverence God and that we are living in the time of judgment. Remember, the standard in which we are judged is the Ten Commandments. **2 Corinthians 5:10** says, "For we must all appear before the judgment seat of Christ; that every one may receive the things *done* in *his* body, according to that he hath done, whether *it be* good or bad." Are you ready to stand before the judgment seat of Christ? This does not mean that you will literally stand before Christ as you are being judged. It means that your name will come up before Christ in the judgment that is going on now. Do you think you are ready?

Before we continue to go to the second angel's message let's get more details of Christ's one true church. Pay close attention to this part of the study because it is extremely important.

True One Church – The Genuine

<u>**What was the main theme of Christ's last prayer for His people before He went to the cross of Calvary?**</u>

John 17:1-4, 17-21
1 "These words spake Jesus, and lifted up his eyes to heaven, and said, Father, the hour is come; glorify thy Son, that thy Son also may glorify thee:
2 As thou hast given him power over all flesh, that he should give eternal life to as many as thou hast given him.
3 And this is life eternal, that they might know thee the only true God, and Jesus Christ, whom thou hast sent.
4 I have glorified thee on the earth: I have finished the work which thou gavest me to do.
17 <u>**Sanctify**</u> them through thy **truth**: **thy word is truth**.
18 As thou hast sent me into the world, even so have I also sent them into the world.
19 And for their sakes I sanctify myself, that they also might be sanctified through the **truth**.
20 Neither pray I for these alone, but for them also which shall believe on me through their word;
21 That they all may be one; as thou, Father, *art* in me, and I in thee, that they also may be one in us: that the world may believe that thou hast sent me."

The main theme of Christ prayer for us is being sanctified or made holy through HIS truth. His truth will make His true church one in Christ. God's truth unifies us with Christ and the people of God to live holy and to do the work of Christ. Unity among the believers of Christ is always based on the truth of God's Word. Lies divide and cause confusion and strife. This is how Satan's counterfeit church operates. More on this later.

Jesus is the center of TRUTH that unifies His church. It is not based on status, wealth, or fame. **Colossians 3:11, 14, 15** says, [11]"Where there is neither Greek nor Jew, circumcision nor uncircumcision, Barbarian, Scythian, bond *nor* free: but Christ *is* all, and in all. [14]And above all these things *put on* charity, which is the bond of perfectness. [15]And let the peace of God rule in your hearts, to the which also ye are called in one body; and be ye thankful."

What is the definition of the word "church" in the Greek?

According to Strong's Greek Dictionary, the New Testament word "church" means a "calling out" or assembly. Dictionary.com has multiple definitions of "church" such as "a building for public Christian worship; public worship of God or a religious service in such a building; the whole body of Christian believers; any division of this body professing the same creed and acknowledging the same ecclesiastical authority (a Christian denomination); that part of the whole Christian body, or of a particular denomination, belonging to the same city, country, nation, etc; or a body of Christians worshipping in a particular building or constituting one congregation; or an ecclesiastical organization, power, and affairs, as distinguished from the state." Do these definitions of a "church" automatically reveal that a "church" is a part of God's true church of the Bible? Of course not. A church denomination or group may call themselves a church, but how do you know if they are part of God's true church? The Bible clearly reveals the true church of Christ and its standards and how to be a member of His true church.

How many "churches" does God have?

Ephesians 4:4-6
4 "*There is* one body, and one Spirit, even as ye are called in one hope of your calling;
5 One Lord, one faith, one baptism,
6 One God and Father of all, who *is* above all, and through all, and in you all."

God only has ONE true church, not multiple churches with various opposing views. God only has one TRUTH that is absolute. As long as ANY denomination or church fellowship follows ALL of God's truth, they are a part of God's true church. Likewise, if a denomination or church fellowship does <u>not</u> follow ALL of God's truth, they are not a part of God's true church. It is that simple.

<u>Who is the "ONE BODY" and who is in charge of it?</u>

Ephesians 5:23 - "For the husband is the head of the wife, even as **Christ is the head of the church**: and he is the **saviour of the body**."

Colossians 1:18 - "And he is the head of the **body, the church**: who is the beginning, the firstborn from the dead; that in all *things* he might have the preeminence."

In **John 14:6** Jesus says, "I am the way, the truth, and the life: no man cometh unto the Father, but by me." **The Truth, Jesus Christ, is the head and neck of the ONE BODY, the true church of God!** Jesus moves the entire body! Jesus and only Jesus is the head. The head of God's true church is not the pastor, bishop, church official, or pope, it's Jesus!

<u>Who established God's one true church?</u>

Matthew 16:16-18
16 "And Simon Peter answered and said, Thou art the Christ, the Son of the living God.
17 And Jesus answered and said unto him, Blessed art thou, Simon Barjona: for flesh and blood hath not revealed *it* unto thee, but my Father which is in heaven.
18 And I say also unto thee, That thou art Peter [Greek: Petros=piece of rock / stone], and upon this rock [Greek: Petra = large rock] I will build my church; and the gates of hell shall not prevail against it."

<u>Who is the rock?</u> God the Father. CHRIST is also the Rock, the Word. Peter is not the rock in which the church was built. Peter's name reveals that he is just a small stone or pebble compared to the petra, the large rock that represents God the Father and Christ.

Christ makes a clear distinction between His church and the others. His church is built on the Rock. His church has been established by Christ

Himself. NO man can duplicate or replicate God's true church. It was founded by Jesus Christ! Jesus Christ is in charge! No human being established God's true church and no human being is in charge of it.

What does the Bible call those who are a part of God's one true church?

Romans 12:4, 5
4 "For as we have many members in one body, and all members have not the same office:
5 So we, *being* many, are one body in Christ, and every one members one of another."

Those who are truly a part of God's one true church are known as members of the one body. The word "member" in the Greek means "limb or part of the body." In other words, all who are members are limbs of the spiritual body of Christ, in which He is the head. Those who are a "limb" of the body are submissive to the brain. They are obedient to the brain, the head. Like a physical body, each limb receives the blood that provide oxygen and nourishment for every limb. As a result, they are active and alive. There are NO inactive limbs of the one body of Christ! All limbs of Christ's one body have an important role to play, they all work! Jesus does not have dead inactive limbs on His body that do not receive the blood. Why can't Jesus afford to have inactive limbs on His body? Like a physical body, inactive limbs that don't receive blood will lead to gangrene. Gangrene is a condition in which a limb of the body dies as a result of not receiving blood. If that limb is not cut off, gangrene will spread damaging other limbs. If it is allowed to spread it can kill the entire body. Christ will not allow His one true church to die. He will cut off all inactive limbs to maintain the health of the entire body. A mere profession that you know the truth does not automatically make you a limb in Christ's one true spiritual church. All members, the limbs, must be obedient and in harmony with the Head in order to remain in the body. This includes church denominations, church ministers, pastors, bishops, deacons, and elders.

How does Jesus make the "ONE BODY" concept even clearer?

John 15:1, 2
1 "I am the **true** vine, and my Father is the **husbandman [farmer]**.
2 Every branch in me that **beareth not fruit he taketh away**: and every *branch* that beareth fruit, he **purgeth** it, that it may bring forth more fruit."

Bible Definition: **Purgeth = Cleanse / prune**

In John chapter 15, Jesus equates the one body of Christ to a grape vine with many branches. Like one church body with many limbs, Jesus clearly reveals in John 15:1 that He is the true vine and God the Father is the farmer. In verse 2, Jesus says that every branch that is not bearing fruit will be cut off by God. In other words, Jesus here reemphasizes that there are no inactive members in His one true church. Jesus continues in verse 2 that those branches who are active will bear fruit, but the Farmer cleanses those active branches through the process of pruning so they can grow even more fruit.

How does God cleanse His church?

John 15:3, 4
3 "Now ye are **clean through the word** which I have spoken unto you.
4 **Abide** in me, and I in you. As the branch cannot bear fruit of itself, except it abide in the vine; no more can ye, except ye abide in me."

Bible Definition: **Abide = to stay, endure, or remain**

Those in God's one true church are cleansed through the Word. Who is the Word? **John 1:1 and 14** says, [1] "In the beginning was the Word, and the Word was with God, and the Word was God. [14]And the Word was made flesh, and dwelt among us, (and we beheld his glory, the glory as of the only begotten of the Father,) full of grace and truth." **Jesus is the Word, but you must be in the Word, the Holy Bible, in order to be cleansed by the Word, Jesus Christ.** In order to remain in the one true church of Christ you must remain in Jesus and Jesus will remain in you. You cannot bear fruit without Christ. If you are disconnected from the vine of Christ it is impossible to bear the fruits of Christ.

What is the fruit produced when you remain or abide in the vine of Christ?

Galatians 5:22, 23
22 "But the fruit of the Spirit is love, joy, peace, longsuffering, gentleness, goodness, faith,
23 Meekness, temperance: against such there is no law."

If you remain in the vine (ONE BODY OF CHRIST) who produces the fruit?

John 15:5 - "<u>I am the vine, ye *are* the branches</u>: He that abideth in me, and I in him, the same bringeth forth <u>much fruit</u>: for <u>without me ye can do nothing</u>."

It is Christ that gives you the power and strength to remain in Him, the Truth, daily. **Philippians 2:13** says, "For it is God which worketh in you both to will and to do of *his* good pleasure."

<u>What happens to those who choose by their actions NOT to remain in the true VINE, the ONE BODY OF CHRIST?</u>

John 15:6 - "If a man abide not in me, he is cast forth as a branch, and is withered; and men gather them, and cast them into the fire, and they are burned."

<u>What will Christ, as the head of His church, do if a church assembly refuses to repent?</u>

Revelation 2:5 - "Remember therefore from whence thou art fallen, and repent, and do the first works; or else I will come unto thee quickly, and **will remove thy candlestick** out of his place, except thou repent."

Revelation 2:16 - "Repent; or else I will come unto thee quickly, and will fight against them with the sword of my mouth."

<u>How do you stay or REMAIN connected to the true vine, the one BODY church of Christ, and be a true disciple of Christ?</u>

John 15:7-11
7 "If ye **abide in me**, and my words abide in you, ye shall ask what ye will, and it shall be done unto you.
8 Herein is my Father glorified, that ye bear much fruit; so shall ye be my disciples.
9 As the Father hath loved me, so have I loved you: continue ye in my love.
10 **If ye keep my commandments, ye shall abide in my love**; even as I have kept my Father's commandments, and abide in his love.
11 These things have I spoken unto you, that my joy might remain in you, and *that* your joy might be full."

All those who want to remain in the vine of Christ, His one true church, must reflect the glory of God. The glory of God is the character of God. The character of God are the fruits of the Holy Spirit. As you allow God to work in you, you will produce the fruits of God; you will keep the commandments of God. As you keep the commandments of God, you will remain in the love of God and live a life of joy even in the midst of difficult times.

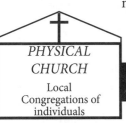

SPIRITUAL CHURCH
ONE HEAD
Jesus

PHYSICAL CHURCH
Local Congregations of individuals

Only faithful & obedient connect to the true church

TRUE CHURCH

ONE BODY

Remember, you cannot be a part of God's true church with just a profession or association. You cannot be voted into God's true church. You must remain in Christ true church daily by faith. ALL those in God's one true church will reflect the character of Christ by keeping all of God's Ten Commandments. This is true love to God and others. They keep the seventh-day Sabbath holy as a memorial of their Creator and Savior. It does not matter what a church assembly or denomination calls themselves. If they are NOT producing the fruits of the Spirit by remaining in Jesus Christ, the Truth, they are not in the one true church of Christ. If they break any of the commandments of God, they are not in the one true church of Christ. If they do not keep the seventh-day Sabbath holy or lightly regard it, they are not in the one true church of Christ.

How pure is Christ's one true church?

Ephesians 5:25-27, 30
25 "Husbands, love your wives, even as Christ also loved the church, and gave himself for it;
26 That he might sanctify and cleanse it with the washing of water by the word,
27 That he might present it to himself a glorious church, **not having spot, or wrinkle, or any such thing; but that it should be holy and without blemish.**
30 For we are members of his body, of his flesh, and of his bones."

Christ's one true church and all the members that abide in His church by faith are pure and holy without spot, wrinkle, or blemish of worldliness and sin - not one taint. They are totally washed by continually abiding in the truth of God's Word. They have severed their relationship with all sinfulness and hold on to Jesus. **Revelation 4:5** says, "And in their mouth was **found no guile [deceit]: for they are without fault before the throne of God**." Are you a member of Christ's one true church by faith? If not, join today.

Detached From The Head

Satan hates God's one true church and the Ten Commandments, especially the seventh-day Sabbath. He hates the Head of the Church and all of His members. Satan has set up a false church system that opposes Jesus and His Commandments. His false church uses a cocktail mixture of truth and error with the philosophies of man to keep people from joining the true body of Christ. Satan also works hard to try to detach members of the true church from Christ, the Head. **Colossians 2:8** says, "Beware lest any man spoil you through philosophy and vain deceit, after the tradition of men, after the rudiments of the world, and not after Christ." "Spoil" in this context means "to lead away from the truth and subject to one's sway" according to the Thayer's Greek Dictionary. Beware! Many are detached from the Head of Christ, because they allowed themselves to be mesmerized and deceived by the philosophies, vanities, and traditions of men rather than holding on to the Truth of God's Word. They become worldly, but still claim to be a part of God's true church. They rely on self and the "human spirit" rather than having faith in God. They have detached themselves from the Head of Christ and become members of Satan's false church system. **Colossians 2:18, 19** warns, [18]"Let no man beguile you of your reward in a voluntary humility and worshipping of angels, intruding into those things which he hath not seen, vainly puffed up by his fleshly mind, [19]And **not holding the Head**, from which all the body by joints and bands having nourishment ministered, and knit together, increaseth with the increase of God." Friends, hold on to the Head, Jesus Christ, and don't let go!

Bible prophecy and history reveals that Satan's false church system has set up a counterfeit weekly sabbath. Who is a part of the false church system? What is its role in the mark of the beast crisis? You need to know. If you are spiritually blind about the mark of the beast and reject God's truth, you will be swept away in the mark of the beast crisis. This is an urgent Bible study. Now that you know what God's true church looks like, let's allow the Bible to expose more about Satan's false church system.

CHAPTER 7
BABYLON IS FALLEN, IS FALLEN

Second Angel's Message

W**hat is the second angel's message that exposes false worship and Satan's false church system?**

Revelation 14:8 - "And there followed another angel, saying, **Babylon is fallen, is fallen**, that great city, because she made all nations drink of the wine of the wrath of her fornication."

The second angel's message in Revelation 14:8 reveals false worship that is connected to Satan's false church system. A very urgent message about the fall of Babylon is given. **Who is Babylon?** Revelation 14:6-11 is a prophetic message that is within the context of the last days. Babylon is not referring to the literal Babylon whose empire fell to the Medo-Persian kingdom in 539 BC as prophesied in Daniel chapter 2 and fulfilled in Daniel chapter 5. After the literal ancient Babylonian kingdom fell it never regained its prominence. Matter of fact, ancient Babylon is a heap of ruins with archaeological evidence of its past. So Revelation 14:8 is referring to Babylon symbolically. The symbol of Babylon is referred to as a woman, "she" as noted in verse 8. In general a woman in Bible prophecy represents either a pure true church of God or an apostate corrupt false church in which Satan stealthily controls. Jesus compares His true church, His woman, to a holy, pure, undefiled, and faithful marriage. **2 Corinthians 11:2** says, "For I am jealous over you with godly jealousy: for I have espoused [married] you to one husband, that I may present *you as* a chaste [pure] virgin to Christ." An apostate and corrupt church is one who has been "sleeping" around, unfaithful to Christ by compromising with sin and worldliness, but still claims to be the "true" church of God. The Bible reveals that sin and worldliness separates us from holiness and righteousness. **1 John 2:15, 16** says, [15]"Love not the world, neither the things *that are* in the world. If any man love the world, the love of the Father is not in him. [16]For all that *is* in the world, the lust of the flesh, and the lust of the eyes, and the pride of life, is not of the Father, but is of the world." When professed people of Christ "fool" around with the world they literally give God a legal separation. **James 4:4** says, "Ye adulterers and adulteresses, know ye not that the **friendship of the world is enmity [hatred]** with God? whosoever therefore will be a friend of the world is the enemy of God." A spiritual adulteress is a perfect description of Babylon.

In **Revelation 17:4-6**, it says, [4]"And the woman was arrayed in purple and scarlet colour, and decked with gold and precious stones and pearls, having a golden cup in her hand full of abominations and filthiness of her fornication: [5]And upon her forehead *was* a name written, MYSTERY, BABYLON THE GREAT, THE MOTHER OF HARLOTS AND ABOMINATIONS OF THE EARTH. [6]And I saw the woman drunken with the blood of the saints, and with the blood of the martyrs of Jesus..." Not only is this Babylonian woman a "filthy" spiritual adulteress, full of abominations, but she is also a murderer of those who are faithful to the truth of Jesus and a part of God's true church. The Babylonian woman hates God's true church with great passion. The name of this woman also reveals the real character of Babylon. Babylon is mysterious and secretive. The name "Babylon the Great" reveals that the corrupt woman spoken of in Revelation chapter 17 is the main leader of Babylon. She is the "Mother of Harlots," implying that she has daughters duplicating herself to spread her abominations and adulteress ways worldwide!

The meaning of the name Babylon is "confusion." This describes the state of mind that all ministers, leaders, and people have who drink the Babylonian "wine of the wrath of her fornication" as revealed in Revelation 14:8. The Babylonian wine is the "adulteress" character and false doctrines of Babylon. Like real alcoholic wine, one sip of Babylonian wine will compromise your spiritual thinking. **Proverbs 20:1** says, "Wine *is* a mocker, strong drink *is* raging: and whosoever is **deceived** thereby is not wise." The more you drink the more spiritually drunk you will become. Also like the real wine, Babylonian wine is extremely addictive to those who drink it because it pleases the "flesh", the sinful and lustful nature of man. Babylonian wine arouses and tickles all the worldly senses, the lust of the flesh, the lust of the eyes, and the pride of life and causes ALL who drink it to compromise God's Word. The more Babylonian wine is consumed, the more people crave it and are overcome by it. The more they drink, the more they become filled with false doctrines which leads them to commit abominations. When they vomit, they spread the contaminating false doctrines to others. Those drunk on Babylonian wine get headaches and hangovers that cause them even more confusion. They remain in a drunken stupor to the spiritual truths of God's Word and will be devoured by the Devil, if they don't sober up! That is why, **2 Peter 5:8** pleads with all in Babylon, "Be sober, be vigilant; because your adversary the devil, as a roaring lion, walketh about, seeking whom he may devour." There is no where in the Bible in which God desires His true followers to be drunk or intoxicated. **1 Peter 1:13** says, "Wherefore gird up the loins of your mind, be sober, and hope to the end for the grace that is to be brought unto you at the revelation of Jesus Christ." In addition to this **1 Peter 4:7** says, "But the end of all things is at hand: be ye therefore sober, and watch unto prayer." Do you see the great need to get sober if you are in Babylon?

There is hope. The only way to break free from the drunken stupor of Babylon is to enroll in a spiritual and Biblical detox program. Jesus, out of His great love, is offering a free Babylonian detoxification program to everyone in Babylon. The only way to truly overcome Babylonian wine through God's power is to stop buying it, drinking it, and socializing around those who drink it. That is why Jesus, in Revelation 14:8, reveals a very urgent last day message to all those in Babylon. The message reveals that Babylon is already in a fallen state. Verse 8 says that Babylon "is fallen, is fallen". The message here repeats the word "fallen" twice not only to reveal the urgency of the message, but also how Babylon fell and its final fate.

The first "fallen" shows that Babylon first fell away from God's truth and compromised with the world. The reason why literal ancient Babylon fell is because they, led by king Belshazzar, rejected the truth of God and embraced rebellion. The prophet Daniel told the story of king Belshazzar in **Daniel 5:22, 23**, [22]"And thou his son, O Belshazzar, hast not humbled thine heart, though thou knewest all this; [23]But hast lifted up thyself against the Lord of heaven; and they have brought the vessels of his house before thee, and thou, and thy lords, thy wives, and thy concubines, have drunk wine in them; and thou hast praised the gods of silver, and gold, of brass, iron, wood, and stone, which see not, nor hear, nor know: and the God in whose hand thy breath *is,* and whose *are* all thy ways, hast thou not glorified." Belshazzar knew the true God. He knew about the true conversion testimony of his grandfather king Nebuchadnezzar; how he was humbled and worshiped the true God of Heaven only. Belshazzar knew all this, but he rejected it. This is the same attitude of symbolical modern day Babylon. The second "fallen" of Revelation 14:8, is the final result of Babylon and all those in Babylon drinking and feasting on her false doctrines.

Babylon is already on "fire" and will soon be totally consumed! The message of Revelation 14:8 is repeated again in Revelation 18:1-4, but with even more urgency before the complete fall of Babylon.

What is that urgent message for all those still in Babylon?

Revelation 18:1-4
1 "And after these things I saw another angel come down from heaven,

having great power; and the earth was lightened with his glory.

2 And he cried mightily with a strong voice, saying, Babylon the great is fallen, is fallen, and is become the habitation of devils, and the hold of every foul spirit, and a cage of every unclean and hateful bird.

3 For all nations have drunk of the wine of the wrath of her fornication, and the kings of the earth have committed fornication with her, and the merchants of the earth are waxed rich through the abundance of her delicacies.

4 And I heard another voice from heaven, saying, **Come out of her, my people**, that ye be not partakers of her sins, and that ye receive not of her plagues."

As we get closer to the end of time Babylon does not get better, it gets worse! It continues its adulteress, corruptible, and abominable ways. Even though those in Babylon claim the name of Jesus, the real true Jesus that created the heavens and the earth is not found there. Those in Babylon are actually serving a false Christ in a false church system full of devils. Even though they teach about "unconditional" love, this is actually a "sentimental" love that excuses and accepts sin and worldliness. Babylonian false love actually loves sin not truth. It excuses the wicked and condemns the true. **Proverbs 17:15** says, "He that justifieth the wicked, and he that condemneth the just, even they both *are* abomination to the LORD." **Isaiah 5:20** continues, "Woe unto them that call evil good, and good evil; that put darkness for light, and light for darkness; that put bitter for sweet, and sweet for bitter!" This is exactly what those in Babylon do. They call good evil and evil good. They call true love of exposing sin hate. They call excusing and allowing sin love. Jesus says in **Revelation 3:19**, "As many as I love, I rebuke and chasten: be zealous therefore, and repent." God in His love reveals sin to us so we will turn from it because there will be no sin in Heaven. If someone was walking backward toward a steep cliff, would it be loving to let that person fall without warning him or her of the danger? No, that is actually hateful. The same is true to excuse and allow others to continue to sin without warning them of its consequence, eternal death, if they don't repent. As a result, Babylon's false love is actually full of hate with leaders and members depicted as "hateful birds" that hate God's truth and those who keep it.

Because of their spiritual drunkenness those in Babylon are led by a false "foul spirit" instead of the Holy Spirit. Many in Babylonian churches believe that its okay to be "drunk" or "slain" in the spirit. This is not the Holy Spirit of the Bible. Jesus says in **John 16:13**, "Howbeit when he, the Spirit of truth, is come, he will guide you into all truth: for he shall not speak of himself; but whatsoever he shall hear, *that* shall he speak: and he will shew you things to come." **The Holy Spirit is all about leading people to truth that will keep them sober. The Holy Spirit leads people out of Babylon into Christ's true church.**

Jesus has sincere people in Babylon who want to know truth for themselves. They study and hear Christ urgently calling them, "Come out of her, my people!" Some obey the call and get out, before it's too late and abide in Christ's one true church. Sadly, many will feel the conviction to come out of Babylon, but they will not obey the call from Jesus because they are afraid of what others may say or do. They would rather trust and respect man's traditions, philosophies, and theories over the Word of God. They would rather please their pastor, family, or church than the Truth revealed in the Bible. It's time to take a personal inventory of your life. What is Jesus calling you to do?

In Summary of Babylon: **Babylon symbolically represents Satan's false church system** in which Revelation chapter 17 reveals is a "mother" with "daughters." Specifically, the mother and the daughters of Babylon will be clearly revealed by the Bible later in this study. However, how do you know if you are in Babylon? In general, **Babylon is a false church system that is filled with confusion by mixing the holy with the profane**; truth with error; righteousness with sin; humility with pride; and godliness with worldliness. Let's make it more practical. Churches in Babylon mix the devil's worldly rhythm of rebellion such as hip hop, rock, rap, jazz, and R&B with the gospel and call it Gospel Hip Hop, Gospel Rock, Gospel Rap, Gospel Jazz, or Gospel R&B. They mix the filth and demonic doctrines of Hollywood with the gospel and call it "Christian entertainment." They mix the worldly pagan dances of ballet, hip hop, etc. with the gospel and call it "praise dance." By the way, who are they truly praising? They take the pagan entertainment of miming with the gospel and call it "gospel miming." Did you know that the pagans used miming to mock Christians? Now it is performed in many "Christian" churches. Babylonian churches take the pagan craft of puppets and ventriloquism mix it with the gospel and call it "gospel ventriloquism or puppetry." They eat the disease causing worldly lustful diet and pray over it hoping for healing and vitality. They are deceiving themselves and deceiving others. They allow themselves to be mesmerized by the world but still claim godliness. They love lustful pleasure more than doing the things of God. There are more people at a fish fry, card night, pool party, movie night, church Super Bowl night, gospel prom, and the church picnic, then at a truth filled Bible study. This is confusion, mixing the world with the church! This is Babylon. Babylon pleases the sinful flesh. **1 Corinthians 10:21 says,** "Ye cannot drink the cup of the Lord, and the cup of devils: ye cannot be partakers of the Lord's table, and of the table of devils." The Bible appeals for us to choose. **Joshua 24:15** says, "And if it seem evil unto you to serve the LORD, choose you this day whom ye will serve; whether the gods which your fathers served that were on the other side of the flood, or the gods of the Amorites, in whose land ye dwell: but as for me and my house, we will serve the LORD." Do you choose to obey the Lord?

Those in Babylon have a "form of godliness" but deny the power of ALL the truths of God's Word, such as God's Ten Commandments. Many treat God's Word like a buffet, they choose only the things that please them. God's Word is a full course meal all by itself. We must eat all of it. Those in Babylon either reject the Ten Commandments all together or believe in some of them. **The main thing that all in Babylon have in common is that they reject or lightly esteem God's holy seventh-day Sabbath.** This rejection of the seventh-day Sabbath truth is a key revelation that exposes Babylon! We will see more proof of this from the Bible as we continue our study. Does this sound like a church assembly or organization that you are a part of? Is God convicting you of truth? Are you in Babylon? Get out before it's too late! Even if your church meets on the seventh-day Sabbath, but it is drinking the wine of Babylon as described above, you better get out because they will soon be in full partnership with Babylon! Think about it. You cannot drink Babylonian wine and expect not to become Babylonian. There is no middle ground. When error is added to truth its total sum is error. In order for truth to remain truth not even a pinch of error can be added. Babylon not only represents all apostate fallen churches that abandon their loyalty to God, but it also includes all false non-Christian religions, such as new age, evolution, humanism, and pop-culture. More details on this later.

What are those in Christ's one true church doing in the last days?

2 Timothy 4:2-5
2 "**Preach the word**; be instant in season, out of season; reprove, rebuke, exhort with all longsuffering and doctrine.
3 For the time will come when they will not endure sound doctrine; but after their own lusts shall they heap to themselves teachers, having itching ears;
4 And they shall turn away *their* ears from the truth, and shall be turned

unto fables.

5 But watch thou in all things, endure afflictions, do the work of an evangelist, make full proof of thy ministry."

With great zeal, faith, and the power of the Holy Spirit the true people of God consistently preach and teach the TRUTH according the Bible even though it may not be popular or accepted by the majority of the world and churches. Even though they are viewed by the world and those in Babylon as extremist they don't flinch, they still give truth. Even though they are persecuted and some killed, they don't back down they still move forward and still give the truth! Even though their relatives, family, and friends reject them, they don't stop; they still give the truth. God's people in these last days have a love for the truth and His Word. They crave God's righteousness and have a great burning need to tell the world of God's Bible truth, straight with no compromise. On the other hand, those who stay in Babylon don't want to hear truth because it pricks the heart and calls to repentance, turning away from sin. They want to hear messages that do not require a full surrender to the will of God. **Babylonians love messages that offer grace, blessings, and eternal life without giving up sinful pleasures.** They only want to hear messages that please their sinful flesh and worldly pleasures. They want to hear from preachers who also indulge in some of the same pleasures they do. They want to feel comfortable wasting countless hours in front of a flat screen watching people run a ball to a line, shooting rubber through a net, acting in a movie, or dancing with the "stars." They want sermons that "tickle" their ears and excuse their selfishness, pride, and vanity. As a result, those who stay in Babylon reject clear Bible truth and continue to drink on the wine of deception.

The following are examples of Bible Truth compared to the excuses that Babylonian ministers and others try to make to refute plain Bible truth.

Bible Truth	Those in Babylon FALSE Excuses & Theories
1 John 5:4 - "For whatsoever is born of God overcometh the world: and this is the victory that overcometh the world, even our faith." **Revelation 3:5** - "He that overcometh, the same shall be clothed in white raiment; and I will not blot out his name out of the book of life, but I will confess his name before my Father, and before his angels."	"It's impossible to overcome sin, it's our nature. It's okay to have some sin in your life as long as you are a good person. Just make sure you keep paying your tithes and offering. You should be alright with God!"

Bible Truth	Those in Babylon FALSE Excuses & Theories
Ephesians 2:8, 9 8 "For by grace are ye saved through faith; and that not of yourselves: it is the gift of God: 9 Not of works, lest any man should boast."	"Our church attendance, shouting, tithing, and gifts to the pastor, hail marys, bead counts, candle vigils, pilgrimages to the holy land should be enough to get me in the kingdom of Heaven!"
John 14:15 - "If ye love me, keep my commandments." **Exodus 20:8-10** 8 "Remember the sabbath day, to keep it holy. 9 Six days shalt thou labour, and do all thy work: 10 But the seventh day is the sabbath of the LORD thy God: in it thou shalt not do any work, thou, nor thy son, nor thy daughter, thy manservant, nor thy maidservant, nor thy cattle, nor thy stranger that is within thy gates."	"The commandments are the old dispensation. Just love each other. Grace is all you need." "The seventh-day Sabbath is for the Jews. We really don't have to keep the old Sabbath. Don't esteem one day above another. The seventh-day Sabbath doesn't matter, keep any day holy."
James 4:4 - "Ye adulterers and adulteresses, know ye not that the friendship of the world is enmity with God? whosoever therefore will be a friend of the world is the enemy of God." **Romans 12:2** - "And be not conformed to this world: but be ye transformed by the renewing of your mind, that ye may prove what is that good, and acceptable, and perfect, will of God." **Psalm 101:3** - "I will set no wicked thing before mine eyes: I hate the work of them that turn aside; it shall not cleave to me."	"We cannot be extreme now. What's wrong with watching a little Hollywood and *Dancing with the Stars*? We pray before we watch the Superbowl? It's the gospel slide not the electric slide. It's gospel hip hop. David danced!" [By the way, David did not do the electric slide, shake, or any worldly dances of our day. David's leaping and whirling was described as a dance but it was not like the dances that have pagan origin. Our only reference point and example of dancing is mainly from the world. This is what is in many churches today. To be safe follow Christ's example. There is not one case in which Christ instructs His disciples to dance.]
Revelation 1:7 - "Behold, he cometh with clouds; and every eye shall see him, and they also which pierced him: and all kindreds of the earth shall wail because of him. Even so, Amen." **Matthew 24:26, 27** 26 "Wherefore if they shall say unto you, Behold, he is in the desert; go not forth: behold, he is in the secret chambers; believe it not. 27 For as the lightning cometh out of the east, and shineth even unto the west; so shall also the coming of the Son of man be."	"The secret rapture of Christ is coming to take us from tribulation. Those "left behind" will go through seven years of tribulation. All the wicked will have a second chance to get it right before Jesus comes again to take them."

Bible Truth	Those in Babylon FALSE Excuses & Theories
Ecclesiastes 9:5, 6 5 "For the living know that they shall die: but the dead know not any thing, neither have they any more a reward; for the memory of them is forgotten. 6 Also their love, and their hatred, and their envy, is now perished; neither have they any more a portion for ever in any thing that is done under the sun." **Psalm 146:4** - "His breath goeth forth, he returneth to his earth; in that very day his thoughts perish." **Psalm 115:17** - "The dead praise not the LORD, neither any that go down into silence." **Acts 2:29** - "Men and brethren, let me freely speak unto you of the patriarch David, that he is both dead and buried, and his sepulchre is with us unto this day." **Acts 2:34** - "For David is not ascended into the heavens." **Daniel 12:2** - "And many of them that sleep in the dust of the earth shall awake, some to everlasting life, and some to shame and everlasting contempt." **1 Thessalonians 4:14-18** 14 For if we believe that Jesus died and rose again, even so them also which sleep in Jesus will God bring with him. 15 For this we say unto you by the word of the Lord, that we which are alive and remain unto the coming of the Lord shall not prevent them which are asleep. 16 For the Lord himself shall descend from heaven with a shout, with the voice of the archangel, and with the trump of God: and the dead in Christ shall rise first. 17 Then we which are alive and remain shall be caught up together with them in the clouds, to meet the Lord in the air: and so shall we ever be with the Lord. 18 Wherefore comfort one another with these words.	"When you die you go straight to heaven or hell." "When you die you continue to live on as a spirit or angel." "When you die you become something else in nature (reincarnated)."

CHAPTER 8
THE BEAST & LITTLE HORN

Third Angel's Message

W**hat is the first part of the message of the third angel that reveals the mark of the beast crisis?**

Revelation 14:9 - "And the third angel followed them, saying with a loud voice, If any man worship the beast and his image, and receive *his* mark in his forehead, or in his hand."

All people worship someone, something, or a belief even if they don't make any profession of religion or worship. For example, atheists worship a belief that there is no god. Evolutionists worship a belief that this world came about through a "big bang." Buddhist worship Buddha. Muslims worship Muhammad. New Age worship spiritualism. And many in between worship "self." The mark of the beast crisis is all about who you worship at the end of time. Do you worship God or Satan, Truth or lies, the Word or man's traditions, Jesus or self? In the end, all those who reject or ignore God's Bible truth, any of God's Ten Commandments including the seventh-day Sabbath, will become by "default" members of Babylon. There is no middle ground. You are either in Christ one true church or Satan's Babylonian church at the end of time.

The Beast, Its Image & The Mark of the Beast

Specifically, who and what does Babylon, the beast, its image, and the mark of the beast represent in the three angel's message?

Since you have a foundational understanding, let's specifically identify Babylon, the beast, its image and the mark of the beast. You need to know so you will not receive the mark of the beast. In the book of Revelation, Babylon, the beast, its image, and the mark of the beast are symbolic imagery that point to reality. Do we have the freedom to guess what each one represents? Absolutely not. Bible prophecy is history told in advanced. You must let the Bible interpret Bible prophecy, but history will confirm its fulfillment and authenticity. The Bible reveals the character of each prophetic symbol in which its fulfillment or identity can be accurately matched to people, things, or events.

Let's first specifically identify the beast. Then we will study the image of the beast and reveal the mark of the beast.

Who is the beast of the third angel's message?

This same symbolic beast spoken about in Revelation chapter 14 is actually introduced in the previous chapter, 13. Here the Bible gives us the characteristic of this beast that can be accurately matched to a real and clearly identifiable system. This is a loaded question with a loaded answer. Dig in God's Word and let's go deeper.

How does the prophet John describe this beast in Revelation chapter 13?

Revelation 13:1, 2
1 "And I stood upon the sand of the sea, and saw **a beast** rise up out of **the sea**, having seven heads and ten horns, and upon his horns ten crowns, and upon his heads the name of blasphemy.
2 And the beast which I saw was like unto a leopard, and his feet were as the feet of a bear, and his mouth as the mouth of a lion: and the dragon gave him his power, and his seat, and great authority."

This description of the beast confirms that the beast of Revelation chapters 13 & 14 is symbolic because there are no beasts in God's literal animal kingdom that have seven heads, ten horns, spots like a leopard, bear's feet,

Revelation 13:1, 2
Leopard-like Beast

and a lion's mouth.

Summary of physical description of leopard-like beast of Revelation 13
- Seven Heads
- Ten Horns with Ten Crowns
- Leopard body
- Feet like bear
- Mouth like a lion

What do beasts in Bible prophecy represent?

To clearly answer this question we must use Revelation's prophetic sister book, Daniel. Note that many prophecies revealed in either books are related and confirm each other. In many cases, comparing prophecies found in both books expand our understanding. Matter of fact, we will see that the beast described in Revelation chapter 13 is directly related to the end time prophecies in Daniel.

In **Daniel 7:2-7**, the prophet Daniel in vision saw four beasts come out of the sea. The first beast was described as a lion with eagle's wings that stood up on two feet. The second was described as a bear with three ribs in his mouth. The third was described as a leopard with four heads and four bird wings. The fourth beast was described as dreadful, terrible, and exceedingly strong with iron teeth and ten horns. You will not find any of these animals at the zoo. The descriptions of the four beasts coming out of the sea in Daniel's vision are symbolic. By the way, when you compare Daniel's description of the four beasts to the leopard-like beast of Revelation chapter 13, you notice that the leopard-like beast has some of the same features as all four beasts in Daniel chapter 7. More on that later. At the end of Daniel chapter 7, Daniel is given the symbolic meaning of what these beasts represent.

Daniel 7:16, 17, & 23
16 "I came near unto one of them that stood by, and asked him the truth of all this. So he told me, and made me know the interpretation of the things.
17 These great beasts, which are four, are **four kings**, which shall arise out of the earth."
23 Thus he said, The fourth beast shall be the **fourth kingdom** upon earth, which shall be diverse from all kingdoms, and shall devour the whole earth, and shall tread it down, and break it in pieces."

Kings are over kingdoms or nations. So, in general, beasts in Bible prophecy are symbolic for kingdoms or nations.

Prophetic Symbol: BEASTS = KINGDOMS / NATIONS

This answers the first clue of the leopard-like beast of Revelation chapter 13: it represents a kingdom or nation. This will be confirmed as we study the other features of the leopard-like beast.

What are the key features of this symbolic leopard-like beast of Revelation chapter 13 and what do they all mean?

Let's look at this prophetic picture of art that Jesus paints and see what is revealed to us based on the clues of Revelation chapter 13. Below is a list of features that we are going to study and analyze in order to unravel the mystery of who is the beast of Revelation chapter 13.

PROPHETIC FEATURES OF THE BEAST

1. Dragon gives him power, seat, and great authority
2. Name of Blasphemy on each head
3. Rise up out of the sea
4. Body like a Leopard, feet like a Bear and mouth like a Lion
5. Seven Heads
6. Ten Horns with Ten Crowns

Let's study these key features in order to accurately identify the leopard-like beast of Revelation chapter 13.

Feature 1: Dragon gives the beast power, seat, and GREAT authority

Who is the Dragon?

Revelation 12:9 - "And the **great dragon** was cast out, that **old serpent**, called **the Devil**, and **Satan**, which deceiveth the whole world: he was cast out into the earth, and his angels were cast out with him."

Satan also known as the Devil is depicted as the great dragon and old serpent. The adjectives "great" and "old" are used to reveal the worldwide size of Satan's reach and his old age on this earth. Satan is that same "old serpent" that deceived Eve in the Garden of Eden almost 6000 years ago (Genesis 3:1-6, 13). Satan has been around for a very long time with a lot of experience developing and implementing his deceptive strategies worldwide. Throughout Bible prophecy when Satan is referred to as a snake, it is pointing to his deceptive character. When Satan is referred to as a dragon, it is pointing to his persecuting character (Revelation 12:13, 17).

So the great dragon that gives the leopard-like beast its power, seat, and great authority is Satan which points to his persecuting character.

Prophetic Symbol: **DRAGON = SATAN / DEVIL**

Below are the "Greek" meanings for power, seat, and great authority:
<u>Definitions</u>
- Power = Force (enforcement)
- Seat = Stately seat which are governmental powers over people
- Great authority = Jurisdiction or territory of rulership with judicial power that is very large or worldwide.

As we already discovered, the leopard-like beast is a kingdom or nation. Satan gives this nation its power, seat, and great authority to enforce its governmental powers as a nation around the world. Since Satan is using his symbol as a dragon, it is obvious that he will use this nation (beast) to persecute God's people.

<u>**Feature 2: Name of Blasphemy on each head**</u>

Blasphemy means slander, wicked speech, or deliberate actions against God. Blasphemy is also applied to humans trying to take on the roles, acts, and privileges of God that only belong to Him. For example, in John 10:31-33 the Jewish leaders falsely charged Jesus for blasphemy because He revealed that He is divine.

John 10:31-33
31 "Then the Jews took up stones again to stone him.
32 Jesus answered them, Many good works have I shewed you from my Father; for which of those works do ye stone me?
33 The Jews answered him, saying, For a good work we stone thee not; but for **blasphemy**; and **because that thou, being a man, makest thyself God**."

The Jewish leaders were wrong in their charge of blasphemy against Jesus, because He is God. **Colossians 2:9** says, "For in him [Christ] dwelleth all the fulness of the Godhead bodily." Even though the Jewish leader's accusation about Jesus were false, they were correct in their definition of blasphemy. Any person that takes on the rights, position, roles, privileges, titles, and worship that only belong to God would be guilty of blasphemy.

On another occasion, Jesus publicly forgave a man from his sins and the Pharisees charged Him of blasphemy again.

Luke 5:20, 21
20 "And when he saw their faith, he said unto him, Man, thy sins are forgiven thee.
21 And the scribes and the Pharisees began to reason, saying, Who is this which speaketh blasphemies? Who can forgive sins, but God alone?"

Again, Jesus is God, so those charges do not apply to Him. Only God can forgive and cleanse us from sin, not man. No man has the power to forgive and cleanse anyone from sin. In addition, according to Webster's Dictionary 1828 series, "Blasphemy is an injury offered to God, by denying that which is due and belonging to him, or attributing to him that which is not agreeable to his nature." So blasphemy is twofold. It is attributing to man the rights that only belong to God and it is also attributing to God things that directly contradict God's character and misrepresent Bible truth.

Notice again that the name of blasphemy is on the heads of the beast of Revelation chapter 13. Behind your forehead is the frontal lobe of the brain. This is where your decisions are made and your character is formed. The name of the beast reveals that its character is blasphemous against God making claims and entitlements that ONLY belong to God.

In summary, the leopard-like beast of Revelation chapters 13 and 14 is a <u>nation</u> and blasphemous <u>religious</u> power, that is empowered by Satan to control and enforce laws on a great territory of people. In other words, the beast has a form of godliness. It is a false church system powered by Satan with religious and governmental power. Let's look at more features of the beast.

<u>**Feature 3: Rise up out of the sea**</u>

What does the sea, a great body of water, represent in Bible prophecy?

Revelation 17:15 "And he saith unto me, The <u>**waters**</u> which thou sawest, where the whore sitteth, are **peoples, and multitudes, and nations, and tongues."**

Prophetic Symbol: SEA = MULTITUDE OF PEOPLE THAT SPEAK MANY LANGUAGES

The leopard-like beast of Revelation chapter 13 rose to power from a territory that has many people and speaks many languages.

Feature 4: Body like a Leopard, feet like a Bear, and mouth like a Lion

These features reveal more about the character and actions of the leopard-like beast.

Leopard's Body
The body of the beast is like the spots of the leopard that can camouflage its deceptive and destructive purposes among people.

Bear's Feet
Bears, especially the polar bears, are known to track and claim large territories. Their feet give off a scent marking their territory. The claws on the feet of a grizzly bear are very intimidating up to 4 inches long! The leopard-like beast of Revelation chapter 13, like the feet of a bear covers large territories; its scent of influence is known everywhere it goes; and its power is very intimidating and destructive like the claws of a grizzly bear.

Lion's Mouth
A lion's roar can be heard up to 5 miles or more. The lion is known as the "king of the jungle" because of his roar and power to kill its prey. Like a mouth of the lion, when the beast of Revelation chapter 13 speaks, its heard by many people. It claims to be the "king" of all, which is another attribute of its blasphemous character. Only Jesus is "King of kings." **Proverbs 28:15** gives us a perfect description of the beast. It says, "*As* a roaring lion, and a ranging bear; *so is* a wicked ruler over the poor people."

The beast who is empowered by Satan has the same characteristics of Satan. Like Satan, the beast is very unassuming, sneaky, and deceptive; covers large territory; is destructive and intimidating; and thinks it is the king over the world.

More Clues and Confirmation

To get more clues and confirmation that the beast is a nation or kingdom
with both governmental and religious authority let's go back to Revelation's
sister book Daniel. In Daniel chapter 7, the same leopard-like beast in
Revelation chapter 13 is depicted as a "little horn" with the same exact
characteristics. In a previous part of this study we summarized Daniel 7:1-7,
now let's read Daniel 7:1-8 in its entirety.

What did Daniel see in Daniel chapter 7 that links to the beast of Revelation 13:1, 2?

Daniel 7:1-8
1 "In the first year of Belshazzar king of Babylon Daniel had a dream and
visions of his head upon his bed: then he wrote the dream, *and* told the sum
of the matters.
2 Daniel spake and said, I saw in my vision by night, and, behold, the four
winds of the heaven strove upon the great sea.
3 And four great beasts came up from the sea, diverse one from another.
4 The first *was* like a lion, and had eagle's wings: I beheld till the wings
thereof were plucked, and it was lifted up from the earth, and made stand
upon the feet as a man, and a man's heart was given to it.
5 And behold another beast, a second, like to a bear, and it raised up itself
on one side, and *it had* three ribs in the mouth of it between the teeth of it:
and they said thus unto it, Arise, devour much flesh.
6 After this I beheld, and lo another, like a leopard, which had upon the
back of it four wings of a fowl; the beast had also four heads; and dominion
was given to it.
7 After this I saw in the night visions, and behold a fourth beast, dreadful
and terrible, and strong exceedingly; and it had great iron teeth: it devoured
and brake in pieces, and stamped the residue with the feet of it: and it *was*
diverse from all the beasts that *were* before it; and it had ten horns.
8 I considered the horns, and, behold, there came up among them another
little horn, before whom there were three of the first horns plucked up by the
roots: and, behold, in this horn *were* eyes like the eyes of man, and a mouth
speaking great things."

Similarities between Revelation 13:1, 2 and Daniel 7:1-8

Now let's compare some similarities between Daniel 7:1-8 and the beast of
Revelation 13:1, 2

Daniel sees **four great beasts come out of the sea** different from one another:

1. Lion with eagle's wings
2. Bear with 3 ribs in its mouth
3. Leopard with four wings and four heads 4
4. A dreadful beast that had 10 horns.
5. Among the 10 horns a little horn grew out of the beast speaking great things.

Remember, **sea or a body of water** in Bible prophecy represent **peoples, multitudes, nations, and tongues.**

The four beasts in Daniel chapter 7 and the beast in Revelation chapter 13 are all kingdoms that rose to power among a body of nations with multitudes of people that speak different languages.

The beast of Revelation chapter 13 is a summarized combination of all four beasts of Daniel chapter 7 in character: the lion, bear, leopard, and dreadful beast with 10 horns. The beast of Revelation chapter 13 is similar. It has a lion's mouth, bear's feet, a leopard's body, and 10 horns.

What do the horns on the "Dreadful Fourth Beast" represent?

Daniel 7:23, 24
23 "Thus he said, The fourth beast shall be the fourth kingdom upon earth, which shall be diverse from all kingdoms, and shall devour the whole earth, and shall tread it down, and break it in pieces.
24 And the **ten horns out of this kingdom are ten kings** *that* shall arise: and another shall rise after them; and he shall be diverse from the first, and he shall subdue three kings."

Like beasts, these horns in Bible prophecy also represent kingdoms or nations.

Prophetic Symbol: HORNS = KINGDOMS / NATIONS

In Daniel 7:8 the little horn that plucks up three of the ten horns on the dreadful fourth beast is a kingdom or nation.

Revelation's Leopard-like Beast & Daniel's Little Horn

This is where it gets very interesting. The little horn in Daniel 7:8 and the beast in Revelation 13:5 have the same exact personality and character. Why? We will see they are actually the same kingdom! Let's compare.

A Mouth Speaking Great Things

In **Daniel 7:8** the little horn on the dreadful beast has "a mouth speaking great things." In **Revelation 13:5** the leopard-like beast also has "a mouth speaking great things." "Great things" in the Hebrew means, "huge" or "domineering." The definition of "domineering" is to force or control the behavior of others as an arrogant bully. Dictionary.com says that domineering means, "inclined to rule arbitrarily or despotically; overbearing; tyrannical." This little horn and beast is a kingdom that rules as a bully monarch that uses tyranny or threats to control the behaviors of all its subjects. The little horn as well as the beast of Revelation chapter 13 represent a kingdom with imperial power.

Blasphemous

In **Daniel 7:25** it says that the little horn, "shall speak *great* words against the most High." The little horn and the beast are both blasphemous against the most High God! In Revelation 13:1 the beast has the name blasphemy on its seven heads and in verse 5 it says that it "blasphemes" with its mouth. Verse 6 says, "And he opened his mouth in blasphemy against God, to blaspheme his name, and his tabernacle, and them that dwell in heaven." Remember blasphemy is claiming the worship, privileges, rights, titles, positions, or roles that only belong to God. Both the beast and the little horn have a blasphemous character claiming the worship, privileges, rights, titles, or roles that only belong to God. Matter of fact, in reference to the whole world, **Revelation 13:4** predicts, "they worshipped the dragon which gave power unto the beast: and they **worshipped the beast**."

War With The Saints

Both the little horn of Daniel 7 and the beast of Revelation 13 make **"war with the saints."** In **Daniel 7:21** the little horn **"made war with the saints, and prevailed against them."** **Daniel 7:25** says that the little horn "shall wear out the saints of the most High." In **Revelation 13:7** the beast also makes "war with the saints." It says, "And it was given unto him to **make war**

with the saints, and to overcome them: and power was given him over all kindreds, and tongues, and nations."

The saints are God's holy and faithful people who truly worship the true God, Creator and Savior Jesus Christ, as revealed in the first angel's message of Revelation 14:6 and 7. They reverence God and worship Him only. They refuse to worship the beast, also known as the little horn, in Daniel chapter 7. As a result, the beast, also known as the little horn, persecutes and kills God's faithful people. The fact that there are people who have remained faithful to God is evidence to the unfaithful that they have no excuse for rejecting the truth. Those who have departed from the faith of God hate the truth and ALL that reveal it and attempt to destroy it. This bitter animosity was displayed by Cain who killed Abel (Genesis 4:3-8) and Joash who killed Zachariah (2 Chronicles 24:18-22). Not only have they "made war with the saints" in the past, but they prophetically "make war with the saints" up to the coming of Jesus.

1260 Years!

Daniel 7:25 reveals how long the little horn reigns as a kingdom and persecute God's people. It says, "...they shall be given into his hand until a time and times and the dividing of time."

In Hebrew, *time* equals one year which is 360 days on the Jewish calendar. *Times* equal two years. *Dividing of time* equals half of a year. Let's add it together.

Time =	1 year	=	360 days
Times =	2 years	=	720 days (360 x 2)
½ Time=	+ ½ year	=	+180 days (360/2)
Total=	**3 ½ years**	=	**1260 days**

Revelation 13:5 also reveals how long the beast reigns as a kingdom and persecute God's people. It says, "...power was given unto him to continue forty *and* two months."

(42 months / 12 months) = 3 ½ years = **1260 days** (360 x 3 ½)

Bible Prophecy: One day = One Year

If the Bible prophecy's context is written in prophetic symbolism the "day =

year" principle <u>must</u> be applied.

Where in the Bible does it confirm that a day equals one year in the context of Bible prophecy?

Ezekiel 4:6 - "And when thou hast accomplished them, lie again on thy right side, and thou shalt bear the iniquity of the house of Judah forty days: **I have appointed thee each day for a year.**"

Numbers 14:34 - "After the number of the days in which ye searched the land, *even* forty days, **each day for a year**, shall ye bear your iniquities, *even* forty years, and ye shall know my breach of promise."

"Each day for a year" principle is only applied to symbolism in the context of Bible prophecy.

So going back to the little horn and the beast, they both reign and persecute God's people for 1260 years!

Little Horn (Daniel 7) = Leopard-like Beast (Revelation 13)

When you put all the characteristics together, it is clear to see that the little horn in Daniel chapter 7 and the beast in Revelation chapter 13 are actually the same bully monarch that had a sovereign kingdom for 1260 years. This sovereign kingdom is also a religious organization that persecutes and kills. This is the same religious-governmental kingdom that the third angel's message warns us about in Revelation 14:9 and 10 that is behind the mark of the beast crisis during the end of time. The "mark of the beast" is a sign of their authority and those who submit to it will receive it.

Remember, when studying Bible prophecy you MUST allow the Bible to be its own interpreter. There is no room for guessing. Guessing will not get you through the mark of the beast crisis. Just taking someone's word for it because he or she has a PhD in religion will keep you in darkness. Study and know for yourself. Those who depend on Hollywood movies to teach them about Bible prophecy and the mark of the beast, will receive the mark. This is the time to cut off Hollywood and the entertainment of the world and embrace the study of God's Word and live it. The mark of the beast crisis is right upon us. How will you know what the mark of the beast is if you do not study? Let's continue on.

CHAPTER 9
DANIEL 2 - HISTORY IN ADVANCE

In this study the Bible has already identified several characteristics that describe this religious-governmental kingdom that is depicted as a little horn in Daniel chapter 7 and the leopard-like beast in Revelation chapters 13 and 14. Before this religious-governmental kingdom is specifically identified, let's first go to Daniel chapter 2 to get more clues about this kingdom.

In Daniel chapter 2, did you know that God predicted the rise and fall of kingdoms that directly affected the people of God even before they came into power? Remember, Bible prophecy is history in advance. But get this, God predicts the rise and fall of these kingdoms until the establishment of His everlasting kingdom in order! This proves the truth and inspiration of the Bible! This brief study on Daniel chapter 2 should build your faith in God and His Word.

Daniel 2 – The Dream

Read **Daniel chapter 2** in its entirety for details. According to **Daniel 1:1, 2**, the kingdom of Babylon, led by King Nebuchadnezzar, was an extremely powerful kingdom that took the people of God captive from Judah. In summary, according to **Daniel 2:1-27**, one night the king had a troubling dream that he knew had meaning, but he could not remember the dream. After his paid magicians, astrologers, and sorcerers were unable to tell him the dream neither its interpretation, King Nebuchadnezzar put out a death decree to kill all his wise men which included God's faithful captives from Judah; Daniel, Hananiah, Mishael, and Azariah. Because of Daniel's faithfulness that was displayed in Daniel chapter 1, God gave Daniel the gift of "understanding in all visions and dreams," according to **Daniel 1:17**. Through the favor of God, Daniel went before the king to request that he would be given time and that he would tell the king the dream and its interpretation. The king honored his request. After a prayer meeting with his three companions of faith, that night God gave Daniel the exact same dream He gave King Nebuchadnezzar and its interpretation. The next day Daniel went before the king and revealed that the God in Heaven told him the dream and its interpretation.

What did Daniel tell the king that clearly reveals that Nebuchadnezzar's dream is prophecy that points to the very end of time?

Daniel 2:28, 29
28 "But there is a God in heaven that revealeth secrets, and maketh known to the king Nebuchadnezzar **what shall be in the latter days.** Thy dream, and the visions of thy head upon thy bed, are these;
29 As for thee, O king, thy thoughts came *into thy mind* upon thy bed, **what should come to pass hereafter**: and he that revealeth secrets maketh known to thee what shall come to pass."

Don't miss it. King Nebuchadnezzar's dream tells us what is going to happen to the very end of time. You need to perk up on this. This is very interesting and exciting. Also God reveals that the prophetic events of the dream "should come to pass hereafter," meaning that prophecy of the dream starts at the time of King Nebuchadnezzar's kingdom and continues forward. The dream does NOT go back in time before King Nebuchadnezzar's Babylonian kingdom. It starts from Babylon and goes forward until the end of time.

Daniel 2 - Metallic Statue

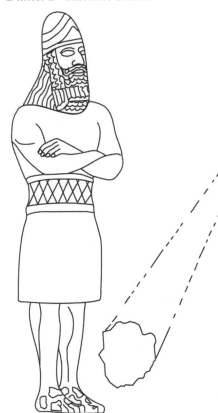

What did Daniel see in the dream?

Daniel 2:31-35
31 "Thou, O king, sawest, and behold a great image. This great image, whose brightness *was* excellent, stood before thee; and the form thereof *was* terrible.
32 This image's head *was* of fine gold, his breast and his arms of silver, his belly and his thighs of brass,
33 His legs of iron, his feet part of iron and part of clay.
34 Thou sawest till that a stone was cut out without hands, which smote the image upon his feet *that were* of iron and clay, and brake them to pieces.
35 Then was the iron, the clay, the brass, the silver, and the gold, broken to pieces together, and became like the chaff of the summer

threshingfloors; and the wind carried them away, that no place was found for them: and the stone that smote the image became a great mountain, and filled the whole earth."

Metallic Statue revealed in Nebuchadnezzar's dream:
1. Head of Gold
2. Chest & Arms of Silver
3. Belly & Thighs of Brass
4. Legs of Iron
5. Feet & 10 Toes of part iron & clay
6. Stone (Everlasting Kingdom)

Daniel 2 – Interpretation

What is the interpretation of the metallic statue; what do the different metals and body parts of the statue represent?

Daniel 2:36-45
36 "This *is* the dream; and we will tell the interpretation thereof before the king.
37 Thou, O king, *art* a king of kings: for the God of heaven hath given thee a kingdom, power, and strength, and glory.
38 And wheresoever the children of men dwell, the beasts of the field and the fowls of the heaven hath he given into thine hand, and hath made thee ruler over them all. Thou *art* this head of gold.
39 And after thee shall arise another kingdom inferior to thee, and another third kingdom of brass, which shall bear rule over all the earth.
40 And the fourth kingdom shall be strong as iron: forasmuch as iron breaketh in pieces and subdueth all *things:* and as iron that breaketh all these, shall it break in pieces and bruise.
41 And whereas thou sawest the feet and toes, part of potters' clay, and part of iron, the kingdom shall be divided; but there shall be in it of the strength of the iron, forasmuch as thou sawest the iron mixed with miry clay.
42 And *as* the toes of the feet *were* part of iron, and part of clay, *so* the kingdom shall be partly strong, and partly broken.
43 And whereas thou sawest iron mixed with miry clay, they shall mingle themselves with the seed of men: but they shall not cleave one to another, even as iron is not mixed with clay.
44 And in the days of these kings shall the God of heaven set up a kingdom, which shall never be destroyed: and the kingdom shall not be left to other

people, *but* it shall break in pieces and consume all these kingdoms, and it shall stand for ever.
45 Forasmuch as thou sawest that the stone was cut out of the mountain without hands, and that it brake in pieces the iron, the brass, the clay, the silver, and the gold; the great God hath made known to the king what shall come to pass hereafter: and the dream *is* certain, and the interpretation thereof sure."

In this interpretation of the dream God is revealing to all the world the rise and fall of kingdoms starting from Babylon until the last everlasting kingdom of God. So each metal or elements on the statue represents the rise and fall of specific kingdoms or nations that have a direct impact on the people of God. Verse 45 repeats verse 29 **"what shall come to pass hereafter"** reemphasizing the fact that the prophecy of the dream starts from the kingdom of Babylon.

Prophetic Symbol: **Metals on Daniel chapter 2 statue = KINGDOMS / NATIONS (Rise & Fall)**

In Daniel chapter 2 God gives us the rise and fall of specific kingdoms in advance. The rise and fall of these kingdoms was prophesied in perfect order. Now, history reveals the accuracy of this prophecy.

The metallic statue of Daniel chapter 2 also tells us how close we are to the end of time and the establishment of God's everlasting kingdom.

What kingdoms are represented on the metallic statue?

What kingdom represents the head of gold? What does Daniel tell king Nebuchadnezzar king of the Babylonian kingdom?

Daniel 2:37, 38
37 "Thou, O king, *art* a king of kings: for the God of heaven hath given thee a kingdom, power, and strength, and glory.
38 And wheresoever the children of men dwell, the beasts of the field and the fowls of the heaven hath he given into thine hand, and hath made thee ruler over them all. Thou *art* this head of gold."

The kingdom of Babylon is the head of gold which rose into power 605 BC and fell in 539 BC.

Prophetic Symbol: **Head of Gold = Babylon (605 to 539 BC)**

What kingdom represents the breast and arms of silver that would arise after Babylon?

In Daniel chapter 8, during the Babylonian reign of King Belshazzar, Nebuchadnezzar's grandson, God prophesied that Babylon would be conquered by a kingdom depicted as a ram with two horns and God gives the name of the kingdom that would conquer Babylon!

Daniel 8:1 - "In the third year of the reign of king Belshazzar a vision appeared unto me, *even unto* me Daniel, after that which appeared unto me at the first."

Daniel 8:20 - "The ram which thou sawest having *two* horns *are* the kings of **Media and Persia**."

The Medes and Persian kingdom conquered Babylon as prophesied in the Bible and confirmed by history. Daniel chapter 5 gives the details of how the Medes and Persian kingdom conquered Babylon.

Daniel 5:28 - "PERES; Thy kingdom is divided, and given to the **Medes and Persians**."

Daniel 5:31 - "And Darius the Median took the kingdom, *being* about threescore and two years old."

The Medes and Persian kingdom represent the chest and arms of silver on the metallic statue. They rose into power in 539 BC and fell in 331 BC.

Prophetic Symbol: **Arms and Chest of Silver = Medes and Persian Kingdom (539 to 331 BC)**

What kingdom represents the belly and thighs of brass that conquered the Medes and Persian kingdom?

In the same vision that the Medes and Persian kingdom was prophetically depicted as a ram with two horns in Daniel chapter 8, it names the kingdom that would conquer the Medes and Persian kingdom. That kingdom is prophetically depicted as a rough goat with a great horn between his eyes that killed the ram with two horns.

Daniel 8:5-7

5 "And as I was considering, behold, an he goat came from the west on the

face of the whole earth, and touched not the ground: and the goat *had* a **notable horn** between his eyes.
6 And he came to the ram that had *two* horns, which I had seen standing before the river, and ran unto him in the fury of his power.
7 And I saw him come close unto the ram, and he was moved with choler against him, and smote the ram, and brake his two horns: and there was no power in the ram to stand before him, but he cast him down to the ground, and stamped upon him: and there was none that could deliver the ram out of his hand."

Daniel 8:21 - "And the rough goat *is* the **king of Grecia**: and the **great horn** that *is* between his eyes *is* the first king."

Bible prophecy is accurate again. Prophecy predicted by name that Greece would conquer the Medes and Persians and history confirms it. The "notable" and "great" horn on the goat is the first king of Greece, Alexander the Great. He is recognized in history as "Great" because of his successful military campaigns. He was the notable king of Greece that conquered over the Media-Persian kingdom as foretold in Bible prophecy!

The Grecian kingdom corresponds with the belly and thighs of brass on the metallic statue. Greece conquered the Medes and Persians in 331 BC and fell in 168 BC.

Prophetic Symbol: **Belly and Thighs of Brass = Grecian Kingdom (331 to 168 BC)**

What kingdom represents the legs of iron on the metallic statue that conquered Greece?

Notice from what you studied thus far that the Bible predicted three kingdoms by name, Babylon, Media-Persia, and Greece. These kingdoms arose in the order as prophesied by Daniel and confirmed by history. So what is the name of the fourth kingdom that conquered Greece? In the Bible, this fourth kingdom was described in detail and we will study those details as we go along in this study. Following the order of the kingdoms on the metallic statue of Daniel chapter 2, the legs of iron is the fourth kingdom that is after Greece. History confirms that the kingdom that arose into power after Greece was the kingdom of Rome, better known as the Roman Empire. The Romans were in power during the ministry of Jesus Christ, the apostles, and throughout the New Testament church. The Roman Empire is also known as Pagan Rome because of the many "pagan" false gods that they worshiped.

Pagan Rome represents the legs of iron of the metallic statue. They conquered Greece in 168 BC and eventually collapsed as a kingdom in 476 AD.

Prophetic Symbol: **Legs of Iron = Pagan Rome (168 BC to 476 AD)**

<u>**Who do the feet of part clay and part iron represent on the metallic statue?**</u>

Pagan Rome was not conquered by a nation or kingdom. Overtime, history reveals that the Roman kingdom grew so large, in the area which is now known as modern Europe, that Rome was not able to successfully manage any rebellion or insurrection within its empire. Tribal faction groups within the empire fought the tyranny of Pagan Rome and was able to establish their own sovereign nations. History also shows that overtime the Roman Empire divided into ten tribal nations. This division into 10 parts perfectly represent the feet with ten toes made of part iron and clay. By the way, the feet of the statue give us more clues of where the religious governmental power of the beast, also known as the little horn, rose up into power.

Below is a list of the ten tribes and modern European nations today. The last three do not exist today. You will learn why later.

10 Tribal Nations	Modern European Nation
Alamanni – Germans	Germany
Burgundians – Swiss	Sweden
Franks – French	France
Lombards – Italians	Italy
Saxons – English	England
Suevi – Portuguese	Portugal
Visigoths – Spanish	Spain
Heruli – Uprooted	N/A
Ostrogoths – Uprooted	N/A
Vandals - Uprooted	N/A

Prophetic Symbol: **Feet with ten toes, part iron and part clay = DIVIDED**

EUROPE (476 AD to present)

Toes of Time!

It has been over 2,600 years since King Nebuchadnezzar's dream of the metallic statue. Where are we in history in relation to the prophecy of Daniel chapter 2? Do any of the first four kingdoms on the statue exist today? Each rose and fell as predicted. Babylon, gone. Media-Persia, gone. Greece, gone. Pagan Rome, gone. The only thing left on the statue is the feet mixed with part iron and clay!

We are in the feet of the prophetic statue of Daniel chapter 2. There are actually three earthly kingdoms that come into focus that are within the feet of the statue of divided Europe. Did you know that two of those kingdoms have already passed? You will see for yourself as you continue to study that we are not only living in the "feet" of time in relation to the prophecy of Daniel chapter 2, but we are living in the "toes" of time! There is only one more earthly kingdom left that will come into power according to the prophecies of Daniel. Who is that kingdom? When will it be formed? Does the last earthly kingdom have anything to do with the mark of the beast crisis? How soon will Jesus set up His everlasting kingdom after the last earthly kingdom is formed? Since the prophecies of God in Daniel have been fulfilled with pinpoint accuracy, don't you think it will be accurate in the future? Jesus is coming extremely soon! Are you ready? Let's learn more straight from the prophetic Word of God!

Daniel's Twelve Chapters

Even though it is not the purpose of this study to give details on the entire book of Daniel, there are some basics about the structure of the book of Daniel that you need to be familiar with before you learn more about the mark of the beast crisis.

There are 12 chapters in the prophetic book of Daniel that are divided into two sections. The first six chapters, Daniel chapters 1 through 6, focus on character lessons that are needed for the last days. Daniel chapter 1 teaches us the lessons of loyalty to God from the story of four young faithful captives from Judah; Daniel, Hananiah, Mishael, and Azariah. They purposed in their heart to serve God and not defile themselves by eating the king's food and drinking the king's wine. Daniel chapter 2 focuses on the importance of prayer, God's power to reveal the future, and the establishment of His everlasting kingdom. Daniel chapter 3 teaches us how to stand for Jesus even when threatened with death through the story of the three Hebrews that were thrown into the fiery furnace. In Daniel chapter 4, we learn lessons of the importance of humility through the testimony of how king Nebuchadnezzar was converted to a true worshiper of God. In Daniel chapter 5 we learn how pride and rejection of God will ruin a nation through the prophetic fulfillment of the fall of Babylon. Daniel chapter 6 re-emphasizes the importance of prayer and true worship to God even when threatened with death. It shows us how to be loyal to God in the face of "lions." The first six chapters of Daniel are very powerful lessons that we all need to read, learn, and apply in our lives in the last days.

The last six chapters of Daniel, 7 through 12, are based on the Daniel chapter 2 prophetic outline of the rise and fall of earthly kingdoms until the establishment of God's eternal kingdom. This is very important. The prophecies of Daniel chapters 7 through 12 repeat some of these same kingdoms revealed in Daniel chapter 2, but give more details of those kingdoms. For example, Daniel chapter 7 reveals more details about the rise and fall of Babylon, Media-Persia, Greece, and Pagan Rome. It also gives us details of a fifth kingdom depicted as a little horn that rises up among the ten horns on the fourth beast which adds more details to the ten toes of the statue of Daniel chapter 2 representing divided Europe. In Daniel chapter 8 it gives more details on the fall of Media-Persia, and the rise and fall of Greece, Pagan Rome, and the fifth empire also depicted as a little horn. Daniel chapters 8 and 9 reveal how close we are to the end of time through a fulfilled prophetic time line that predicts the baptism of Jesus, His death, the end of the Jewish nation's probationary time, and the time of judgment. Daniel chapters 10 and 11 give more details of the kingdom of Media-Persia and its fall. Then as with a magnifying glass, it gives more details of the rise and fall of Greece, Pagan Rome, and Papal Rome. Near the end of Daniel chapters 11 and 12 more details are given of the seventh earthly kingdom and its climatic end. Each prophecy in Daniel chapters 2 and 7-12 of the rise and fall of kingdoms move progressively forward in time. So by time you get to Daniel chapter 12 it does NOT go back in time, it continues to move forward until the end of time.

The next page is a summary of prophetic symbols of Daniel 2, 7, and 8 with its corresponding kingdom.

Summary of prophetic symbols of Daniel 2, 7, and 8 with its corresponding kingdom.

Daniel 2	Daniel 7	Daniel 8	Kingdom
Head of Gold	Lion with eagle's wings	N/A	Babylon [605-539 BC]
Arms & Chest of Silver	Bear with three ribs in mouth	Ram with two horns	Medes and Persian [539-331 BC]
Belly & Thighs of Brass	Leopard with four heads and four wings	He-Goat with a great horn that broke, four horns grew in its place	Greece [331-168 BC]
Legs of Iron	Dreadful Beast	1st Phase Little Horn grows	Pagan Rome [168 BC - 476 AD]
Ten Toes part iron & clay	Ten Horns on Dreadful Beast & Little Horn	2nd Phase Little Horn mature	Divided Europe [476 AD to present]
Stone (Everlasting Kingdom)	Everlasting Kingdom	Prince of princes	God's Everlasting Kingdom

CHAPTER 10
BEAST LITTLE-HORN IDENTIFIED!

At this point in the study you should have a basic understanding of the fulfilled prophecies of the rise and fall of kingdoms in Daniel starting from Babylon. Now let's focus again on the little horn as revealed in Daniel chapters 7 and 8. Remember the little horn in Daniel is the same religious-governmental kingdom depicted as a leopard-like beast in Revelation chapters 13 and 14. This kingdom is the fifth kingdom within the feet of the statue in Daniel chapter 2. In this study we already identified several characteristics of this religious-governmental kingdom. Now let's go ahead and identify exactly who it is? Are you ready for this? Let's look at each clue already identified and match it with historical facts to verify its prophetic fulfillment. Plus, we will look at some more clues from Daniel chapters 7 and 8. (If you need a refresher review Chapter 8: Beast & Little Horn)

Clue 1: Rose up into power from among multitudes of people with many languages (modern European region) & a religious-governmental power

According to history, what kingdom rose into power among many nations with several languages after the fall of Pagan Rome?

History reveals that by 538 AD, Papal Rome, head of the Roman Catholic Church, also became a dominating governmental monarch that ruled a large portion of what used to be the Roman Empire. "Catholic" means "universal." Papal Rome believes they are the head of the "Universal" Church.

By 476 AD much of the western Roman Empire, which is now known as modern Europe, was divided into ten tribal factions or barbarous states (see chart on page 98). These ten divisions represent the ten toes on the statue in Daniel chapter 2 and they also correspond with the ten horns that are on the dreadful fourth beast of Daniel 7:7.

Daniel 7:7 - "After this I saw in the night visions, and behold a fourth beast, dreadful and terrible, and strong exceedingly; and it had great iron teeth: it devoured and brake in pieces, and stamped the residue with the feet of it: and it *was* diverse from all the beasts that *were* before it; and it had **ten horns**."

Remember, this fourth beast represents the Roman Empire. The ten horns on the beast represents the ten divisions of the Roman Empire (western territory - modern Europe) by 476 AD. In Daniel 7:8 and 24 it predicted that the little horn (Papal Rome) would grow out of the Roman Empire and "pluck up" three of the ten tribal states as prophesied in Daniel 7:8 and 24.

Daniel 7:8 - "I considered the horns, and, behold, there came up among them another little horn, before whom there were **three of the first horns plucked up by the roots**: and, behold, in this horn *were* eyes like the eyes of man, and a mouth speaking great things."

Daniel 7:24 - "And the ten horns out of this kingdom *are* ten kings *that* shall arise: and another shall rise after them; and he shall be diverse from the first, and he shall subdue three kings."

History records that Papal Rome, also known as the papacy, deceitfully and with craft took control over the collapsed Roman Empire. As predicted in Daniel 7:7 and 24, the papacy orchestrated the defeat of three of the ten barbarian tribal nations that gave them absolute monarchical governmental power over the former Roman Empire. They cleverly uprooted the Heruli in 493 AD, the Vandals in 534 AD, and the Ostrogoths in 538 AD.

The head of the papacy, known as the pope, was given absolute and "kingly" authority. As the Roman Empire was collapsing, the papacy whose headquarters were established in Rome, had control and a strong grip on the majority of the Christian churches throughout the empire through compromise, bullying, and deceit. Even though the Christian church was in an apostate condition, they had grown steadily throughout the empire with strong political influence.

Many historians credit Roman Emperor Constantine as the one who helped Papal Rome to gain political prominence after his questionable conversion experience to Christianity in 312 AD during the battle of the Milvian Bridge. In 313 AD he made Christianity an official religion of the Roman Empire, led by the papacy. The papacy was also given the right to receive gifts from the citizens of Rome in which Constantine personally donated large sums of money and land that greatly enriched the papacy. What added to the papacy's power was when Constantine relocated the capital of Rome to the eastern part of the Roman Empire, Constantinople, in 330 AD. This move allowed the papacy to fill the political void that Constantine left behind in Rome and to freely operate and grow in the western part of the Roman

Empire. The pope, the leader of the papacy, was not only seen as one with supreme spiritual authority, but also of great political influence.

Below are historical quotes concerning Papal Rome's rise out of the Roman Empire as a religious governmental monarchical power:

"Long ages ago, when Rome through the neglect of the Western emperors was left to the mercy of the barbarous hordes, the Romans turned to one figure for aid and protection, and asked him to rule them; and thus commenced the temporal sovereignty of the popes. And meekly stepping to the throne of Caesar, the vicar of Christ took up the scepter to which the emperors and kings of Europe were to bow in reverence through so many ages." - American Catholic Quarterly Review, April, 1911

"Under the Roman Empire the popes had no temporal powers. But when the Roman Empire had disintegrated and its place had been taken by a number of rude, barbarous kingdoms, the Roman Catholic church not only became independent of the states in religious affairs, but dominated secular affairs as well. At times, under such rulers as Charlemagne (768-814), Otto the Great (936-973), and Henry III (1039-1056), the civil power controlled the church to some extent; but in general, under the weak political system of feudalism, the well-organized, unified, and centralized church, with the pope at its head, was not only independent in ecclesiastical affairs but also controlled civil affairs." - Carl Conrad Eckhardt, The Papacy and World-Affairs, The University of Chicago Press, 1937, p. 1

"The removal of the capital of the Empire from Rome to Constantinople in 330, left the Western Church, practically free from imperial power, to develop its own form of organization. The Bishop of Rome, in the seat of the Caesars, was now the greatest man in the West, and was soon [when the barbarians overran the Empire] forced to become the political as well as the spiritual head." - A.C. Flick, The Rise of the Mediaeval Church, p. 168

Referring to the papacy's rise during the time that the Roman Empire was crumbling around 500 AD, "No, the [Catholic] Church will not descend into the tomb. It will survive the Empire. At length a second empire will arise, and of this empire, the Pope will be the master—more than this, he will be the master of Europe. He will dictate his orders to kings who will obey them." - Andrea Lagarde, The Latin Church in the Middle Ages, 1915 p. vi

Clue 2: Eyes like the eyes of man, and a mouth speaking great things." - (Daniel 7:8 & Revelation 13:5)

Remember, a mouth "speaking great things" refers to a kingdom that is a "domineering" monarchical system that controls the behavior of others as an arrogant bully. At the height of the Roman Empire's power, the emperors were revered as "Pontifex Maximus" which means "Chief bridge builder" or "constructor of ways." They assumed this title "Pontifex Maximus" because they had power as an absolute monarch and head of the pagan religion of Rome. When Papal Rome grew into power the popes assumed the same title of "Pontifex Maximus" as absolute ruler over civil and religious affairs. Their supremacy and power spoke as "a mouth speaking great things" to all under their control. "Eyes like the eyes of man" is referring to the pope as human leader of the papacy who is controlled by man's "wisdom" rather than God's wisdom.

Clue 3: Blasphemous Character

Papal Rome's "mouth speaking great things" not only applies to its civil and religious powers, but it also points to its arrogant and blasphemous character as revealed by the beast in Revelation 13:1, 5 and 6. **Revelation 13:6** says, "And he opened his mouth in blasphemy against God, to blaspheme his name, and his tabernacle, and them that dwell in heaven." Similarly the little horn in **Daniel 7:25** says that "he shall speak *great* words against the most High..." Also **Daniel 8:11** says that "he magnified *himself* even to the prince of the host." The "prince of the host" is Jesus who is also known as the "Prince of peace" in Isaiah 9:6. Remember, blasphemy is any person who claims privileges, rights, titles, positions, or roles that only belong to God. Also, those who misrepresent the character of God are guilty of blasphemy.

The pope and Papal Rome blaspheme God's name by claiming titles, roles, rights, and privileges that ONLY belong to God.

Historical quotes that refer to the blasphemous character of the pope and Papal Rome as the little horn in Daniel 7 & 8 and the leopard-like beast of Revelation 13 & 14:

"The Pope is not only the representative of Jesus Christ, but he is Jesus himself, hidden under the veil of flesh." - The Catholic National 1895

"He is the infallible ruler... the supreme judge of heaven and earth, the judge of all, being judged by no one, God himself on earth." - The New York Catechism (Taken from Roman Catholicism, p. 127)

"We hold upon this earth the place of God Almighty." - Pope Leo XIII, in an Encyclical letter, June 20, 1894

"The pope is supreme judge of the law of the land. He is the vicegerent of Christ, and is not only a priest forever, but also King of kings and Lord of lords." - La Civilta Catholica, March 18, 1871

"All the names which in the Scriptures are applied to Christ, by virtue of which it is established that he is over the church, all the same names are applied to the Pope." - Robert Bellarmine, On the Authority of the Councils, chapter 17, 1628 ed., vol. 1, p. 266

"All the faithful must believe that the Holy Apostolic See and the Roman Pontiff [Pope] possesses the primacy over the whole world, and the Roman Pontiff is the successor of Blessed Peter, Prince of the Apostles, and is true vicar of Christ, and head of the whole church, and father and teacher of all Christians; and that full power was given to him in blessed Peter to rule, feed and govern the universal Church by Jesus Christ Our Lord:" - First Dogmatic Constitution on the Church of Christ, *Eternal Pastor*, published in the fourth session of the Vatican Council, 1870, chap. 3, in Philip Schaff, Creeds of Christendom, vol. 2, p. 262

"In the beautiful expression of St. Ignatius of Antioch, the bishop is *typos tou Patros*: he is like the living image of God the Father." - www.vatican.va/ archive/ccc_css/archive/catechism/p2s2c3a6.htm / St. Ignatius of Antioch, Ad Trall. 3,1:SCh 10,96; cf. Ad Magn. 6,1:SCh 10, pp. 82-84

All these statements are blasphemous! Papal Rome and the pope are literally trying to take the place of God! The pope is not God nor the head of the church, Jesus is the head.

What does Jesus say about church leaders using titles that belong only to God?

Matthew 23:8-10
8 "But be not ye called Rabbi: for one is your Master, *even* Christ; and all ye

are brethren.

9 And call no *man* your father upon the earth: for one is your Father, which is in heaven.

10 Neither be ye called masters: for one is your Master, *even* Christ."

Father in this context is not referring to someone's biological father, but another human being who has elevated himself to the place of God. Using titles that only belong to God is blasphemous.

Blasphemous Titles of the head of the papacy
1) Pope (Italian for "papa" which is an abbreviation of *pater patruum* which means father of fathers or principal father)
2) Most Holy Father
3) Vicar of Christ ("vicar" = a person who acts in place of another; substitute. Dictionary.com)
4) Supreme Pontiff (Latin = Pontifex Maximus = greatest "bridge builder" or "constructor of the way")
5) His Holiness

Blasphemous Titles of the Pope's clergy
1) Reverend
2) Father
3) Monsignor (meaning "my lord")
4) Grand Master
5) His Eminence (Cardinals)

According to the Bible no human being should be given titles that belong only to God such as "Reverend" or "Your Holiness." "Reverend" meaning "worthy to be revered; entitled to reverence." - Dictionary.com "Revered" refers to devotion or worship. Jesus says in **Matthew 4:10**, "Thou shalt worship the Lord thy God, and him only shalt thou serve." No man should be worshiped or revered. **Psalm 111:9** says, "...holy and reverend *is* his [God's] name." No man's name is holy, only God's name. Many who assume titles that only belong to God are trying to assert their authority to try to control the conscience or belief of others. We are all on the same level, brothers and sisters, in the family of God. No one should try to control the conscience of another. God, His Word, and the Holy Spirit should be our only guide for our beliefs and conscience.

Confession of Sins to Priest - Blasphemous

Papal Rome blasphemes God by claiming that the pope and its priests have the power to forgive people from sin. They believe that Jesus gave them the "Sacrament of Reconciliation" also known as Penance or Confession which allows people to confess their sins to a Catholic priest because a priest stands "in Persona Christi" meaning that "he is in the person of Christ." - lifeteen. com/blog/why-do-catholics-confess-to-a-priest/

This is what the papacy says about its priest's power to forgive sins, "Seek where you will, through heaven and earth, and you will find one created being who can forgive the sinner, who can free him from the chains of hell. That extraordinary being is the priest, the Roman Catholic priest." - The Catholic Priest, p. 78

Only God, Jesus Christ, can forgive and cleanse people from sin (1 John 1:9; Psalm 32:5). We are to go directly to God the Father through Jesus Christ for the forgiveness of sin.

Hebrews 4:14-16
14 "Seeing then that we have a great high priest, that is passed into the heavens, Jesus the Son of God, let us hold fast *our* profession.
15 For we have not an high priest which cannot be touched with the feeling of our infirmities; but was in all points tempted like as *we are, yet* without sin.
16 Let us therefore come boldly unto the throne of grace, that we may obtain mercy, and find grace to help in time of need."

Eucharist, Mass – Extremely Blasphemous!!!

The Eucharist known as the Catholic Mass also speaks to the blasphemous character of the papacy. It is a ceremony and a sacrifice that is suppose to commemorate the Lord's Supper in the New Testament. All priest believe that they are given ecclesiastical powers as a man to call Jesus down from heaven and slay him as a "victim" on the "altar" and literally turn the bread and the wine served in the mass into the actual flesh and blood of Christ. Through the mass they believe they are the "creator of the Creator." This is blasphemous and Satanic. No man has power to call Jesus from heaven every mass and sacrifice Him over again and turn the bread into the literal flesh of Jesus and the wine into the literal blood of Jesus.

Christ died only once for the sins of the world. **Romans 6:9, 10** says, [9]"Knowing that Christ being raised from the dead dieth no more; death hath no more dominion over him. [10]For in that he died, **he died unto sin once**: but in that he liveth, he liveth unto God." **Hebrews 9:28** adds, "So Christ **was once offered** to bear the sins of many; and unto them that look for him shall he appear the second time without sin unto salvation." Jesus teaches that communion is a time to reflect and remember what Jesus has done for us on Calvary. The bread (unleavened) and wine (unfermented) are only symbols that Jesus uses to point us to the work of His sacrifice and plan of salvation.

It must be emphasized that the papacy does not believe that the bread and wine in the Catholic Mass are symbolic. Again, they believe it is literal or the actual flesh and blood of Jesus. The references below confirm what the papacy of the Roman Catholic Church teaches about the Eucharist:

"343. What is the Holy Eucharist? The Holy Eucharist is a sacrament and a sacrifice. In the Holy Eucharist, under the appearances of bread and wine, the Lord Christ is contained, offered, and received. (a) The whole Christ is really, truly, and substantially present in the Holy Eucharist. We use the words "really, truly, and substantially" to describe Christ's presence in the Holy Eucharist in order to distinguish Our Lord's teaching from that of mere men who falsely teach that the Holy Eucharist is only a sign or figure of Christ, or that He is present only by His power. 350. What is the change of the entire substance of the bread and wine into the body and blood of Christ called? The change of the entire substance of the bread and wine into the body and blood of Christ is called Transubstantiation." - www.ewtn.com/faith/teachings/eucha1a.htm

"Transubstantiation is, according to the teaching of the Catholic Church, the change of substance by which the bread and the wine offered in the sacrifice of the sacrament of the Eucharist during the Mass, become, in reality, the Body and Blood of Jesus the Christ" - en.wikipedia.org/wiki/Transubstantiation

Alphonsus de Liguori, a bishop of the papacy who lived during the mid 1700's wrote the book Dignity and Duties of the Priest or Selva that presents an official position on the powers and duties of the Roman Catholic priests.

Please note, the following quotations from Liguori's book concerning the

Catholic Mass are extremely blasphemous and arrogant:

"The dignity of the priest is also estimated from the power that he has over the real and the mystic body of Jesus Christ. With regard to the power of priests over the real body of Jesus Christ, it is of faith that when they pronounce the words of consecration the Incarnate Word has obliged himself to obey and to come into their hands under the sacramental species... But our wonder should be far greater when we find that in obedience to the words of his priests Hoc EST CORPUS MEUM God himself descends on the altar, that he comes wherever they call him, and as often as they call him, and places himself in their hands, even though they should be his enemies. And after having come, he remains, entirely at their disposal; they move him as they please, from one place to another; they may, if they wish, shut him up in the tabernacle, or expose him on the altar, or carry him outside the church; they may, if they choose, eat his flesh, and give him for the food of others." - Alphonsus de Liguori, Dignity and Duties of the Priest or Selva, pp. 26, 27

"The saint assigns the reason of the superiority of the priesthood over Mary; she conceived Jesus Christ only once; but by consecrating the Eucharist, the priest, as it were, conceives him as often as he wishes, so that if the person of the Redeemer had not as yet been in the world, the priest, by pronouncing the words of consecration, would produce this great person of a Man-God. 'O wonderful dignity of the priests'; cries out St. Augustine; 'in their hands, as in the womb of the Blessed Virgin, the Son of God becomes- incarnate.' Hence priests are called the parents of Jesus Christ: such is the title that St. Bernard gives them, for they are the active cause by which he is made to exist really in the consecrated Host."- Ibid p. 32

"Thus the priest may, in a certain manner, be called the creator of his Creator, since by saying the words of consecration, he creates, as it were, Jesus in the sacrament, by giving him a sacramental existence, and produces him as a victim to be offered to the eternal Father. As in creating the world it was sufficient for God to have said, Let it be made, and it was created He spoke, and they were made? So it is sufficient for the priest to say, 'Hoc est corpus meum,' and behold the bread is no longer bread, but the body of Jesus Christ. 'The power of the priest,' says St. Bernardine of Sienna, 'is the power of the divine person; for the transubstantiation of the bread requires as much power as the creation of the world.' And St. Augustine has written, 'O venerable sanctity of the hands! O happy function of the priest! He that created (if I may say so) gave me the power to create him; and he that created me without me is himself created by me!' As the Word of God created heaven and earth, so, says St. Jerome, the words of the priest create Jesus Christ." - Ibid pp. 32, 33

Do you see the blasphemy, arrogance, and error of the Eucharist / Roman Catholic Mass? They believe that the powers "invested" to the priest to give the mass makes them the "parents of Jesus" and also "the creator of his Creator." They believe that "the words of the priest create Jesus Christ." How much more blasphemous and arrogant can the papacy be? The Catholic Mass is blasphemous, arrogant, and full of pride which are befitting characteristics of Satan and the little horn in Daniel chapters 7 and 8.

Not only is this blasphemous character of Papal Rome revealed in Daniel and Revelation but it is also prophesied by Paul in 2 Thessalonians 2:3, 4.

What warning did Apostle Paul give to all Christians and how blasphemous is Papal Rome revealed in 2 Thessalonians 2:3, 4?

2 Thessalonians 2:3 - "Let no man deceive you by any means: for *that day shall not come,* except there come a falling away first, and that man of sin be revealed, the son of perdition."

Who is the "man of sin," the son of perdition? Verse 4 reveals who it is.

2 Thessalonians 2:4 - "Who opposeth and exalteth himself above all that is called God, or that is worshipped; so that he as God sitteth in the temple of God, shewing himself that he is God."

This is a perfect description of the blasphemous character of Papal Rome. The "man of sin" is no other than Papal Rome who fell away from the Truth, detaching itself from the Head, Jesus Christ. He is also the son of perdition. Perdition means utter destruction. Since he is the son of perdition, who is the father of it? That is not hard to know. It is the same one who gives Papal Rome her power, seat, and authority described in Revelation 13:2 as the dragon. This great dragon was clearly identified in **Revelation 12:9** as "that old serpent, called the Devil, and Satan, which deceiveth the whole world." Satan is the father of perdition, utter destruction. Satan uses Papal Rome to destroy millions of lives worldwide through its deceptions and lies. Satan is behind it all.

Moreover, all people who ignore or reject God's truth have the spirit of Satan and are the sons and daughters of perdition. Jesus explains this plainly in

John 8:44, 45, [44]"Ye are of your father the devil, and the lusts of your father ye will do. He was a murderer from the beginning, and abode not in the truth, because there is no truth in him. When he speaketh a lie, he speaketh of his own: for he is a liar, and the father of it. [45]And because I tell you the truth, ye believe me not." **1 John 3:9, 10** adds, [9]"Whosoever is born of God doth not commit sin; for his seed remaineth in him: and he cannot sin, because he is born of God. [10]In this the children of God are manifest, and the children of the devil: whosoever doeth not righteousness is not of God, neither he that loveth not his brother." If we are children of God, **Romans 8:17** says that we will be "heirs of God, and joint-heirs with Christ." Who do you want to be a child of?

The Antichrist

The apostle John warns us in **1 John 2:18,** "Little children, it is the last time: and as ye have heard that antichrist shall come, even now are there many antichrists; whereby we know that it is the last time."

The Greek meaning for "antichrist" is an **opponent or adversary of the Messiah**, according to Strong's & Thayer's dictionaries. The blasphemous character of Papal Rome and its Mass is clearly against the truth of Jesus. They are an adversary or enemy of Christ. It is clear that Papal Rome is an antichrist, but you will see as you study that they are the main antichrist in the last days.

The blasphemous character of Papal Rome has been clearly exposed. All the clues we studied so far clearly identifies Papal Rome as the little horn of Daniel chapters 7 and 8 and the beast of Revelation chapters 13 and 14. What are more clues that confirm this?

Clue 4: Ruled for 1260 Years!

Remember, in Daniel 7:25 and Revelation 13:5 we learned that the little horn-beast kingdom would rule for 1260 years. Daniel 7:25 says, "...they shall be given into his hand until a time and times and the dividing of time." Revelation 13:5 says, "...power was given unto him to continue forty and two months." Each description of time is equal to 1260 days as previously taught (see pages 90 & 91). Since the context is symbolic, the day for a year principle is used. So the 1260 days equal 1260 years. Does Papal Rome match this clue too?

History shows us that the Papal Roman Empire led by the pope, began its reign in 538 AD. In 1798, its power as a political government ended. French general, Napoleon, ousted the Papal Roman monarchical ruler. General Berthier took Pope Pius VI captive and the pope died as a captive eighteen months later. Papal Rome lost their position as the political ruler over the Roman Empire but not as a church. Even though Papal Rome still functioned as a religious church, it appeared that it would be off the political scene forever. The Papal Roman Empire ruled from 538 to 1798 AD. How many years is that? It is 1260 years exactly as the Bible predicted! But does the Bible predict that Papal Rome would get its political and governmental power back? How much power will they have? You will learn more as you continue to study this lesson. It is not by chance that Papal Rome fulfills all the clues of the little horn and the beast.

Clue 5: "War With The Saints" - Persecute God's Faithful

Recall in Daniel 7:21 that the little horn "**made war with the saints**, and prevailed against them," and in **Daniel 7:25** it "shall wear out the saints of the most High." In **Revelation 13:7** the beast also made "war with the saints." Since we know that the Papal Roman Empire is clearly identified as the little horn-beast power, does history reveal that they persecuted God's faithful during the 1260 years of their monarch?

History records that the Papal Roman Empire thought it was their ecclesiastical and governmental right to penalize, imprison, torture, or kill anyone who defied their beliefs, laws, and traditions. Papal Rome outlawed the Bible because it exposed their greed, abominations, and errors. Papal Rome hated all forms of protest against its authority. They thought it had the right to force the consciences of people that were under its rule. As a result, throughout the history of the Papal Roman Empire millions of God's faithful people who held on to the truths of God's Word were persecuted and killed. Those who protested against the laws, actions, and beliefs of Papal Rome that conflicted with the Bible were known as "Protestants."

Historical quotes that confirm that the Papal Roman Empire persecuted and killed millions of God's faithful people:

The British historian, William Edward Lecky wrote: "That the Church of Rome has shed more innocent blood than any other institution that has ever existed among mankind, will be questioned by no Protestant who has a competent knowledge of history."- The History of the Rise of the Spirit of Rationalism in Europe, Vol. 2, p. 32

"For professing faith contrary to the teachings of the Church of Rome history records the martyrdom of more than one hundred million people. A million Waldenses and Albigenses [Swiss and French Protestants] perished during a crusade proclaimed by Pope Innocent III in 1208. Beginning from the establishment of the Jesuits in 1540 to 1580, nine hundred thousand were destroyed. One hundred and fifty thousand perished by the Inquisition in thirty years. Within the space of thirty-eight years after the edict of Charles V against the Protestants, fifty thousand persons were hanged, beheaded, or burned alive for heresy. Eighteen thousand more perished during the administration of the Duke of Alva in five and a half years." - Brief Bible Readings, p. 16

Historical quotes from Roman Catholic publications that admit and try to "justify" Papal Roman's persecution of millions of Christians:

"The Catholic has some reason on his side when he calls for the temporal punishment of heretics, for he claims the true title of Christian for himself exclusively, and professes to be taught by the never-failing presence of the Spirit of God...it is not more 'morally' wrong to put a man to death for heresy than for murder,... [and] in many cases persecution for religious opinions is not only permissible, but highly advisable and necessary." - *The Lawfulness of Persecution*, in The Rambler, 4, June, 1849, pp. 119, 126

"The [Catholic] Church has persecuted. Only a tyro [novice] in church history will deny that... Protestants were persecuted in France and Spain with the full approval of the [Catholic] Church authorities...When she thinks it good to use physical force the Church will use it." - Western Watchmen December 24, 1908

The persecuting and deceptive nature of Papal Rome is not the ministry of Jesus Christ. Jesus never ministered in this way. Jesus never forces anyone to accept His truth. The Bible makes it very clear that Jesus came to save people from their sins (Matthew 1:21). He does not want anyone to perish and that is why He came. He understands the deadly nature of sin and how it is contaminating and contagious and that is why He has to cleanse us from sin. If sin was not deadly Jesus would not have had to die, but the fact that He did reveals to us the awfulness of sin. He does everything He can do to free us from sin. He has made provision so that no one has to perish. That is why Jesus pleads with people to let go of sin and to take hold of His strength to overcome sin. But if a person chooses to hold on to sin that person will inevitably perish. **Romans 6:23** says, "For the wages of sin *is* death; but the gift of God *is* eternal life through Jesus Christ our Lord." All have the invitation to receive the gift before God executes His judgment. This is not persecution, but the final result of choosing to reject the gift. The execution of final judgment or punishment is NOT the duty of man, but ONLY done by Jesus. No man or organization on earth is given that Divine responsibility. Jesus offers life to all; He does not force man to receive life. If a person rejects the gift of life and decides to remain in sin, his or her end will be eternal death. Force is the spirit of Satan, not Jesus.

Matter of fact, in **Luke 9:52-56** when a Samaritan village refused to receive the messengers and the message of Jesus, the disciples, James and John told Jesus, [54]"Lord, wilt thou that we command fire to come down from heaven, and consume them, even as Elias did?" James and John thought that the whole town should be killed for refusing them to come in and present the "gift" of salvation.

What was the response of Jesus?

Luke 9:55, 56
55 "But he turned, and rebuked them, and said, Ye know not what manner of spirit ye are of.
56 For the Son of man is not come to destroy men's lives, but to save *them.* And they went to another village."

It is clear from our study thus far that Satan, the great Deceiver like a snake and Persecutor like a dragon, is the power behind the system of Papal Rome. Papal Rome is truly the son of perdition (destruction) and deception. Jesus and His true followers never used deception or persecution to win others to Jesus in the past, present, or future.

What are some more clues that Paul prophesied that fit the character and beliefs of Papal Rome in the "latter times"?

1 Timothy 4:1-4
1 "Now the Spirit speaketh expressly, that in the latter times some shall depart from the faith, giving heed to seducing spirits, and doctrines of devils;

2 Speaking lies in hypocrisy; having their conscience seared with a hot iron;
3 Forbidding to marry, *and commanding* to abstain from meats, which God
hath created to be received with thanksgiving of them which believe and
know the truth.
4 For every creature of God *is* good, and nothing to be refused, if it be
received with thanksgiving."

In the latter days a great majority of people will follow seducing demonic
spirits and their teachings! The word "hypocrisy" according to the Strong's
Greek Dictionary, means "*acting under* a feigned [deceitful] part." Thayer's
Greek Dictionary makes it even clearer, hypocrisy is "the acting of a stage
player." It is clear from the usage of the word "hypocrisy" that Satan uses a
religious-political "actor" on the world's "stage" that appears to follow Jesus,
to be holy, and do charitable works on the outside, but is used to spread his
lies and deceit. Jesus warns us in **Matthew 7:15**, "Beware of false prophets,
which come to you in sheep's clothing, but inwardly they are ravening
wolves." All those who reject the clear plain word of Bible truth and believe
and teach lies to others while still professing to be Christians are Satan's
actors. Their conscience is seared. In other words, the conscience mind,
where we have the ability to know truth from error, right or wrong with the
leading of the Holy Spirit and the Word of God is gone. It will no longer
respond to the conviction of the Holy Spirit and Bible truth.

1 Timothy 4:3 gives two more clues of Satan's "actor" that clearly point to
Papal Rome: 1) Forbidding to marry, and 2) Abstaining from meats. Let's
examine this carefully.

Clue 6: Forbidding to marry

It is a well known fact that Papal Rome forbids their Catholic priests,
bishops, monks, and nuns to get married in general. "Celibacy [forbidden
to marry] is one of the most widely recognized characteristics of a Roman
Catholic priest... Technically, celibacy is the commitment not to marry. In
the Latin (Roman) Catholic Church, it is a prerequisite for ordination to
the priesthood. The candidate must freely assume this obligation publicly
and for life. Because church teaching reserves sexual activity to marriage,
celibacy also requires abstinence." - *Why Are Priest Celibate?*, Santiago
Cortes-Sjoberg, www.uscatholic.org/glad-you-asked/2009/08/why-are-
priests-celibate

There is no mandate or teaching in the Bible that says that workers of Jesus are forbidden to marry. Matter of fact, **Hebrews 13:4** says, "Marriage *is* honourable in all, and the bed undefiled..." Peter, a disciple of Jesus, was married (Matthew 8:14). Also, what is one of the Biblical requirements for a bishop, church overseer, such as an elder or pastor? **1 Timothy 3:2** says, "A bishop then must be blameless, the **husband of one wife**, vigilant, sober, of good behaviour, given to hospitality, apt to teach."

Clue 7: Abstaining from "meats" = food

The word "meat" in our modern English usually refers to flesh, but the old English word "meat" in the context of 1 Timothy 4:3 is talking about food in general. Paul reveals that it is good to eat God's wonderful creation of foods that God permitted to eat. Food is good. There are times when fasting is needed in the Christian journey, but a mandate abstaining from food as a public show of repentance and devotion to God is not Biblical.

According to Jesus, how should a true follower "fast"? Should it be a public outward show or private?

Matthew 6:16-18
16 "Moreover when ye fast, be not, as the hypocrites, of a sad countenance: for they disfigure their faces, that they may appear unto men to fast. Verily I say unto you, They have their reward.
17 But thou, when thou fastest, anoint thine head, and wash thy face;
18 That thou appear not unto men to fast, but unto thy Father which is in secret: and thy Father, which seeth in secret, shall reward thee openly."

Fasting is a private matter between God and His followers. Even though Jesus fasted 40 days in the wilderness, He never mandated His followers to schedule a public fast as a show of repentance or devotion to God. Plus, when Jesus fasted for 40 days He was not in public showing His fast, He was in the wilderness. It was in preparation for His challenging public ministry that would lead Him to the cross of Calvary.

Papal Rome mandates that Catholics abstain from certain foods during 40 days of fasting known as Lent for the "purpose of doing penance, repentance of sins, almsgiving, atonement, and self-denial" as a outward display of their devotion to God. - Wikipedia. In centuries past, it was a very serious endeavor. Many devoted followers went several days without eating any food. Overtime there have been many variations on what could be eaten and when from culture to culture. Today, in many Catholic cultures, it is mandated to mainly abstain from flesh meat during Lent.

Papal Rome again is clearly exposed as the religious-political "actor" forbidding its priest and nuns to marry and requiring a mandate of abstaining from food as prophesied would happen in the "latter times."

Prophetic Symbol: **Little Horn (Daniel 7 & 8) and Beast (Revelation 13 & 14) = Papal Rome**

Papal Rome clearly fulfills all the characteristics of both the little horn in Daniel chapters 7 and 8 and the leopard-like beast in Revelation chapters 13 and 14. The little horn and the beast are the same. The Papal Roman Empire's religious-governmental monarch was in power from 538 AD to 1798 AD, 1260 years as predicted in the Bible. At the height of its empire it covered much of modern Europe such as Germany, Netherlands, Belgium, Switzerland, Austria, as well as parts of France, Italy, Czechoslovakia, and Poland. Its governmental monarch was broken in 1798 during the French Revolution, but it still functioned as a religious church. It appeared that the "glory" days of papal monarchical supremacy were over. If this is an "actor" powered by the dragon and the serpent, Satan, will it ever get its power back to influence and deceive billions of people in the world?

What does Jesus tell you to do as you see the time of the end approaching?

Luke 21:36 - "**Watch** ye therefore, and **pray always**, that ye may be accounted worthy to escape all these things that shall come to pass, and to stand before the Son of man."

Mark 13:35-37
35 "**Watch** ye therefore: for ye know not when the master of the house cometh, at even, or at midnight, or at the cockcrowing, or in the morning:
36 Lest coming suddenly he find you sleeping.
37 And what I say unto you I say unto all, **Watch**."

In **Matthew 25:13** Jesus says, "**Watch** therefore, for ye know neither the day nor the hour wherein the Son of man cometh." We may not know the exact "day nor the hour" when Jesus is coming, but Jesus reveals to us the "season."

<u>**According to Jesus how do you know the "season" of His soon return?**</u>

Mark 13:28, 29
28 "Now learn a parable of the fig tree; When her branch is yet tender, and putteth forth leaves, ye know that summer is near:
29 So ye in like manner, when ye shall see these things come to pass, know that it is nigh, *even* at the doors."

It is just about "summer time!" In Mark 13:28, 29, referring to the fulfilling of the all the prophecies in the Bible that point to His soon return, Jesus said when you see all these things being fulfilled as the Bible accurately predicted know that we are near summer time prophetically of the soon coming of Jesus. From all that you studied thus far can you see that we are close to the soon coming of Jesus!

Before we move on in this study, pause, and think about where we are in prophetic time according to all that you have studied so far. Can you see that the "branch is yet tender, and putteth forth leaves?" Summer time is near! Reflect again on the prophetic metallic statue and the pinpoint accuracy of the fulfilled prophecies of the rise and fall of earthly kingdoms. What part of the statue are we in today? Remember, we are in the feet of part iron and clay that represent divided Europe. What kingdom rose up out of the "feet" according to Daniel chapter 2? The Little Horn, Papal Rome from 538 to 1798. What part of the image does the stone cut without hands strike? The feet! Remember, this is the final blow to ALL earthly kingdoms. That stone grows into a great mountain representing the eternal kingdom of God. It is clear that Jesus is very soon to come.

As mentioned earlier you will see that we are not only at the feet of the prophetic image but at the edge of the toes. Jesus stone kingdom is about to strike! Pay attention to the next question.

CHAPTER 11
HEALING OF THE DEADLY WOUND

Which kingdom will be the last earthly kingdom before the "stone" strikes, representing the second coming of Jesus and the establishment of His Eternal Kingdom? Hint: Will Papal Rome, the beast described in Revelation chapter 13, get its "power back" in the near future? How will the world react?

Let's go back and look at the prophecy of the leopard-like beast in Revelation chapter 13:

Revelation 13:3 - "And I saw one of his heads as it were wounded to death; and his **deadly wound was healed: and all the world wondered after the beast.**"

We must pay great attention to this prophecy. It reveals that the beast, Papal Rome, will strike back with world dominance. All the world will **wonder after**, or admire greatly with reverence, Papal Rome. The Papal Roman Empire in the past mainly covered modern day Europe. The prophecy reveals that the new Papal Roman Empire will include the entire world. It will be given a new lease on life, "his deadly wound" will be healed.

Does Papal Rome exist today? What kind of power and influence does it have? In 1798 it appeared that Papal Rome was dead. It appeared that it would never have its monarchical power back. Another blow happened when its capital of Rome was overtaken by Italian forces in 1870 including Papal Rome's beloved Vatican City, except the Apostolic Palace, the home of the papacy. Over the next 59 years the papacy refused to leave the Apostolic Palace in Vatican and declared itself "a prisoner in Vatican." As the prophecy says they "were wounded to death." From all appearances they would be like other empires who lost their dominance like Babylon, Medo-Persia, Greece, and Rome, never to come back. How could Papal Rome come back into world dominance as "a prisoner in Vatican" living under the shadows of Italy? Is this even possible? Remember again, Bible prophecy is extremely accurate. Let's continue to study.

What happened in 1929 that began "healing" the wound of Papal Rome?

As you can imagine since 1870 Papal Rome worked with persistence to get its governmental sovereignty back. In 1929, the papacy negotiated a treaty with the government of Italy and its dictator Benito Mussolini known as the Lateran Treaty, also called the Lateran Pact. This treaty gave Papal Rome its monarchical governmental sovereignty back within the territory of Vatican, approximately 109 acres. The treaty also recognizes that the Catholic religion is the only official religion within the government of Papal Rome.

It is interesting to note that after the Lateran Treaty was signed the *San Francisco Chronicle*, February 12, 1929, wrote an article entitle "MUSSOLINI AND GASPARRI SIGN HISTORIC ROMAN PACT." In part of the article it speaks about "healing the wound" of Papal Rome:

"The Roman question tonight was a thing of the past and the Vatican was at peace with Italy. The formal accomplishment of this today was the exchange of signatures in the historic Palace of St. John Lateran by two noteworthy plenipotentiaries, Cardinal Gasparri for Pope Pius XI and Premier Mussolini for King Victor Emmanuel III.

In affixing the autographs to the memorable document, **healing the wound** which has festered since 1870, extreme cordiality was displayed on both sides." - *The San Francisco Chronicle*, February 12, 1929, p. 1

Did the *San Francisco Chronicle* know about the Bible prophecy of Revelation chapter 13? Not sure, but it is quite interesting that they would use those words that points to the "healing" of the wound of Papal Rome. Even though Papal Rome's "wound" was not completely healed in 1929 it surely started the healing process.

What is the status of Papal Rome since 1929?

Today, Papal Rome's headquarters of the Catholic Church is still in Vatican. It is a religious governmental monarch on 109 acres surrounded by Rome, Italy. The Pope is both the leader of the church and sovereign leader of the Papal government also known as the Holy See. In other words, he is the "king". He is both priest and absolute king. It is still the smallest nation on earth, but is growing in worldwide power and influence.

Quick Facts:
1. Vatican is Papal Rome's Headquarters

2.   109 Acres (surrounded by Rome, Italy)
3.   Vatican's population is approximately 1,000 citizens
4.   Pope is sovereign leader or king
5.   Religious head of an estimate 1.2 billion Catholics worldwide

The papacy's power and influence to "shape men's minds" worldwide has grown very much since 1929 into the modern 21st tech century. Remember, according to Revelation's prophecy the beast, Papal Rome, will once again have an empire, but this time it will cover the entire globe. It will be the head of the seventh empire, the last earthly kingdom.

How can a small nation rise to world power as prophesied?

The answer is found in its organizational system. Ellen White, who has written much on this subject in her classic book entitled, The Great Controversy says, "The Roman Catholic Church, with all its ramifications throughout the world, forms one vast organization under the control, and designed to serve the interests, of the papal see. Its millions of communicants, in every country of the globe, are instructed to hold themselves as bound in allegiance to the pope. Whatever their nationality or their government, they are to regard the authority of the church as above all other. Though they may take the oath pledging their loyalty to the state, yet back of this lies the vow of obedience to Rome, absolving them from every pledge inimical to her interests. History testifies of her artful and persistent efforts to insinuate herself into the affairs of the nations; and having gained a foothold, to further her own aims, even at the ruin of princes and people." - Ellen White, Great Controversy, p. 580

How much has Papal Rome healed since 1929? Is Papal Rome fulfilling prophecy of being the last worldly empire on this Earth with the pope as king?

Since 1929 until the present time, the papacy has been very intentional in creating formal governmental relationships and diplomacy worldwide. Over the years the papacy has been a key negotiator and diplomat at United Nations. Its most prized diplomatic relationship and direct political influence has been the United States of America, a world superpower after War World II. The current cozy relationship between the United States of America and the papacy would be shocking and appalling to many immigrants from the "old world," Europe, who escaped the religious persecution of Papal Rome to the "new world," America. They risked their lives to protest against the atrocities and errors of the papacy. The word "Protestant" refers to individuals and churches that oppose or "protest" the doctrines and influence of the papacy in all its forms. When the founders established the United States of America, it was based on Christian Protestant principles without the influence of the papacy. They saw Papal Rome as a danger to their religious freedom and the American's way of life. John Adams, Second President of the United States, sums up the America's thoughts of Papal Rome, "I have long been decided in opinion that a free government and the Roman Catholic religion can never exist together in any nation or Country." - John Adams to Thomas Jefferson, December 3, 1813. *Cappon, Adams-Jefferson Letters*, 2: p. 571. Adams continues, "Liberty and Popery cannot live together." - John Adam to Louisa Catherine Adams, May 17, 1821, Adams Papers (microfilm), reel 451, Library of Congress. General Marquis de LaFayette (1757-1834) who served in the American Continental Army concurs with Adams, "It is my opinion that if the liberties of this country – the United States of America – are destroyed, it will be by the subtlety of the Roman Catholic Jesuit priests, for they are the most crafty, dangerous enemies to civil and religious liberty. They have instigated most of the wars of Europe."

To combat the Protestant principles of true religious freedom in America, Papal Rome deployed its most feared, diabolical, secretive, insidious, corrupt, ruthless, and murderous order of the Catholic church, the Jesuits, also known as the Society of Jesus. The order was founded in 1534 by Ignatius Loyola as a specialized "army" of priests to combat the Protestant Reformation. In general, a Jesuit will become whoever it needs to be in order to accomplish their goal. Not many years after America was established, the Jesuits covered themselves in Protestant "robes". For example they became Baptist or Methodist students, teachers, preachers, and administrators, secretively inserting the papacy's principles and errors. They successfully created schools in America that attracted even Protestant students. They established their first American Jesuit University in the heart of the nation's capital, Georgetown University. Overtime the Jesuits were successful in infiltrating American politics, government, schools, and religious denominations.

Ellen White, who also researched and wrote about the Jesuits stated, **"When appearing as members of their order [Jesuits], they wore a garb of**

sanctity, visiting prisons and hospitals, ministering to the sick and the poor, professing to have renounced the world, and bearing the sacred name of Jesus, who went about doing good. But under this blameless exterior the most criminal and deadly purposes were often concealed. It was a fundamental principle of the order that the end justifies the means. By this code, lying, theft, perjury, assassination, were not only pardonable but commendable, when they served the interests of the church. Under various disguises the Jesuits worked their way into offices of state, climbing up to be the counselors of kings, and shaping the policy of nations. They became servants to act as spies upon their masters. They established colleges for the sons of princes and nobles, and schools for the common people; and the children of Protestant parents were drawn into an observance of popish rites. All the outward pomp and display of the Romish worship was brought to bear to confuse the mind and dazzle and captivate the imagination, and thus the liberty for which the fathers had toiled and bled was betrayed by the sons. **The Jesuits rapidly spread themselves over Europe, and wherever they went, there followed a revival of popery."** - Ellen White, Great Controversy p. 235

"There was no crime too great for them to commit, no deception too base for them to practice, no disguise too difficult for them to assume. Vowed to perpetual poverty and humility, it was their studied aim to secure wealth and power, to be devoted to the overthrow of Protestantism, and the re-establishment of the papal supremacy." - Ibid, p. 234

By the time Abraham Lincoln became the 16th president of the United States, he could see the stealthy moves of Papal Rome and its future influences on America. He said, "I do not pretend to be a prophet; but though not a prophet, I see a very dark cloud on our horizon, and that cloud is coming from Rome. It is filled with tears of blood. The true motive power is secreted behind the thick walls of the Vatican, the colleges and schools of the Jesuits the convents of the nuns and the confessional boxes of Rome." - Charles Chiniquy, Fifty Years in the Church of Rome, p. 115

Even though the Jesuits and Papal Rome were successful in setting up institutions in the U.S., American presidents resisted Papal Rome politically and kept a great distance away from the pope. However in 1919 that all changed when President Woodrow Wilson became the first U.S. President to visit Pope Benedict XV in Vatican on January 4, 1919. Forty years after the first U.S. president's visit with the pope, the visits became more frequent.

On December 6, 1959, President Dwight Eisenhower met with Pope John XXIII in Vatican. On July 2, 1963, the first Roman Catholic President John F. Kennedy met with Pope Paul VI in Vatican. On October 4, 1965, Pope Paul VI was the first pope ever to be allowed to set foot on American soil to meet with President Lyndon B. Johnson in New York City. On December 23, 1967, President Lyndon Johnson met with Pope Paul VI for the second time in Vatican becoming the first U.S. president to meet with the pope twice. Matter of fact, every single U.S. president since Eisenhower to our current day has met with the pope, multiple times in many cases. On October 6, 1979, Pope John Paul II met President Jimmy Carter in the White House. Pope John Paul II was the first pope to meet with the President of the United States in the White House.

By the 1980's Papal Rome and the United States had formed a very engaging and comfortable relationship with each other. In 1984 President Ronald Reagan was the first U.S. president to establish a formal diplomatic relationship with the papacy when he officially appointed a U.S. Ambassador to Papal Rome. As a result of the bond that the U.S. has formed with the Vatican, both President Reagan and John Paul II are credited with the fall of the communist world superpower, Union of Soviet Socialist Republics (USSR). Over the last fifty years the United States and the papacy have developed a strong diplomatic and political relationship. On September 24, 2015, there was another major first time event. Pope Francis was the first pope ever to publicly address U.S. Congress lawmakers. This influence that the papacy now has on America's lawmakers was the "dark cloud" that Abraham Lincoln referred to that will be filled with "tears of blood," persecution. More about persecution later in this study.

This formal relationship with a world superpower and host of the United Nations General Assembly in New York City has opened up many doors to the papacy worldwide. The four popes over the last fifty years have spoken to the United Nations General Assembly. Pope Paul VI made an address to the UN in 1965. Pope John Paul II spoke twice, once in 1979 and again on the 50th anniversary of the UN in 1995. Pope Benedict addressed UN in 2008. Twenty years after Pope John Paul II spoke at UN's 50th anniversary, Pope Francis spoke to many attentive ears at the UN General Assembly on their 70th anniversary on September 25, 2015. At that time it was the largest gathering of presidents and world leaders ever at the United Nations General Assembly to hear a pope speak.

Even though the papacy never applied to be a member of the UN, they were granted permanent observer state on April 6, 1964. "In that capacity, it has the right to attend all sessions of the United Nations General Assembly, the United Nations Security Council, and the United Nations Economic and Social Council to observe their work. Accordingly, the Holy See has established permanent observer missions in New York and in Geneva and has been able to influence the decisions and recommendations of the United Nations." - en.wikipedia.org/wiki/Holy_See_and_the_United_Nations

The papacy currently has the power to "influence decisions and recommendations" worldwide. The pope has personally met with many heads of nations over the last 50 years. Leaders and lawmakers from around the world have kissed the ring of the pope. Papal Rome has gained popularity worldwide as a star, key diplomatic negotiator, and peace maker. In our modern times popular popes such as John Paul II and Francis have been on the cover of several magazines and even listed as the person of the year. In 2004, U.S. President George W. Bush presented John Paul II with United States' highest civilian honor, the President Medal of Freedom. When John Paul II died in 2005, his funeral attracted the largest gathering of the heads of state in history! History records four kings, five queens, at least seventy presidents and prime ministers, and more than fourteen religious leaders from around the world *(en.wikipedia.org/wiki/Pope_John_ Paul_II#Criticism)*. Three former U.S. Presidents who where in attendance, George Bush, Sr., George W. Bush, and Bill Clinton along with Secretary of State, Condoleezza Rice, were pictured together kneeling in worship before the dead body of John Paul II. Is the world "wondering" or "admiring" after the beast as predicted in the Bible? Is the wounded head healed?

Pope Francis has broken attendance records in many places around the world that he has visited. He has been called, "The people's pope," "A new world pope," and "Pope for a new world." Did you know that Pope Francis was the first Jesuit pope in the papacy history? Do you think that is by chance or design?

The world media outlets are picking up on the clues that the papacy wants to lead the world both spiritually and politically. On September 15, 2015 just prior to Pope Francis' historic visit to the United States, Time magazine had a picture of him on its cover holding up a golden monstrance used for mass with the title *"New Roman Empire: The global reach of Pope Francis."* Just a few hours after Pope Francis spoke to the U.S. Congress, Howard Fineman,

Global Editorial Director of the Huffington Post, wrote an article entitled, *"Pope Francis Wants To Be The President Of The World."* Does Fineman know about the prophecies of Revelation chapters 13 and 14? Not sure, but it is interesting to note what he writes about Pope Francis first visit to the U.S. Here are a few quotes from that article:

"But shrewdly, methodically and with a showman's flair, the soft-spoken, 78-year-old Argentinian Jesuit priest named Jorge Mario Bergoglio - Pope Francis - showed Thursday that he is running to become president of the planet. He did so in a congressional ceremony of secular civic pomp in a massive legislative building that, after all, harks back to ancient Rome. As devout as he is, and as focused on the faith and practice of the Catholic Church, Francis is also campaigning to lead public, secular, political discourse worldwide...The pope wants to win that battle, and Washington was one more stop on the campaign tour." - Howard Fineman, *Pope Wants To Be President Of The World*, September 24, 2015, Huffington Post (www.huffingtonpost.com/entry/pope-francis-world-leader_us_56041e79e4b00310edfa4d0f)

Friend, can't you see that prophecy is fast fulfilling? All these things that are currently transpiring in our world today is not by chance. Jesus is soon to come. Are you ready? The head that was wounded to death is almost completely healed! The whole world is becoming more and more mesmerized by the leopard-like beast, Papal Rome. The papacy is moving with rapid speed to become the world's king as the Bible predicts or it is already moved into that position after the print of this book. Revelation 13:3 predicts that after the head of Papal Rome is completely healed that "all the world wondered after the beast." Verse 4 reveals that they have not only wondered or admired the beast, but "they worshipped the dragon which gave power unto the beast: and they worshipped the beast, saying, Who is like unto the beast? Who is able to make war with him?"

Satan is behind the entire papacy, but there are many innocent and sincere Catholics and others who are a part of that system or admire it who are not aware of whose behind it. God is calling them from darkness to His marvelous light of Truth. It is time to sound the alarm and blow the trumpet of truth around the world! Wake up! Wake up! Time is almost over as revealed in God's Word. Why does God reveal truth? Because He loves us and does not want anybody to be lost. Let's continue to study.

CHAPTER 12
IMAGE OF THE BEAST

Third Angel's Message Warning Continues

Now let's go back to the Third Angel's Message in Revelation 14:9.

Revelation 14:9 - "And the third angel followed them, saying with a loud voice, If any man worship the beast and his image, and receive *his* mark in his forehead, or in his hand."

Prophetic Symbol: **The Beast = Papal Rome**

Since it has clearly been revealed from the Bible and historical evidence that Papal Rome is the beast, who is his image (image of the beast)?

"Image" is "eikōn" in the Greek which means a "*likeness, statue, profile,* or (figuratively) *representation, resemblance,*" according to the Strong's Greek Dictionary.

It is clear from the definition that the image of the beast is one who is in the likeness or resembles Papal Rome. In other words, the image of the beast mirrors the beast with some of the same characteristics of the beast, but it is not the original. Like Papal Rome, the image of the beast is a religious group of people who profess to be Christians but have apostatized from God's truth. Like Papal Rome, they are religious-hypocrites who have apostatized from God's truth. Like Papal Rome, the image of the beast uses its "religious authority" or church beliefs to influence multitudes of people and governments. Not only does the image of the beast look like Papal Rome, but they have made an alliance to unify with the pope and Papal Rome's objectives and goals. Also, like the beast, they have political power.

Revelation 14:9 asserts that if any man worships the beast and his image, that person will receive the mark of the beast. **It is clear from this text that the mark of the beast is a centralizing doctrine that unifies them together.** You will find what doctrine that is as you continue this study. **Simply, the image of the beast is any Christian religious church or organization that unites with the doctrine of the mark of the beast.** This includes Protestant Christian churches or denominations who at one time in their history protested against the apostasy of Papal Rome, but have compromised God's truth and joined her in her apostasy!

Prophetic Symbol: **Image of the Beast = All Apostate Christian Churches**

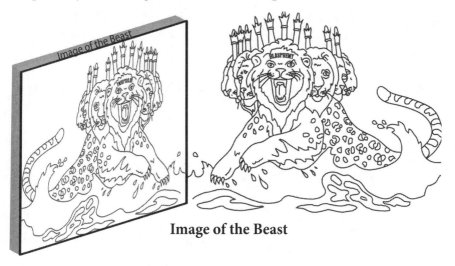

Image of the Beast

Is your "image" original or self made?

This may surprise you, but your "image" is not really your own. It's NOT original. In other words, your "image" is actually a reflection of a collection of ideas, beliefs, and experiences gathered from your family and your past and present environment. This may be a concept that is hard for our "self" driven society to accept. We were not created to be "self" driven. We CANNOT self make an original image. It is literally impossible for us to create our own original image. We learn from those teaching and training us and reflect that image to others. We are learning all the time and our environment and what we choose to watch and listen to will determine whose image we reflect.

Whose image do you reflect, Christ's or Satan's?

You were made in the image of God to reflect the character of God. Sin and disobedience has marred and corrupted that image. Sin has made us into the image of Satan, but Jesus came to this world to restore us back to His original image. If you partake in the worldly things of Satan you will reflect the image of Satan. But if you partake, turn your eyes upon the Word of God, and have faith in the Truth of God you will reflect the image of Jesus. In other words, what you "behold" you are.

CHAPTER 13
LAMB-LIKE BEAST WITH TWO HORNS

Whithat nation will Satan use to make all the world worship the beast, Papal Rome, and make an image of the beast, apostate Christian churches?

Revelation 13:11 - "And I beheld another beast coming up out of the earth; and he had two horns like a lamb, and he spake as a dragon."

LAMB-LIKE BEAST

You already learned earlier in this study that beast in Bible prophecy represents a kingdom or nation. Now let's study the clues of this nation to find out who it is.

Clue 1: Comes up out of the earth

Who is this nation that is "coming up out of the earth?" Going back to Revelation 13:1, the leopard-like beast representing Papal Rome came up out of the sea. Remember, "sea" in Bible prophecy represents, a multitude of people or territory that speak many languages. Papal Rome, as prophesied, rose up out of a highly populated area of several languages. So what does the earth represent here in Bible prophecy? If the "sea" in Bible prophecy represents a heavily populated region of the world we can conclude that the "earth" represents the very opposite. "Earth" in Revelation 13:11

symbolically represents a sparsely populated region of the world which mainly consist of wilderness or woods. The Bible also gives us clues on this in Revelation 12:6, 14, and 16.

Prophetic Symbol: **Earth = Sparsely populated world region that is mainly wilderness**

Clue 2: Like a lamb

A lamb is a young sheep. Figuratively, a lamb is used as a symbol of meekness, innocence, or gentleness. The "like a lamb" description of this nation represents its youthful and meek character.

Who does a "lamb" generally represent in the Bible?

1 Peter 1:19 - "But with the precious blood of Christ, as of a lamb without blemish and without spot."

John 1:29 - "The next day John seeth Jesus coming unto him, and saith, Behold the Lamb of God, which taketh away the sin of the world."

Jesus Christ is depicted as a meek and innocent lamb that died for the sins of the world. Those who claim to be followers of the Lamb, Christ, they are known as Christians.

So based on these clues it can be concluded that this lamb-like beast represents a young and innocent Christian nation.

Clue 3: Two horns

This lamb-like beast not only is young and innocent, but it has two horns on its head. Remember, horns in general in Bible prophecy also represent a nation.

What else can horns represent?

Habakkuk 3:4 - "And *his* [God's] brightness was as the light; he had horns *coming* out of his hand: and there *was* the hiding of his **power**."

Horns also represent power. Horns on a Christian nation represents

God's power.

Based on world history, what nation on earth rose into power in a land that was a sparsely populated wilderness; started as a meek nation; historically known as a Christian nation; relatively a young nation; and has become a world superpower? Think about it. Could it be a country in Europe such as the Germany or France? No, because those countries have been in existence for a very long time, plus they are in very populated regions of the world and none of them profess to be a Christian nation. No nation in the ancient world, Europe or the eastern part of the world fits the characteristics of Revelation 13:11. The only nation that fits the characteristics of Revelation 13:11 is found in the western part of the world and that is the United States of America. The United States of America is relatively a young nation, less than 250 years old. America grew out of a sparsely populated wilderness. Historically, America was founded on Protestant Christian principles. Many of the first settlers to America were Christian Protestants who escaped religious persecution from the church of England and Papal Rome. They wanted to live in a land free from forced religion. They wanted to worship God according to the dictates of their own hearts in freedom. Though the United States started off relatively small it has now grown into a young world superpower.

Prophetic Symbol: **Lamb-like beast with two horns = UNITED STATES OF AMERICA**

<u>**As a Christian nation, what main principle does Christ want all His followers to have?**</u>

Galatians 5:1 - "Stand fast therefore in the <u>**liberty**</u> wherewith Christ hath made us free, and be not entangled again with the yoke of bondage."

Liberty! Freedom is the main foundational principle that the United States of America was founded upon. America's most cherished symbol of liberty is its Declaration of Independence. It states, "We hold these truths to be self-evident, that all men are created equal, that they are endowed by their Creator with certain unalienable Rights, that among these are Life, Liberty and the pursuit of Happiness." In 1776 America declared its freedom from the monarch of England. Americans would rather die than be under the dictatorship of England. "Give me liberty or give me death" was the rallying cry for many who fought for freedom in the Revolutionary War against the monarch of England. **Freedom is what gives the United States its power.**

<u>**How is this power of freedom represented as the two horns on the lamb-like beast revealed in the governance of the United States of American?**</u>

The power of freedom in the governance of the United States of America is outlined in its U.S. Constitution. Its basic principle is that it is a government "by the people and for the people," a republic. A republic is "a state in which supreme power is held by the people and their elected representatives, and which has an elected or nominated president rather than a monarch." - Dictionary.com. Also, a constitution within a republic protects basic human and religious rights that cannot be removed by the government nor by a majority in order to protect the basic rights of a minority. The government of the United States was built on a republic. A republic is not a kingly power. The U.S. Constitution gives details on how its legislative power is spread out through a system of checks and balances between its three branches of government, 1)The Executive Branch – President's Administration; 2) Congress – House of Representatives and Senate; and 3) Judicial branch. The Constitution builds a government that is designed to govern and protect things that all its citizens have in common such as freedom, justice, environment, and general welfare, but not to govern or force religion. The preamble of the U.S. Constitution says, "We the people of the United States, in order to form a more perfect union, establish justice, insure domestic tranquility, provide for the common defense, promote the general welfare, and secure the blessings of liberty to ourselves and our posterity, do ordain and establish the Constitution for the United States of American." The Constitution establishes, the separation between church and state. A Republic and Protestantism are the two fundamental principles of the United States of America. They are the two separate horns on the lamb-like beast that give this nation its power.

Prophetic Symbol: **Two horns on the lamb like beast = A Republic and Protestantism (separation of church and state)**

Let's briefly look at more historical details of why the founding fathers of the United States thought that it was important to separate church and state. In America's humble beginnings it was known to the rest of the world as the "New World." Many settlers from the "Old World," Europe, such as the Puritans, also known as the pilgrims, came to America to escape the religious persecution from the Church of England. It is also critical

to note here that the power that many of the Puritans were escaping from
was a Protestant power. The Church of England that developed out of the
reformation movement was a Protestant church which eventually became
a part of the government of England. Remember, Protestants are those
who protested against the power and religious doctrines of Papal Rome. In
England, many of the church members practiced some of the truths that they
were exposed to by Protestant reformers such as Martin Luther and John
Huss, but they failed to continue to explore and live by the many other truths
of the Bible. As as result, the Church of England held on to many practices
of Papal Rome and began to institute laws in their government to force
the Protestant Christian religion on its people. They thought that making
laws that forced all its citizen to become a Protestant Christian or at least
practice its principles would make it a great and "holy" nation. They were
not tolerant to any other forms of religion. Those who refused to conform
to the religious practices of the Church of England were persecuted by the
government of England. At that time in England it was illegal to hold private
religious meetings, they were only allowed to meet at the Protestant churches
that England's government approved. The Puritans in England thought
this was wrong and refused to follow the unbiblical legislative religious laws
formed by the Church of England. As a result, many were persecuted and
many fled the country and settled in American to practice their Puritan
Christian religion freely without the fear of the Church of England.

It is interesting that history records that when the Puritans began to settle
in America and develop colonies, like Papal Rome and the Church of
England, the Puritans developed laws and government policies that fined or
imprisoned all its citizens in their colonies who did not follow the official
Puritan religion. It was not until Roger Williams, a Puritan pastor who
settled in America, protested and spoke up against the Puritan government
enforcing Christian obedience that things began to change. Roger Williams
believed that God gave all people the freedom to worship based on the
convictions of their own mind. God does not force us to worship Him. He
invites us to choose to serve Him freely. Roger Williams was ridiculed by
the Puritans for his belief in religious freedom. As a result of his protest, he
was not permitted to be part of the their colonies and expelled. Through
God's providence and leading, Roger Williams started a small colony known
as Rhode Island. This young pastor created a colony in which all Americans
are indebted. He established a colony in which all men and women had the
true freedom to worship God or not. His government separated church and
state. Roger Williams did not believe church or religious matters should

dictate civil government. He believed that a church or religion should not control the government because it would endanger freedom of religion and infringe on the rights of others who may believe differently. So when the United States began to become a united body in 1776, the framers of the Constitution agreed and adopted the views of Roger Williams and created a nation in which one religion does not control how people are governed and how laws are made.

The foundation of the religion of the United States is based on Protestant Christian principles. Even though America was founded upon these principles, the government has no right to force all its citizens to be Christian. The founding fathers saw the disaster of a government that forced religion through lessons of Papal Rome and the Church of England. History shows that governments that force religion leads to bondage and persecution of its citizens. The first amendment of the U.S. Constitution guarantees the freedom to worship according to the dictates of each citizen's conscience without government interference or force. It says, "Congress shall make no law respecting the establishment of religion, or prohibiting the **free** exercise thereof..." This is the reason why millions flocked to the shores of America. **This was the greatest power of America to the world, religious freedom!**

The Everson v. Board, U.S. Supreme Court Decision makes the separation of church and state very clear. It says, "The 'establishment of religion' clause of the First Amendment means at least this: Neither a state nor the Federal Government can set up a church. Neither can pass laws which aid one religion, aid all religions, or prefer one religion over another. Neither can force nor influence a person to go to or to remain away from church against his will or force him to profess a belief or disbelief in any religion. No person can be punished for entertaining or professing religious beliefs or disbeliefs, for church attendance or nonattendance. No tax in any amount, large or small, can be levied to support any religious activity or institutions whatever they may be called, or whatever form they may adopt to teach or practice religion. Neither a state nor the Federal Government can, openly or secretly, participate in the affairs of any religious organizations or groups and vice versa. In the words of Jefferson, the clause against establishment of religion by law was intended to erect 'a wall of separation between Church and State."
- *US. Supreme Court Decision, Everson v. Board of Education*, 330 U.S. 1 (Feb. 10, 1947), in U.S. Reports, pp. 15-16

Clue 4: U.S.A. Speaks as a dragon!

How does the U.S. Government speak as a dragon?

The separation of church and state, a Republic and Protestantism, is the power that blessed America and has given it prosperity and influence worldwide. It is a young nation that has risen into the world's foremost superpower. There is no other nation on earth like it, but Revelation 13:11 predicts that this lamb-like nation with two horns will speak as a dragon! Remember, the dragon is Satan himself. Satan uses nations such as Papal Rome to attack the true people of God through deception as a snake or persecution as a dragon. It is clear that Satan, the dragon, will use the U.S. to persecute God's people. How does a nation speak? Through its laws. During the 1260 years of the Papal Roman Empire, the papacy persecuted millions of faithful Christians based on its laws. In Revelation 13:11, the lamb-like beast, United States of America will soon create laws that oppress and persecute the true believers of Jesus Christ. This is the reason why all Americans need to be concerned about the eroding away of the U.S. Constitution and the merging of church and state. Since the "terror attacks" on September 11, 2001, and declaration of war on "terror" in America, there has been a rapid erosion of the U.S. Constitution. Millions are willing to give up their freedoms for "safety." Terrorism laws have eroded away many freedoms in America. This is no play matter. We must be aware and take heed to what the Bible reveals prophetically.

What text confirms that Satan will use the United States' power and laws to persecute God's faithful followers?

Revelation 13:12 - "And he [U.S.A.] exerciseth all the power of the first beast before him, and causeth the earth and them which dwell therein to worship the first beast, whose deadly wound was healed."

Revelation 13:12 says that the U.S.A. will do exactly what the "first beast before him," Papal Rome, did in the past. What did Papal Rome do in the past? Remember, they used their laws as a religious-government monarch to oppress and persecute God's faithful. Revelation 13:12 just confirms that this is exactly what the United States government will do in the future as it erodes away the Constitution and the separation of church and state.

CHAPTER 14
LAMB-LIKE BEAST FORCES WORSHIP

Revelation 13:12 - "And he [U.S.A.] exerciseth all the **power** of the first beast before him, and **causeth** the earth and them which dwell therein to worship the first beast, whose deadly wound was healed." America will also use their **"power"**, global economic influence, legislative actions and/ or judicial decisions, to force or **"causeth"** the world to worship Papal Rome, whose deadly wound was healed. Remember, the power of the U.S. government has applied more healing "agents" to heal the "wounds" of Papal Rome! Papal Rome's head is almost completely healed!

Papal Rome has not changed. Their policies and doctrines are still the same as they were centuries ago. They may appear to have adopted to American principles, but historically they believe that church and state should not be separate. They believe that they are the "true universal church" in which both church and state should be under their control in order for the world to experience "true freedom."

Pope Leo XIII writes in his 1879 Encyclical, "The Church of Rome is one monarchy over all the kingdoms, as the mind and soul of the body of a man, or as God in the world. Therefore, the Church of Rome must not only have the spiritual power, but also the Supreme temporal power." - Grant, M.R. Americanism vs. Roman Catholicism. Gulfport, MA: Truth Publishing, 1921, p. 29

Papal Rome can try to make these blasphemous claims, but Jesus is the head of His true church, not man. God has not given any organization the religious power that Papal Rome claims. Papal Rome does not like the U.S. Constitution and its fundamental principles of separation of church and state.

What does Papal Rome say about the U.S. Constitution and its principles of separation of church and state?

"This shameful font of indifferentism gives rise to that absurd and erroneous proposition which claims that liberty of conscience must be maintained for everyone. It spreads ruin in sacred and civil affairs, though some repeat over and over again with the greatest impudence that some advantage accrues to religion from it." - Pope Gregory XVI, Encyclical Letter: On Liberalism and Religious Indifferentism, August 15, 1832

Pope Pius IX in his August 15, 1854, Encyclical Letter says, "The absurd and erroneous doctrines, or ravings in defense of liberty of conscience, are a most pestilential error, a pest of all others, to be dreaded in the State." - Brandt, John, America or Rome: Christ or the Pope, Toledo: The Loyal, 1895, p. 416

Pius also believed that it was an error that "the church ought to be separate from the state and the state from the church." - Ibid, p. 417

In June 1991 after the fall of communism, Pope John Paul visited his homeland of Poland who was freed from under the USSR regime. *Time* magazine published its commentary of John Paul's visit. It noted the pope's thoughts on the separation of church and state: "This time the crowds were smaller and more muted, while the Pope's message was aimed not at repression, but at the **danger of unchecked freedom**. In sermons based on the Ten Commandments, John Paul **denounced** excessive materialism, divorce, contraception and **the separation of church and state**, imploring Poles." - TIME June 17, 1991 *"The Gift Of Life"* p. 47 *Sermons from A Native Son*. John Paul was a modern day pope. Even though Polish people were free from oppressive rule of communism John Paul believed that there is a "danger of unchecked freedom" and denounced "the separation of church and state."

According Pope Leo XIII encyclical of November 7, 1885, he says, "Every Catholic should rigidly adhere to the teachings of the Roman pontiff, especially in the matter of modern liberty, which, already, under the semblance of honesty of purpose, leads to destruction. We exhort all Catholics to devote careful attention to public matters, and to take part in all municipal affairs and elections, and all public services, meetings, and gatherings. All Catholics must make themselves felt as active elements in daily political life in countries where they live. All Catholics should exert their power to cause the constitutions of states to be modeled on the principles of the true church." - Liberty, Second Quarter 1909, Volume 4, No. 2, *Cardinal Gibbons' s Views on Church and State p.6*

"The textbook on public ecclesiastical law used at the Pontifical University in Rome, where the elite of the American clergy are trained, makes the duty of Catholics in the United States very clear: 'Catholics must make all possible efforts to bring about the rejection of this religious indifference of the State and the instauration [restoring], as soon as possible, of the wished-for union and concord of State and Church... Whether tolerance of non-Catholic religions is promised under oath by statutory law or not, it can never be admitted." - James Hastings Nichols, *Democracy and the Churches*, Philadelphia: The Westminster Press, 1951, p. 266. Nichols took the original quote from, La Piana, Shane Quarterly, April, 1942, pp. 92ff.

This study has already revealed the historical evidence of how the U.S. government and its presidents have developed a very close and intimate relationship over the years with the papacy in our modern time "healing the wound" while at the same time eroding away the U.S. Constitution.

All Catholics are taught that their main loyalty is to the pope and the papacy first. See the following quotes:

"The Roman Catholic citizens of the United States owe no allegiance to any principles of the Government which are condemned by the Pope," says The Tablet - Grant, M.R. *Americanism vs. Roman Catholicism*. Gulfport, MA: Truth Publishing, 1921, p. 29

"Nationalities must be subordinate to religion and must learn that we are Catholics first and citizens next," says Bishop Gilmore in the *Lenten Letter*, March, 1873 - Ibid p. 28

Within our modern new millennium era, did you know that the papacy through its Catholic and Jesuit "agents" have successfully secured powerful and influential positions in the U.S. government, Congress, judicial systems, and military defense?

"Undoubtedly it is the intention of the Pope to possess this country [U.S.A.]. In this intention, he is aided by the Jesuits and all the Catholic prelates and priests," says Catholic writer, Dr. O. A. Bronson – Ibid p. 29

The Catholic Register, April 16, 1914, records, "There is no crime that the doting warrior (General Miles) charges against us to which we must not plead guilty. He says that we are trying to make the United States a Catholic country. We most certainly are doing all in our power to accomplish it." - Ibid p. 29

The 113th Congress had a historic high of 163 Catholics in Congress. According to the National Catholic Reporter, "Since at least the 1960s, Catholics have been the single largest denomination in Congress. Although when Protestant denominations are counted together, they still constitute the largest number of members, at 56 percent. Another analysis finds that alumni of Jesuit colleges and universities account for almost 10 percent of all members of Congress." - Patricia Zapor Catholic News Service: Jan. 8,

2013 *Catholics still largest Congress denomination; 10 percent Jesuit grads*
(ncronline.org/news/politics/catholics-still-largest-congress-denomination-
10-percent-jesuit-grads)

According to the Association of Jesuit Colleges and Universities (AJCU),
"Graduates of Jesuit institutions well represented in the 112th U.S. Congress
and Obama Administration ten percent of the 112th U.S. Congress are Jesuit
college and university alumni. Among the 535 Members of this Congress,
53 of them are alumni of Jesuit institutions. At least 30 alumni also serve in
appointed positions in the Obama Administration."

There were 12 Jesuit alumni in the Senate and 41 in the House of
Representatives. Among the top leadership, Congressmen John Boehner
(R-OH) was the first Jesuit alumnus to serve as the Speaker of the House
of Representatives. Did you know that John Boehner was the one who was
able to get Pope Francis, a Jesuit, to speak to U.S. Congress in 2015? Do you
think that was by chance? Of course, not. It was all by the crafty design
of the papacy. Did you know that Boehner was overjoyed that he got the
pope to speak to Congress? There were times in which Boehner was seen
shedding tears of joy during the pope's speech. After Boehner's success the
next day he abruptly "retired" from one of the most powerful positions in the
world. Why? Mission accomplished! His successor as speaker of the house,
Paul Ryan is also a Catholic. This is all pushed by the papacy to execute their
agenda.

<u>Top positions in the Obama Administration who were Jesuit trained:</u>
Members of the Obama administration from AJCU institutions included
Department of Defense Secretary Robert M. Gates (Georgetown University,
1974, PhD), Department of Homeland Security Secretary Janet A.
Napolitano (Santa Clara University, 1979, BA), Central Intelligence Agency
(CIA) Director Leon E. Panetta (Santa Clara University, 1960, BA), Office
of Management and Budget Director Jacob Lew (Georgetown University,
1983, JD), and White House Chief of Staff William Daley (Loyola University
Chicago, 1970, BA).

Before the death of Justice Antonin Scalia in 2016, six out of nine Supreme
Court Justices would have been Roman Catholics, the remaining three
Jewish. Do you think the shift to a majority Catholic Supreme Court, the
highest court in the land, is also by chance? Of course, not.

The Missionary, an old Catholic publication, in June 1909 says, "Many non-Catholics fear us as a political organization and are afraid that the Catholic Church will dominate and rule; we are working quietly, seriously and I may say effectively, to that end." - M.R. Grant, *Americanism vs. Roman Catholicism*. Gulfport, MA: Truth Publishing, 1921, p. 29

The Shepherd of the Valley, the official journal of the Bishop of St. Louis, November 23, 1851 edition reports, "If Catholics ever gain a sufficient numerical majority in this country, religious freedom is at an end-so our enemies say - so we believe." - Thompson, Slason and Hobart C. Taylor, America: *Journal For Americans, Volume 2*, Chicago: Slason Thompson and Co Publishers, 1889, p. 82

Should all Americans and true Protestant Christians worldwide be concerned about this? Yes. "We the people" must wake up to what the Bible is warning us about. The end is extremely near! Let's continue to study.

Remember, Papal Rome, the beast, has a replica of itself known as the image of the beast who symbolically represent all apostate Christian churches who have unified with Papal Rome on key doctrines and principles that ignites the mark of the beast crisis.

What nation makes an image of the beast?
The following verses is a continuation of Revelation 13:11 and 12 which speaks of the lamb like beast with two horns which represents the U.S.A.

Revelation 13:13, 14
13 "And he [U.S.A.] doeth great wonders, so that he maketh fire come down from heaven on the earth in the sight of men,
14 And deceiveth them that dwell on the earth by the means of those miracles which he had power to do in the sight of the beast; saying to them that dwell on the earth, that they should make an image of the beast, which had the wound by a sword, and did live."

The lamb-like beast of Revelation 13:11 has been clearly identified as the United States of America. Revelation 13:14 makes it very clear that the U.S.A. will make an image of the beast! How? Revelation 13:13 says through "great wonders" even making fire come down from heaven. "Wonders" in the Greek also means "signs" or "mark." These great signs will be used as proof to the world that they should worship the beast. These signs will have the power to deceive the world in the "sight" or face of Papal Rome. This shows you the great success of Papal Rome's infiltration in the U.S. Government and its institutions. Their agents will literally be in America to witness this. Remember, in Revelation 13:2 it is the dragon that is behind Papal Rome and in Revelation 13:11 the U.S.A. "speaks as a dragon." It is very clear that the dragon, Satan, is behind the whole operation. He will use the influence of America to deceive the world and make an image of the beast.

You need to beware and study God's Word carefully knowing the truth so you can detect error. **2 Thessalonians 2:9, 10** asserts that this great worldwide deception will be by "the working of Satan with all power and signs and lying wonders, and with all deceivableness of unrighteousness." Right before the coming of Jesus Christ, Satan will come as an "angel of light" to the world. **2 Corinthians 11:14** says, "And no marvel; for Satan himself is transformed into an angel of light." Be not deceived. Jesus says in **Matthew 24:24**, "For there shall arise false Christs, and false prophets, and shall shew great signs and wonders; insomuch that, if it were possible, they shall deceive the very elect." The only ones who are not deceived in the last days are those who are faithfully studying God's Word and abiding in Christ denying all worldliness. If you are not doing this, you will be deceived. There is no middle ground. By the way, in **1 Thessalonians 4:16, 17** the Bible teaches that Jesus at His second coming will descend from heaven to get those who are saved, they will "meet the Lord in the air." Jesus will not touch this earth at His second coming and walk around on the earth.

U.S.A.'s Death Penalty?

Not only will the U.S. make an image of the beast through deceptive signs and wonders, but it will eventually legislate and enforce a death penalty for those who refuse to worship the image of the beast.

Revelation 13:15 - "And he had power to give life unto the image of the beast, that the image of the beast should both speak, and cause that as many as **would not worship the image of the beast should be killed.**"

Remember, America "speaks" through its laws and "causes" through the enforcement of those laws using the police, military, and other law enforcement. In the last days a great number of people will worship the image of the beast because they don't want to be killed. On the other hand, many of God's faithful who refuse to bow down to the image of the beast will be killed. They must stand firm in faith like the three Hebrew young men recorded in Daniel chapter 3 who refused to bow down to the golden image that the king of Babylon set up.

Who will worship the Beast?

Revelation 13:8, 9
8 "And all that dwell upon the earth shall worship him, **whose names are not written in the book of life** of the Lamb slain from the foundation of the world.
9 If any man have an ear, let him hear."

It does not matter if a person is wealthy or broke, popular or not, religious or atheist, on a church role or not, if his or her name is NOT written in the book of life in Heaven that person WILL receive the mark of the beast. All whose names are written in the book of life are covered by the blood of Christ, abiding in Him daily with victory over sin and obeying all the commandments of God out of love.

What is God's promise and reminder for those going through persecution for Christ sake?

Matthew 5:10-12
10 "Blessed are they which are persecuted for righteousness' sake: for theirs is the kingdom of heaven.
11 Blessed are ye, when men shall revile you, and persecute you, and shall say all manner of evil against you falsely, for my sake.
12 Rejoice, and be exceeding glad: for great is your reward in heaven: for so persecuted they the prophets which were before you."

Mark 13:13 - "And ye shall be hated of all *men* for my name's sake: but he that shall endure unto the end, the same shall be saved."

Revelation 3:5 - "He that overcometh, the same shall be clothed in white raiment; and I will not blot out his name out of the book of life, but I will confess his name before my Father, and before his angels."

Those who have to go through the "fire" faithfully endure persecution. They live in Christ in obedience to His word by faith in His name and will be written in the Lamb's book of life. If you are living by the truth expect persecution. **2 Timothy 3:12** says, "Yea, and all that will live godly in Christ Jesus shall suffer persecution." Live the truth, endure to the end!

CHAPTER 15
BACK TO THE THREE ANGELS' MESSAGE

Let's briefly review what you have learned so far about the three angels' messages of Revelation chapter 14:

1st Angel's Message (Revelation 14:7) - Fear (reverence) God, judgment is now, and only worship the Creator God who gives us His blessed and holy seventh-day Sabbath.

2nd Angel's Message (Revelation 14:8) - Babylon is fallen! Babylon means confusion and represents all who teach and live by the doctrines and commandments of men rather than God. Papal Rome, including all apostate Christian religions, false non-Christian religions, and pop-culture are all part of "Babylon."

3rd Angel's Message (Revelation 14:9) - All those who are in Babylon will worship the beast and his image, and will receive the mark of the beast. The beast, represents Papal Rome. The image of the beast represents all apostate churches who unite with the beast in principle and the main doctrine of the mark of the beast. United States of America is the lamb-like beast in Revelation 13:11-17 that will make the image of the beast.

Babylon includes the Mother, Daughters, & Others

This is worth repeating, **all those in spiritual Babylon, drinking the wine of false doctrine, WILL worship the beast and its image and receive the mark of the beast.** Both the beast and the image of the beast are automatically a major part of Babylon. As you already know, the image of the beast looks like the original, like a daughter. This mother and daughter relationship is confirmed in Revelation chapter 17. In summary, there is a woman sitting on a red beast that fits the description of the dragon in Revelation 12:3 and the leopard-like beast of Revelation 13:1, 2. This woman is a corrupt and false church system. This false church system is easily identified as Papal Rome, in its religious role. This red beast is Papal Rome in its governmental monarchical role empowered by Satan. This woman is known as a mother. In Revelation 17:5, this woman is known as the "MOTHER OF HARLOTS." This means that this woman has daughters who are harlots or who have also forsaken the true worship of God. Isaiah 1:21 says, "How is the faithful city become an harlot! it was full of judgment; righteousness lodged in it; but now murderers."

What are the names of the woman sitting on the beast?

Revelation 17:5 - "And upon her forehead *was* a name written, MYSTERY, BABYLON THE GREAT, THE MOTHER OF HARLOTS AND ABOMINATIONS OF THE EARTH."

The forehead again denotes the character. The character of Papal Rome is mystery. They are very secretive. Papal Rome is affiliated with many secret societies. They are Babylon the Great, because they are the head of Babylon, confused false doctrine. They also are the mother of harlots. Harlots are all apostate churches who have "fallen away" from Bible truth. They have disconnected themselves from the Head, Jesus Christ. **The daughters of Babylon are those who look like their "mother" Babylon; they are the image of the beast, all apostate Christian churches.** Papal Rome believes that they are the "universal" church of all Christian religions. Papal Rome views Protestants as wayward "children" who left their "mother." But today many Protestants are no longer protesting the apostasy and false doctrines of Papal Rome, they have unified with her.

Counterfeit Three Angels' Message & Babylon!

To understand the counterfeit message you must understand the true message found in Revelation 14:6-12. In summary, the message is about the true worship of God and giving glory to God our Creator who made the heaven, earth, and the sea. It is a message about the everlasting gospel, and a calling out of God's people from those who have fallen away or rejected truth, and making known the results of those who stay in false worship will be the wrath of God.

Did you know at the very end of time there will be a counterfeit three angels' message that will come from all those in Babylon? This false system is described in Revelation 16:13 and 14 during the "seven last plagues."

Revelation 16:13, 14

13 "And I saw three unclean spirits like frogs come out of the mouth of the dragon, and out of the mouth of the beast, and out of the mouth of the false prophet.
14 For they are the spirits of devils, working miracles, which go forth unto the kings of the earth and of the whole world, to gather them to the battle of that great day of God Almighty."

This is a perfect description of many of the things you already learned about the dragon, the beast, image of the beast, and Babylon. The three unclean (not pure) spirits like frogs are the false three angels' message that leaps out the mouth of the dragon, the beast, and the false prophet. All three make up Babylon. In the Greek, a false prophet is a "pretended foreteller" or "religious impostor." - Strong's Greek Dictionary

Symbolic Spiritual Babylon - Summarized
1. **Dragon** = All of Satan's other false non-Christian religions and beliefs that he uses for example Buddhism, Hinduism, Muslims, New Age, Humanism, Atheism, Satanism, and pop-culture
2. **Beast** = Papal Rome the mother of Babylon
3. **False Prophet** = Image of the Beast – All Apostate Christian churches fallen away from Bible truth

There is no middle ground. You are either following Bible truth or in Babylon. Those who are not abiding in Christ and are not obedient to all of His commandments will be in one of the three parts of Babylon; the beast, image of the beast, or the dragon's other non-Christian systems.

All those in Babylon try to counteract the true three angels' message by working miracles in order to deceive the world leaders and the people on the Earth. In **2 Timothy 3:8, 9,** Paul compares those who are opposing God's true work in the last days to those who opposed Moses. It says, [8]"Now as Jannes and Jambres withstood Moses, so do these also resist the truth: men of corrupt minds, reprobate concerning the faith. [9]But they shall proceed no further: for their folly shall be manifest unto all men, as theirs also was." Just like Satan used the magicians to counteract the work of Moses to Pharaoh, Babylon will try to counteract the work of God's servants in the last days. But in the end the folly of those in Babylon will be manifest to the world and God's truth will continue to go forward with even greater power.

Opposing God's truth is foolish. When the Pharisees were trying to stop the disciples from giving the gospel, Gamaliel told them in **Acts 5:38, 39,** [38]"And now I say unto you, Refrain from these men, and let them alone: for if this counsel or this work be of men, it will come to nought: [39]But if it be of God, ye cannot overthrow it; lest haply ye be found even to fight against God." Only fools think they can fight with God and stop HIS truth from going forward. Their attempts to oppose God's servants is fighting against God. **Deuteronomy 3:22** let's all God's servants know not to fear their persecutors because "the LORD your God he shall fight for you." God will fight for His servants and the folly of their persecutors will become manifest to all. So do not be afraid to stand for the truth.

CHAPTER 16
MARK OF GOD VS. MARK OF THE BEAST

Now let's complete the study on the third angel message and the mark of the beast crisis. Here it is! At this point you should have a foundational understanding of Babylon, the beast, image of the beast, and the lamb-like beast with two horns. All of these are key players in the mark of the beast crisis.

The first part of the third angel's message in Revelation 14:9 warns that if ANY person worships the beast and the image of the beast, that person WILL receive the mark of the beast in his forehead or hand.

Before we move on there are some basics that we have already uncovered about the mark of the beast:

1) The mark of the beast is a "mark" of Papal Rome
2) The mark of the beast is a unifying doctrine that brings all in Babylon together led by Papal Rome (the beast) and all apostate fallen churches (image of the beast).

Now it is time to completely learn and understand the mark of the beast crisis. Are you ready? You must be in humble prayer as God continues to expose you to Bible truth.

Why is the mark of the beast in the forehead or in hand (not both)?

FOREHEAD: What's behind the forehead? The frontal lobe of the brain. This is the reasoning control center of the brain. This is where we make conscious decisions. Those who have the mark of the beast in the foreheads, have the character of the beast. They wholeheartedly believe in the deceptions of the beast as fact.

HAND: The mark of the beast in the hand represents conforming to the demands of the beast because of fear of persecution, hunger, or death.

Satan's counterfeit church system is connected to Babylon, the beast, and its image. **The mark of the beast is her official identifying "mark" on ALL those who worship the beast and its image.** The mark of the beast crisis is connected to false worship. A micro-chip under your skin or a bar code on your literal forehead or hand is not the mark of the beast.

What is the meaning of the "mark"?

According to Strong's Greek dictionary, "mark" is "charagma" which means "a *scratch* or *etching*, that is, *stamp* (as a *badge* of servitude), or *sculptured* figure (*statue*): - graven, mark." The Greek word "charagma" is where we get the English word "character." In Greek, a "kharaktēr" spelled as "character" in English "was a stamping tool, used to give something a distinctive mark." - www.vocabulary.com/dictionary/character. In the Greek, "character" literally means "an engraved mark," something that cannot be easily changed or erased like letters engraved in stone. This "engraved mark" reveals who you are. The way your character is formed begins with your thoughts. Your thoughts influence your feelings; happy, sad, excited, or depressed. Your feelings directly influence your behavior or actions. Your behavior develops habits. Your habits, the things you do over and over again, form or "stamps" your character. This is the reason why it is very important to guard your thoughts, feelings, habits, and actions. Remember, each one is the "etching" or "stamping" tool that forms your character.

What is the "natural" condition of all our characters?

Psalm 1:5 - "Behold, I was shapen in iniquity; and in sin did my mother conceive me."

Romans 3:23 - "For all have sinned, and come short of the glory of God."

Romans 5:12 - "Wherefore, as by one man sin entered into the world, and death by sin; and so death passed upon all men, for that all have sinned."

Sin, the disobedience of God's Ten Commandments, is "stamped" in all of our characters naturally. It takes a "supernatural" stamping tool to change our character. That stamping tool of course is our wonderful Savior and Creator, Jesus Christ!

Jesus came to transform "re-stamp" our characters in the likeness of Him.

Romans 12:2 - "And be not conformed to this world: but be ye transformed by the renewing of your mind, that ye may prove what *is* that good, and acceptable, and perfect, will of God."

2 Corinthians 5:17 - "Therefore if any man *be* in Christ, *he is* a new creature: old things are passed away; behold, all things are become new."

Jesus came to save us from our sin. He came to totally transform our characters. Satan wants our characters to remain in sin. Those who remain in sin, who are stamped with the character of sin, worship the one who is responsible for sin, Satan. Your character will determine who you truly worship. Your character will determine if you will receive the mark of the beast or not. **Who is "stamping" your character?**

Where will God "stamp" His character on those who are faithful to Him and saved into His kingdom?

Revelation 14:1 - "And I looked, and, lo, a Lamb stood on the mount Sion, and with him an hundred forty *and* four thousand, having his **Father's name written in their foreheads.**"

"Name" in Greek is "onoma" which means, authority or character. God's faithful will have His character "engraved" within them. As a result, **Revelation 14:5** says, "And in their mouth was **found no guile**: for they are **without fault** before the throne of God." Those who have the character of God will be found perfect through the blood of Jesus Christ, standing before the throne of God.

Distinctive Mark Owned By Papal Rome, A Counterfeit

The mark of the beast reveals the true character of the Papal Rome and the dragon it truly worships. **The "mark" of the beast is a distinctive mark of Papal Rome that cannot be claimed by anyone else.** Remember, Satan always has a counterfeit to everything that God has that is genuine. Satan's counterfeit may look like the truth, it may smell like the truth, even taste like the truth, but if one word does not line up with the Truth of God's Word it is still a lie. Satan is the master of mixing truth and lies. He may add a lot of truth to his counterfeits, but his one drop of lie makes the whole thing a lie. **The mark of the beast is a counterfeit "mark" to God's genuine "mark."** This genuine "mark" is a distinctive mark claimed by God's faithful people.

What is God's genuine identifying "mark" that reveals that you are a true follower of Jesus Christ?

If we clearly identify God's mark on His people, we know that Satan has a counterfeit mark close behind. Let's briefly go to Revelation 7:1-3.

Revelation 7:1-3
1 "And after these things I saw four angels standing on the four corners of the earth, holding the four winds of the earth, that the wind should not blow on the earth, nor on the sea, nor on any tree.
2 And I saw another angel ascending from the east, having the seal of the living God: and he cried with a loud voice to the four angels, to whom it was given to hurt the earth and the sea,
3 Saying, Hurt not the earth, neither the sea, nor the trees, till we have sealed the servants of our God in their foreheads."

Revelation 7:1-3 is a response to **Revelation 6:17** which ask a very profound question, **"For the great day of his wrath is come; and who shall be able to stand?"** In Revelation 7:1 the "wind" in this prophetic context is strife and chaos in the very last days. More specifically it is the seven last plagues described in Revelation chapter 16. The seven last plagues are also known as the great time of trouble that will happen right before the coming of Jesus Christ. God instructs His four angels to hold these "winds" of destruction until all the "servants of our God" are sealed with the **"seal of the living God"** in their foreheads. The ONLY ones who are going to be able to stand during the seven last plagues and at the second coming of Jesus are those who are sealed with the living seal of God.

Notice that God only seals or marks his faithful symbolically in their foreheads. It is not a literal stamp, but they have been "stamped" with the character of Christ because they are faithfully abiding in Him and are obedient to His Ten Commandments.

<u>**Seal of the Living God, A Seal of Authentication & Preservation**</u>

"Seal" according to Strong's Greek Dictionary is "sphragis" which means "a si*gnet* (as *fencing* in or protecting from misappropriation); by implication the *stamp* impressed (as **a mark** of privacy, or **genuineness**), literally or figuratively: - seal."

Governments use a seal as a mark of authenticity of an official document or law. According to Wikipedia.com, "A seal is a device for making an impression in wax, clay, paper, or some other medium, including an embossment on paper, and is also the impression thus made. The original purpose was to authenticate a document." For example, a notary uses a stamp that makes an official impression on a document to authenticate and certify that you personally signed for the title of your car that proves that you own it.

When you want to complete a deal such as buying a house you cannot "seal the deal" without your unique signature that is seen as a mark or seal that you agree with this contract or deal. You are said to have "sealed the deal" with your signature.

The Greek definition of "seal" also implies that it protects as a fence from "misappropriation" or being unlawful. The seal protects it from corruption or spoilage. Those who are sealed with the seal of the living God in their forehead have the law of God stamped and etched in their hearts. It is a part of their characters. All who are sealed with the seal of the living God live by **Psalm 40:8**, "I delight to do thy will, O my God: yea, thy law *is* within my heart." This invitation is to all people who believe and are true followers of Jesus. God says in **Jeremiah 31:33,** "But this *shall be* the covenant that I will make with the house of Israel; After those days, saith the LORD, I will put my law in their inward parts, and write it in their hearts; and will be their God, and they shall be my people."

What is the seal of the living God that officially marks the faithful people of God as a sign of their loyalty and obedience?

Ezekiel 20:12 - "Moreover also I gave them **my sabbaths**, to be a **sign** between **me and them**, that they might **know that I am the LORD that sanctify them**."

It's repeated again in verse 20, but notice a slight difference.

Ezekiel 20:20 - "And hallow **my sabbaths**; and they shall be a **sign** between **me and you**, that ye may **know that I *am* the LORD your God**."

In verse 12, the keeping of the sabbath is a sign between Him and "them", His faithful followers as a whole. But notice in verse 20 God makes it very personal; the sabbath is a sign between Him and YOU!

Exodus 31:13-17

13 "Speak thou also unto the children of Israel, saying, Verily **my sabbaths** ye shall keep: for it is a **sign** between me and you throughout your generations; that ye may know that I am the LORD that doth sanctify you.

14 Ye shall keep the sabbath therefore; for it is holy unto you: every one that defileth it shall surely be put to death: for whosoever doeth any work therein, that soul shall be cut off from among his people.

15 Six days may work be done; but in the seventh is the sabbath of rest, holy to the LORD: whosoever doeth any work in the sabbath day, he shall surely be put to death.

16 Wherefore the children of Israel shall keep the sabbath, to observe the sabbath throughout their generations, for a **perpetual** covenant.

17 It is a **sign between me and the children of Israel for ever:** for in six days the LORD made heaven and earth, and on the seventh day he rested, and was refreshed."

"Sign" in the Hebrew, "ôth", means "a *signal* (literally or figuratively), as a *flag, beacon, monument, **evidence**,* etc.: - **mark**, miracle, (en-) sign, token."
- Strong's Hebrew Dictionary

<u>So based on our study, sign, seal, and mark are the same.</u> **They are synonymous in their meaning. Remember, keeping the seventh-day Sabbath is a sign or mark that proves your loyalty to God in which you keep ALL of His Commandments as an expression of your love for Him. This sign is the evidence that you rather keep the commandments of God rather than the commandments men.** Do you want to please God rather than man? Do you really love Jesus? Faithfully keeping the Sabbath really separates the "sheep" from the "goats"; the faithful from the unfaithful. Choose you this day who you are going to serve. Remember the seventh-day Sabbath to keep it holy. God has already given you evidence of who He is. Are you going to give Him evidence that you truly love Him and believe His Word by being obedient to His holy Ten Commandments including the seventh-day Sabbath?

The Ten Commandments found in Exodus 20:1-17, is the only official document that is written on two tables of stone by the finger of God. It stands forever and cannot be changed.

<u>**What is the seal or mark of the living God within the Ten Commandments that authenticates the document?**</u>

4th Commandment:

Exodus 20:8-11

8 "Remember the sabbath day, to keep it holy.

9 Six days shalt thou labour, and do all thy work:

10 But the seventh day is the sabbath of the LORD thy God: in it thou shalt not do any work, thou, nor thy son, nor thy daughter, thy manservant, nor thy maidservant, nor thy cattle, nor thy stranger that is within thy gates:

11 For in six days the LORD made heaven and earth, the sea, and all that in them is, and rested the seventh day: wherefore the LORD blessed the sabbath day, and hallowed it."

There are three elements of a legal seal: 1. Name; 2. Title; 3. Territory. For example, on the official seal of the president of the United States, it has the name of the president; title, President; and territory, the United States of America. The fourth commandment reveals the seal or mark of the living God. It reveals His name, the Lord which means Jehovah or self existent one; His title, Creator; and His territory, the heaven, earth and sea.

The seal of the living God or official mark of God that authenticates His Ten Commandments is the seventh-day Sabbath. In other words, the seventh-day Sabbath commandment is the signature of God. It not only authenticates the Ten Commandments, but clearly identifies the Author of the commandments. The seventh-day Sabbath is a holy and distinct mark that comes from the Creator and no one else. It cannot be duplicated or copied to another day. The seventh-day Sabbath is established forever.

All those who are sealed with the mark of God before the "winds" of chaos and strife are let loose, keep the seventh-day Sabbath holy. Satan knows this. This is why he has an all out assault on God's holy day.

Prophetic Symbol: **Seal of the Living God = Seventh-day Sabbath Commandment that authenticates the Ten Commandments.**

Now that we know the true mark or seal of God that is the seal of His authority and supremacy, let's look at the mark of the beast, Satan's counterfeit.

Remember, the "mark" reveals who you truly worship. If you know that the mark of God is His seventh-day holy Sabbath, the mark of the beast, Satan's counterfeit, **has to do with a day of worship** that opposes God's true day according to the Bible.

What is the "Mark of the Beast"?

Remember: **Revelation 14:9** says, "If any man worship the beast and his image, and receive *his* mark in his forehead, or in his hand."

It is clear that the "mark of the beast" is connected to false worship. **It is a doctrine that unifies both the beast, Papal Rome, and his image, apostate Christian churches. The mark of the beast is a counterfeit compared to the genuine seal of God.** Since the genuine seal of the living God is God's holy seventh-day Sabbath, what do you think is the "mark of the beast?" Let's hear what the beast has to say about this.

What does the beast, Papal Rome, say is its distinctive "mark" of authority?

"**Sunday is our Mark of authority**....The church is ABOVE the Bible, and this transference of Sabbath observance is proof of that fact." - Catholic Record, September 1, 1923

"Of course the Catholic Church claims that the change [of the Sabbath to Sunday] was her act. It could not have been otherwise, as none in those days would have dreamed of doing anything in matters spiritual and ecclesiastical and religious without her. And **THE ACT IS A MARK** of ecclesiastical power and authority in religious matters." - James Cardinal Gibbons, in a letter to J .F. Snyder of Bloomington, Illinois, dated November II, 1895, and signed by H.F. Thomas, Chancellor for the Cardinal

Did you get it? **Papal Rome claims that they have "ecclesiastical" power and authority to change God's holy seventh-day Sabbath to the first day of the week, Sunday.** Sunday, is a counterfeit Sabbath that the beast has set up, not God. No one has the right to change God's law. Since Jesus did not come to change His law, how blasphemous and arrogant of Papal Rome to believe that they have a right to change God's law.

Does God predict in Bible prophecy that Papal Rome would "think" to change God's holy seventh-day Sabbath?

Let's go back to Daniel chapter 7 where it talks about the little horn, Papal Rome.

Daniel 7:25 - "And he [little horn/Papal Rome] shall speak great words against the most High, and shall wear out the saints of the most High, and **think to change times and laws**: and they shall be given into his hand until a time and times and the dividing of time."

The Bible predicts that Papal Rome "shall wear out the saints of the most High, and think to change times and laws." The fourth commandment, the seventh-day Sabbath, is the only Ten Commandment law that has to do with time. Papal Rome "thinks" they have authority to change God's Holy Day to another day of the week. Think about it. Can anyone change your birthday to another day? Absolutely not! It is absurd for anybody to think that they have a right to change God's weekly seventh-day Sabbath that He established at Creation.

Papal Rome believes that this change of the Sabbath from the seventh day of the week, Saturday, to the first day of the week, Sunday, is their "mark" of authority. This "change" is their distinctive mark that distinguishes them from all other Christian religions. Here are some more quotes from Papal Rome concerning his "mark":

"Sunday is a Catholic Institution, and its claims to observance can be defended only on Catholic principles... From beginning to end of Scripture there is not a single passage that warrants the transfer of weekly public worship from the last day of the week to the first." - The Catholic Press, Sydney, Australia, August, 1900

"God simply gave His (Catholic) Church the power to set aside whatever day or days, she would deem suitable as Holy Days. The Church chose Sunday, the first day of the week, and in the course of time added other days, as holy days." - Vincent J. Kelly, Forbidden Sunday and Feast-Day Occupations, p. 2

"Question: 'Which day is the Sabbath?'
Answer: 'Saturday is the Sabbath.'
Question: 'Why do we observe Sunday instead of Saturday?'
Answer: 'We observe Sunday instead of Saturday because the Catholic Church in the Council of Laodicea (A.D. 336) transferred the solemnity from Saturday to Sunday.' " - The Convert's Catechism of Catholic Doctrine, by Peter Geiermann, p. 50

There are many more quotes throughout Papal Rome's history just like these. Not only does Papal Rome "think" to change God's Holy Sabbath, but they have also tempered with the Ten Commandments as a whole in order to fit their man-made traditions and commandments. Papal Rome's ten commandments are NOT a summarized version. They literally delete whole passages of the Ten Commandments! They added "strange" gods in the first commandment and deleted the second commandment because they worship idols. They don't think their idols are "strange" gods. Because of the removal of the original second commandment, they made the original third commandment the second commandment and so on. In order to keep "ten" commandments they split the tenth commandment into two parts. As a result of this re-ordering, they made the fourth commandment about God's Sabbath their third commandment. They deleted about 90% of the seventh-day Sabbath commandment and made it very general. There is no mention that the Sabbath is the seventh day of the week. See for yourself.

Below is a comparison of God's original Ten Commandments and the Catholic's man-made commandments:

God's Ten Commandments Exodus 20:1-17	Papal Rome Catholic Ten Commandments
1st Thou shalt have no other gods before me.	1st I am the Lord thy God. Thou shalt not have strange gods before Me.
2nd Thou shalt not make unto thee any graven image, or any likeness of anything that is in heaven above, or that is in the earth beneath, or that is in the water under the earth. Thou shalt not bow down thyself to them, nor serve them: for I the LORD thy God am a jealous God, visiting the iniquity of the fathers upon the children unto the third and fourth generation of them that hate me; And shewing mercy unto thousands of them that love me, and keep my commandments.	**Please note: Papal Rome removed the 2nd Commandment because they worship idols and made the 3rd commandment the 2nd.**
3rd Thou shalt not take the name of the LORD thy God in vain; for the LORD will not hold him guiltless that taketh his name in vain.	2nd Thou shalt not take the name of the Lord the God in vain.

4th Remember the Sabbath day, to keep it holy. Six days shalt thou labour, and do all thy work: But the seventh day is the Sabbath of the LORD thy God: in it thou shalt not do any work, thou, nor thy son, nor thy daughter, thy manservant, nor thy maidservant, nor thy cattle, nor thy stranger that is within thy gates: For in six days the LORD made heaven and earth, the sea, and all that in them is, and rested the seventh day: wherefore the LORD blessed the Sabbath day, and hallowed it.	3rd Remember that thou keep holy the Sabbath day. (Note: Where is the rest of the text? Deleted!)
5th Honour thy father and thy mother: that thy days may be long upon the land which the LORD thy God giveth thee.	4th Honor thy father and thy mother.
6th Thou shalt not kill.	5th Thou shalt not kill.
7th Thou shalt not commit adultery.	6th Thou shalt not commit adultery.
8th Thou shalt not steal.	7th Thou shalt not steal.
9th Thou shalt not bear false witness against thy neighbor.	8th Thou shalt not bear false witness against thy neighbor.
10th Thou shalt not covet thy neighbour's house, thou shalt not covet thy neighbour's wife, nor his manservant, nor his maidservant, nor his ox, nor his ass, nor any thing that is thy neighbour's.	(Note: Papal Rome split tenth commandment into two parts to keep "ten") 9th Thou shalt not covet thy neighbor's wife. 10th Thou shalt not covet thy neighbor's goods.

The change of the seventh-day Sabbath to Sunday and the altering of the Ten Commandments is a complete fulfillment of Daniel 7:25. Papal Rome did "think to change times and laws." How much more proof does a person need to see that Satan is behind this system of religious fraud. Again, there are sincere people who are Catholic and non-Catholic who do not know this truth. Out of love, God is revealing the lie. They have to make their own decision to follow, TRUTH or LIES. At the end of times all who follow the Truth will receive the "seal of the living God", but those who choose to stay in darkness and believe the lies will receive the mark of the beast.

The Sunday "sabbath" and worship is clearly a man-made Papal Roman Catholic institution. It was exclusively established by the papacy as their distinctive "mark" in which no other Christian religious church can claim. Sunday sacredness is the papacy's "trademark."

Papal Rome's current official *"Catechism of The Catholic Church"* on Vatican's website says:

"2189 - Observe the sabbath day, to keep it holy (Deut 5:12). The seventh day is a sabbath of solemn rest, holy to the Lord (Ex 31:15). 2190 - The sabbath, which represented the completion of the first creation, has been replaced by Sunday which recalls the new creation inaugurated by the Resurrection of Christ. 2191 - The Church celebrates the day of Christ's Resurrection on the "eighth day," Sunday, which is rightly called the Lord's Day." - www.vatican.va/archive/ccc_css/archive/catechism/p3s2c1a3.htm

Again, Papal Rome admits that the Bible says that the seventh day is the Sabbath but they believe they had authority to change it to Sunday.

It has to be puzzling why the great majority of Protestants, evangelicals, and non-Catholic Christians honor and worship on Sunday when the Bible is VERY clear that Sunday, the first day of the week, is NOT the holy seventh-day Sabbath that Jesus set up at Creation. Sunday worship is a counterfeit.

Millions of non-Catholic Christians who worship on Sunday do not realize that they are honoring the papacy. Is Papal Rome aware of this? What do they say about other Protestants and non-Catholics honoring and worshiping on Sunday instead of the seventh day of the week, Saturday?

"If Protestants would follow the Bible, they should worship God on the Sabbath day. In keeping the Sunday, they are following a law of the Catholic Church." - Chancellor Albert Smith for Cardinal of Baltimore Archdiocese, letter dated February 10, 1920

"The Sabbath was Saturday, not Sunday. The Church altered the observance of the Sabbath to the observance of Sunday. Protestants must be rather puzzled by the keeping of Sunday when God distinctly said, 'Keep holy the Sabbath Day.' The word Sunday does not come anywhere in the Bible, so, without knowing it they are obeying the authority of the Catholic Church." - Canon Cafferata, The Catechism Explained, p. 89

"I have repeatedly offered $1000 to anyone who can prove to me from the Bible alone that I am bound to keep Sunday holy. There is no such law in the Bible. It is a law of the holy Catholic Church alone. The Bible says,

'Remember the Sabbath day to keep it holy.' The Catholic Church says: 'No. By my divine power I abolish the Sabbath day and command you to keep holy the first day of the week.' And lo! The entire civilized world bows down in a reverent obedience to the command of the holy Catholic Church" - Priest Thomas Enright, CSSR, President of Redemptorist College, Kansas City, Missouri, in a lecture at Hartford, Kansas, and printed in the American Sentinel, June 1883, a New York Roman Catholic Journal

"The observance of Sunday by the Protestants is an homage they pay, in spite of themselves, to the authority of the [Catholic] Church." - Louis Segur, 'Plain Talk About the Protestantism of Today', 1868, p. 213

"Sunday is founded, not of scripture, but on tradition, and is distinctly a Catholic institution. As there is no scripture for the transfer of the day of rest from the last to the first day of the week, Protestants ought to keep their Sabbath on Saturday and thus leave Catholics in full possession of Sunday."- Catholic Record, September 17, 1893

"Sunday is a Catholic institution, and can be defended only on Catholic principles... From beginning to end of Scripture there is not a single passage that warrants the transfer of weekly public worship from the last day of the week to the first." - Catholic Press, Aug. 25, 1900

"Reason and sense demand the acceptance of one or the other of these alternatives: either Protestantism and the keeping holy of Saturday, or Catholicity and the keeping holy of Sunday. Compromise is impossible." - John Cardinal Gibbons, The Catholic Mirror, December 23, 1893

This may be a shock for some, but it is the truth. **Millions of Christian worshipers who go to church on Sunday do not realize that they are NOT following a scriptural doctrine, but a doctrine of Papal Rome.** Many Sunday keepers are blindly obeying the authority of Papal Rome. **The papacy sees that Sunday worship unifies others to them as long as they keep the Sunday institution that they established.** This is the beast and little horn power who has "cast down the truth to the ground" according to **Daniel 8:12**. Christian churches and individuals need to wake up to the truth. Are you going to pick up the truth and follow it?

CHAPTER 17
MARK OF THE BEAST CRISIS REVEALED

W<u>hen will the mark of the beast crisis take place?</u> Let's revisit Revelation 13:11-14 and look at it carefully.

Revelation 13:11-14
11 "And I beheld another beast coming up out of the earth; and he had two horns like a lamb, and he spake as a dragon. [Review: Who is this lamb-like beast? U.S.A]
12 And he exerciseth all the power of the first beast before him, and **causeth the earth** and them which dwell therein to **worship the first beast**, whose deadly wound was healed.
13 And he doeth great wonders, so that he maketh fire come down from heaven on the earth in the sight of men,
14 And deceiveth them that dwell on the earth by the means of those miracles which he had power to do in the sight of the beast; saying to them that dwell on the earth, that **they should make an image of the beast**, which had the wound by a sword, and did live."

There are two key things that the lamb-like beast, America, does to build the platform for the mark of the beast crisis:
1) Causes the world to <u>WORSHIP the beast</u>, Papal Rome.
2) <u>Makes an image of the beast</u>, apostate Christian churches.

How? Remember, it will be done through deception and **ENFORCEMENT** of laws. These laws will be primarily pushed by apostate Christian churches in America who have gained political power with the support of Papal Rome. **The Sunday counterfeit Sabbath is the <u>main unifying doctrine</u> that brings the beast, Papal Rome, and the image of the beast, apostate Christian churches, together. This unifying doctrine of Sunday sacredness will ignite and inflame the mark of the beast crisis in America and around the world.**

<u>What does the image of the beast cause or force?</u>
Revelation 13:15-17
15 "And he had **power to give life** unto the image of the beast, that the **image of the beast** should both **speak, and cause** that as many as would not worship the image of the beast **should be killed**.
16 And he **causeth all**, both small and great, rich and poor, free and bond,

to receive **a mark in their right hand, or in their foreheads:**
17 And that **no man might buy or sell**, save he that had the mark, or the
name of the beast, or the number of his name."

Revelation 13:15-17 prophetically records the mark of the beast crisis. Look
at its key components starting with verse 15. "He" representing America has
authority to give "life" to the apostate Christian churches. How is "life" given
to the image of the beast when the principle of the U.S. Constitution is the
separation of church and state and liberty for all? Notice in the middle of
verse 15 it says that "the image of the beast should both SPEAK and CAUSE."
"SPEAK" reveals that the apostate Christian churches who have become
a reflection of Papal Rome, have gained significant political power in the
United States' legislative systems. In addition to the papacy's "agents" who
are already in legislative and judicial positions, the image of the beast will
add even more. As a result, America with the approval of the majority of its
citizens, gives legislative "life" to the apostate Christian churches, like Papal
Rome. With the merging of church and state, they have power to legislate
"religious" laws for the "common good" and "liberty." These legislations with
the political influence of the image of the beast "CAUSE" or make people
"worship" them. How? It is through **ENFORCEMENT. Those who refuse
to worship as they have legislated are characterized as a small minority
of "trouble-makers", "extremist", "terrorist", and "hateful."** They are not
able to buy or sell and eventually receive the death penalty. These "religious"
laws are passed in the midst of MAJOR economic, social, political, moral,
environmental, and violent crises.

Currently, many Christian churches in America have unified to build a
formidable and powerful political infrastructure to influence elections and
laws within the U.S. government. For example, *The Gathering*, a popular
conference movement for the purpose of unifying Christians throughout
America from various denominations, churches, and ministries says, "The
church must again become the **conscience of the government.** Through
its national solemn assembly it should clearly and respectfully call political
leadership to God's principles for government... It also means we must begin
speaking with one voice so that the nation might see a unified church and
not one that is fractured and scattered by differences in how we practice
our faith." - thegathering2016.com/about. There are many other Christian
conferences and strategy sessions like these sweeping America to gain more
political power.

We must keep in mind the prophecy of Revelation 13:15-17. When the popular and influential churches and ministries in America put away their differences and unite on doctrines that they have in common to influence the U.S. government to enforce their religious decrees and support their institutions, "then Protestant America will have formed an image of the Roman hierarchy, and the infliction of civil penalties upon dissenters will inevitably result." - Ellen White, Great Controversy, p. 445

Don't forget that the major unifying religious doctrine that brings both the beast and its image together is the Sunday counterfeit sabbath that was established by Papal Rome. This is the "mark" of Papal Rome's authority. Sunday Sacredness along with it's Eucharist is extremely serious to the papacy.

Let's examine some excerpts from their "Catechism Of The Catholic Church" which is online at their official website, www.vatican.va/archive/ccc_css/ archive/catechism/p3s2c1a3.htm, concerning "ARTICLE 3 - THE THIRD COMMANDMENT" referring the sabbath commandment:

"2177 The Sunday celebration of the Lord's Day and his Eucharist is **at the heart of the Church's life**. 'Sunday is the day on which the paschal mystery is celebrated in light of the apostolic tradition and is to be observed as the foremost **holy day of obligation in the universal Church**.' "

"2181 The **Sunday Eucharist** is the **foundation and confirmation** of **all Christian practice**... Those who deliberately fail in this obligation **commit a grave sin**."

Based on these two excerpts, Sunday holiness and the Eucharist (Mass) are two key components "at the heart" of Papal Rome's "Lord's Day" sabbath. **They believe that ALL Christians, not just Catholics, are obligated to keep their day of worship and the Eucharist. If not it is a "grave sin."** As mentioned before, the Eucharist is extremely blasphemous and disrespectful to God. No true Christian should have anything to do with it. When the papacy uses the term "universal" with lower cased "u" which is the same word for "catholic," they are referring to all Christians regardless of what affiliation or denomination a person belongs to. Remember Papal Rome believes that they are the only true original church in which they have "universal" authority over ALL Christians.

Let's briefly look at a few more excerpts:
"2187 Sanctifying Sundays and holy days requires a **common effort. Every Christian** should avoid making unnecessary demands on others that

would hinder them from observing the Lord's Day... In spite of economic constraints, **public authorities should ensure citizens** a time intended for rest and divine worship. Employers have a similar obligation toward their employees."

"2188 In respecting **religious liberty** and the **common good of all**, Christians should seek recognition of Sundays and the Church's holy days as **legal holidays**. They have to give everyone a public example of prayer, respect, and joy and **defend their traditions** as a precious contribution to the **spiritual life of society**."

"Sanctifying Sundays and holy days requires a common effort" is a call for governments to legislate Sunday "sabbath" laws for "religious liberty and the common good of all." "Public authorities should ensure a time off intended for rest and divine worship." These public authorities include the legislators or judges who make and interpret the law and law enforcement who ENFORCE the law. For Sundays to be recognized as "legal holidays" also requires the government to legislate a religious doctrine. Papal Rome believes that a Sunday holy day legislation will not only benefit Christians but all people including non-Christians. It will be a time to "defend their tradition" and contribute to the "spiritual life of society." This is extremely dangerous and a violation of the freedom of religion. But the legalization and enforcement of Sunday "sabbaths" is the goal of Papal Rome.

Pope John Paul II believed that the historical Sunday civil legislation of the Empire of Rome around the fourth century, that required Sunday as a legal weekly day off of work, was a great benefit to Christians. In his Apostolic letter entitled, Dies Domini (May 31, 1998) "On Keeping the Lord's Day Holy", he stated, "Christians rejoiced to see thus removed the obstacles which until then had sometimes made observance of the Lord's Day heroic. They could now devote themselves to prayer in common without hindrance." Then he continued to imply in the letter that Sunday legislation should not only be a thing of the past, but enforced in our modern times. He stated, "It would therefore be wrong to see in this legislation of the rhythm of the week a mere historical circumstance with no special significance for the Church and which she could simply set aside. Even after the fall of the Empire, the Councils did not cease to insist upon the arrangements regarding Sunday rest." - Pope John II, Dies Domini, May 31, 1998, Section 64

Ellen White who also wrote much on this topic says, "The dignitaries of church and state will unite to bribe, persuade, or compel all classes to honor the Sunday. The lack of divine authority will be supplied by oppressive enactments. Political corruption is destroying love of justice and regard for truth; and even in free America, rulers and legislators, in order to secure public favor, will yield to the popular demand for a law enforcing Sunday observance. Liberty of conscience, which has cost so great a sacrifice, will no longer be respected. In the soon-coming conflict we shall see exemplified the prophet's words: 'The dragon was wroth with the woman, and went to make war with the remnant of her seed, which keep the commandments of God, and have the testimony of Jesus Christ.' Revelation 12:17." - Ellen White, Great Controversy, p. 592

The legalization and the enforcement of Sunday "sabbaths" is the mark of the beast crisis in which both the beast, Papal Rome, and the image of the beast, apostate Christian churches, will push for in America and around the world. **According to the prophecy, no one has the "mark of the beast" until the Sunday law is passed and enforced.**

Going back to Revelation 13:16, the image of the beast will cause ALL to receive the mark of the beast, which is the legislation and enforcement of Sunday "sabbath" worship, in their "forehead" or "hand." They will "cause" all to submit, rich or poor, through deception or pressure to "worship" the beast and his image and accept the Sunday counterfeit "sabbath." Remember, the mark of the beast is not a physical mark in the forehead or hand. The "forehead" represents a group of people who have the character of the beast. They believe in the deceptions of the beast, accept the counterfeit Sabbath over God's true seventh-day Sabbath, and teach it to others. The "hand" represents a group of people who conform to the enforcement of Sunday legislation because of the fear of persecution, hunger, pain, or death.

Revelation 13:17 predicts that those who refuse the mark of the beast, the name of the beast, or the number of his name will not be able to buy or sell. In other words, those who do not "bow down" in obedience to the enforcement of the Sunday sabbath and who reject the doctrines, traditions, and character of Papal Rome, will be imposed with economic sanctions. This will be reality. Think about it. Our present economic society is almost cashless. Just about every money transaction we make today is done electronically through the Internet, bank card, credit card, or check. Cash and coins are gradually being phased out now and will soon be worthless. During the mark of the beast crisis it is apparent that the government will have centralized control over ALL money transactions electronically, making it easy to stop individuals from buying or selling.

In addition, the "name of the beast" in verse 17 is the "character" of Papal

Rome and the "number of his name" is another characteristic that confirms the identity of the beast.

What is the "number" or another identifying characteristic of the beast?

Revelation 13:18 - "Here is wisdom. Let him that hath understanding **count the number of the beast**: for it is the number of a man; and his number *is* **Six hundred threescore and six**."

666 is the identifying "number of the beast." The beast is clearly identified as Papal Rome. In other words, 666 cannot be applied to anyone else or position that is NOT within Papal Rome. Presidents of the U.S. may have met with the pope, but presidents cannot fit this description. The same for famous people or other controversial figures, they do not fit. "The number of a man" points to a specific position within Papal Rome. The main character of the beast is extremely blasphemous. The papacy take on the roles, right, titles, and worship that only belong to God. They believe that the pope is infallible and is God on earth, the "Vicar of Christ." One of the ancient titles of the popes that was used for centuries is "Vicarius Filii Dei" which is Latin for "Representative of the Son of God." Verse 18 says, "**count the number of the beast.**" When you count and add the Latin numerals to "Vicarius Filii Dei" it equals, 666. (See table below)

"Vicarius Filii Dei" = 666

V	= 5	F	=0	D	=500
I	= 1	I	=1	E	=0
C	=100	L	=50	I	=1
A	= 0	I	=1		
R	= 0	I	=1		
I	= 1				
U(V)	= 5				
S	=0				
Total	= 112		= 53		=501

Add together: 112+53+501 = **666**

Papal Rome has tried to refute this claim, but there is no doubt that 666 applies to the "man" who is head of that system, the pope. 666 cannot be applied to any other system. Again, the Bible says that 666 is "**the number of the beast**" - period.

The prophecy of the mark of the beast crisis, the enforcement of the

Sunday counterfeit "sabbath," is worldwide at the end of time.

<u>**Have there been laws in the past that were made to force people to worship on Sunday?**</u> Let's briefly look at a couple examples.

The Roman Emperor Constantine, a pagan priest sun-worshiper and professed convert to Christianity, named himself Bishop of the Catholic Church and enacted the first civil law regarding Sunday observance in 321 AD. His "conversion" appeared to be more of a political move than a genuine heart change.

Excerpts of the Sunday Law said, "On the venerable day of the sun let the magistrate and people residing in cities rest, and let all workshops be closed. In the country however, persons engaged in agricultural work may freely and lawfully continue their pursuits; because it often happens that another day is not so suitable for grain growing or for vine planting; lest by neglecting the proper moment for such operations the bounty of heaven should be lost." - Schaff's History of the Christian Church, vol. III, chap. 75

The Roman Emperor made this law at the time when the Christian church of Rome, now known as the papacy had already compromised God's seventh-day Sabbath truth and honored the first day of the week, Sunday. It was no coincidence that Sunday was also revered by the pagan sun-worshipers in Rome. It was a day that they gathered together for public worship of their sun god. In order to unite the pagans and Christians for the "common good," Constantine set up a "legal holiday" on Sunday. This was pleasing to both the pagans and Christians. They put away their conflicting interests and became a united religious-power, known as Papal Rome. Papal Rome kept the name "Christian" but adopted many of the traditions, customs, and idol worship of paganism and sun-worship.

"Later, the pope gave directions that the parish priest should admonish the violators of Sunday, and wish them to go to church and say their prayers, lest they bring some great calamity on themselves and neighbors. An ecclesiastical council brought forward the argument, since so widely employed, even by Protestants, that because persons had been struck by lightning while laboring on Sunday, it must be the Sabbath. 'It is apparent,' said the prelates, 'how high the displeasure of God was upon their neglect of this day.' " - Ellen White, Great Controversy, p. 575

<u>Did you know that there were Sunday Laws in American's past?</u> Let's look at a few excerpts from the "American Papers: Bearing on Sunday Legislation," by William Blakely, original print 1800 currently in New York Public Library or online archive.org/details/americanstatepap00blak. This book features Sunday Laws that were at one time enforced in many states:

"Whosoever shall profane the Lords-day, by doing unnecessary servile work, by unnecessary travailing, or by sports and recreations, he or they that so transgress, shall forfeit for every such default forty shillings, or be publickly whipt: But if it clearly appear that the sin was proudly. Presumptuously and with a high hand committed, against the known Command and Authority of the blessed God, such a person therein despising and reproaching the Lord, **shall he put to death or grievously punished** at the Judgment of the Court." (Page 37)

"That from and after the publishing of this law, no person or persons for whatsoever within this Province, shall work or do any bodily labor or occupation upon the Lord's Day, commonly called Sunday, ... (the works of absolute necessity and mercy always excepted)." (Page 45)

"Within recent years, under its Sunday laws, have occurred numerous **prosecutions of conscientious observers of the seventh day, with fines and imprisonments following.**" (Page 78)

These are only a few examples of the past, but it will happen again on a larger scale in America and around the world very soon. The mark of the beast crisis may have already begun after the print of this book. **Remember the Sunday "sabbath" is the rallying cry of Papal Rome and apostate churches that unify them together. They are both promoting legal Sunday "sabbaths".** The Lord's Day Alliance of the U.S., a coalition of Christian Protestant, evangelical, and Catholic churches, confirms that the Sunday "sabbath" is what unifies all Christians. On their website and "Sunday" magazine Spring 2015 edition, they published an article entitled, *Sunday as a Mark of Christian Unity*" written by Scott Brill. He says, **"I also believe that our communal Sunday practices are a sign of unity (something we share as fellow believers) that what unites us is stronger and more profound than what divides us."** - *"Sunday as a Mark of Christian Unity."* The Lord's Day Alliance of the United States, Spring 2015, Vol 102, No. 1: p. 9

According to Deseret News National poll in 2016, sixty-two percent of Americans agree that it is important for society to have one day a week set aside for (spiritual) rest. Only eleven percent disagreed. - Deseret News

Sabbath Day Observance Survey

According to a United Kingdom poll in 2005, NOP Consumer Poll, **"87% of people think it is important for family stability and community life to have a common day off each week."** - UK NOP Consumer Poll, 2005

The people are primed and ready. This is serious.

<u>Are both Papal Rome and modern apostate churches promoting Sunday as a day of rest that will lead to the mark of the beast crisis? If so, how are they promoting it?</u>

There are many modern examples, but let's take a look at a few and read for yourself how the Sunday counterfeit sabbath is being promoted globally:

1) Pope John Paul II: APOSTOLIC LETTER, DIES DOMINI, May 31, 1998:

"The coming of the Third Millennium, which calls believers to reflect upon the course of history in the light of Christ, also invites them to rediscover with new intensity the meaning of Sunday: its 'mystery', its celebration, its significance for Christian and human life."

"Therefore, also in the particular circumstances of our own time, Christians will naturally strive to ensure that civil legislation respects their duty to keep Sunday holy." - Pope John II, Dies Domini. May 31, 1998. Sections 3 & 67.

2) Pope Benedict: *"Sundays must be a day of rest dedicated to God, family, pope says,"* Catholic News Service, June 6, 2012:

" 'The demands of work can't bully people out of needed time off,' Pope Benedict XVI said. 'Sunday must be a day of rest for everyone, so people can be free to be with their families and with God,' the pope said, **'By defending Sunday, one defends human freedom.'** The pope said when he met government representatives in Milan, he reminded them of the importance of policies and laws that protect the family. The most essential is the right to life, 'whose its deliberate suppression can never be allowed.' " - Carol Glatz, *"Sundays must be a day of rest dedicated to God, family pope says."* Catholic News Service, June 6, 2012.

Notice that the papacy believes that "defending Sunday [worship], one defends human freedom." Is that really "freedom"? Force is never freedom, but the papacy believes it is "freedom." You will see the same emphasis on "freedom" in the next quote.

3) Pope Francis: *"Keeping stores open on Sunday is not beneficial for society"* NY Daily News, July 6, 2014:

"Pope Francis lamented Saturday the abandoning of the traditionally Christian practice of not working on Sundays, saying it has a negative impact on families and friendships.

While he said poor people need jobs to have dignity, he indicated that opening stores and other businesses on Sundays as a way to create jobs wasn't beneficial for society.

'Maybe it's time to ask ourselves if working on Sundays is true freedom,' the Pope said." - www.nydailynews.com/news/world/pope-francis-sundays-article-1.1856433

4) Pope Francis believes that Sunday needs to be recovered – in keeping with John Paul II "Dies Domini":

"Pope Francis replies: 'Together with a culture of work, there must be a culture of leisure as gratification. To put it another way: people who work must take the time to relax, to be with their families, to enjoy themselves, read, listen to music, play a sport. But this is being destroyed, in large part, by the elimination of the Sabbath rest day. More and more people work on Sundays as a consequence of the competitiveness imposed by a consumer society.' In such cases, he concludes, 'work ends up dehumanizing people.' The Catholic Church has been recovering this teaching [Sunday "sabbath"] at least since 1998, when Pope John Paul II published his apostolic letter Dies Domini... Last October, about 250 bishops met in Rome for a conference on the movement called the New Evangelization, which focuses on reawakening faith in those already baptized. One of their conclusions was, 'Even though there is a tension between the Christian Sunday and the secular Sunday, Sunday needs to be recovered' - in keeping, they wrote, with John Paul's Dies Domini." - Mark Oppenheimer, *"Pope Francis Has a Few Words in Support of Leisure"* The New York Times. April 26, 2013

5) Francis **promotes Sunday rest and the Eucharist in his Encyclical Letter on climate change:** "On Care For Our Common Home." May 25, 2015:

"On Sunday, our participation in the Eucharist has special importance...

And so the day of rest, centered on the Eucharist, sheds it light on the whole week, and motivates us to greater concern for nature and the poor." - Ibid, Section 237, p. 172-173.

The promotion of Sunday rest and the Eucharist was weaved into Francis' letter to address "climate change. Leaders, legislators, and policy makers from around the world have applauded Francis' letter and have used it to develop policies and legislations worldwide. Along with the persuasion of Pope Francis, it has been the catalyst behind the "Climate Change Paris Agreement" in which the majority of the world governments have adopted.

6) Lord's Day Alliance of the U.S.
Purpose: "The Lord's Day Alliance of the United States exists to encourage Christians to reclaim the [Sunday] Sabbath–the Lord's Day–as a day of spiritual and personal renewal, enabling them to impact their communities with the Gospel." - www.ldausa.org/lda/about/

7) Day One Christian Ministries in the United Kingdom
Purpose: "Day One Christian Ministries campaigns for Sunday to be a day of worship and rest particularly as it is increasingly under threat from retail businesses, sports events and entertainment and as people seek to use Sunday as just another day to make money." - dayone.co.uk/pages/about-us

8) National Back to Church Sunday Movement
"Back to Church Sunday is a campaign strategically designed to help churches reach out and invite everyone to try church again. This powerful movement encourages church attendance by inspiring and empowering church members to invite their neighbors, friends and loved ones to a special Sunday service designed just for them." According to their website, approximately 30,000 churches in America and 1,500 churches worldwide from various denominations and traditions have joined the campaign. It is promoted by many church leaders, pastors and celebrities. - backtochurch.com/about

As you can see, the Sunday "sabbath" movement is real and is gaining in popularity worldwide. **There are also labor and trade unions, businesses, and government and church alliances who are also pushing for Sunday's off for worship and rest.** Let's take a look at a few more examples.

European Sunday Alliance: "The European Sunday Alliance is a network of national Sunday Alliances, trade unions, civil society organizations and religious communities committed to raise awareness of the unique value of synchronised free time for our European societies. Sunday and, more general, decent working hours, are the focus of our campaigns." - www. europeansundayalliance.eu/site/whoweare

The following excerpt from a Huffington Post article, sheds more light on the purpose of the European Sunday Alliance and its supporters:

"In Brussels, dozens of religious groups -- including the Catholic Church -- unions and business associations from 27 countries have formed the 'European Sunday Alliance' to lobby the European Union to keep Sunday as a continent-wide day of rest, at least in principle. Johanna Touzel, the alliance's spokeswoman, said that setting Sunday aside is not necessarily a religious issue, and not discriminatory towards Jews and Muslims. 'We need one day when everyone can rest -- this is the origin of Shabbat. And in fact, even Muslim organizations support us.'" - Speciale, Alessandro. "*Vatican Works To Stop Sunday Shopping In Italy*." Huffington Post, December 20, 2012.

The European Sunday Alliance has also been successful in influencing the European Union Parliament and political European candidates. At a 2014 conference at the European Union Parliament they officially launched a pledge to political candidates that is "aimed at committing European politicians to the promotion of a common weekly day of rest as well as a legal framework guaranteeing sustainable working time patterns based on the principle of decent work." - www.europeansundayalliance.eu/site/ sundayconference2014

The pledge states, "A work-free Sunday and decent working hours are of paramount importance for citizens and workers throughout Europe and are not necessarily in conflict with economic competitiveness. Especially in the present time of socio-economic crisis, the adoption of legislation extending working hours to late evenings, nights, bank holidays and Sundays has direct consequences for the working conditions of employees and for small and medium sized enterprises. Competitiveness needs innovation, innovation needs creativity and creativity needs recreation!" - Ibid

"By signing this pledge, current members of the EU Parliament and candidates in the upcoming European elections commit themselves :

1. To ensure that all relevant EU-legislation both respects and promotes the protection of a common weekly day of rest for all EU citizens, which

shall be in principle on a Sunday, in order to protect workers' health and promote a better balance between family and private life and work;

2.   To promote EU-legislation guaranteeing sustainable working time patterns based on the principle of decent work benefiting society as well as the economy as a whole." - Ibid

Keep Sunday's Special: This is an United Kingdom alliance of trade unions, churches, political parties, business, and other religions that operates as a conventional secular civil society organization to campaign "to retain the existing Sunday Trading regulations" and promote Sunday as "a special day, allowing families and communities to spend time together." - www. keepsundayspecial.org.uk/

Sunday trading law reform "will damage fabric of society" - The Telegraph, August 8, 2105: "Churches, trade unions and retailers have claimed that changing Sunday trading laws will undermine 'the fabric of society' in an open letter published by The Telegraph. Overhauling Sunday trading laws will damage the 'fabric of our society' and threaten family life for no economic gain, churches, trade unions and retailers insist today.

The Church of England has joined forces with Union of Shop, Distributive and Allied Workers (USDAW) and small businesses in a combined attack on ministers' [government officials] plans to overhaul Sunday trading laws.

But, more fundamentally, they insist that the move would trigger the end of a common day of rest and recreation, cherished far more widely than simply those motivated by religious beliefs." - Bingham, John, and Edward Malnick (www.telegraph.co.uk/news/society/11792237/Sunday-trading-law-reform-will-damage-fabric-of-society.html)

European Trade Union Confederation - Pushes for Sunday law in Europe: "The protection of a work-free Sunday is of paramount importance for workers' health, and has a greater impact on workers health and well-being compared to any other work-free day. Sunday work impacts negatively on work-life balance, and results in higher levels of stress, ill-health and absenteeism than other work-free days." - ETUC. *"Fact Sheet: Working Time In The Commerce Sector."* - petition.etuc.org/IMG/pdf/A_TT_secteur_com_EN.pdf

Vatican Works To Stop Sunday Shopping In Italy: "The Roman Catholic

Church, trade unions and small business associations have joined forces in a bid to save Sundays. In a bid to spur economic growth, outgoing Italian Prime Minister Mario Monti backed a new law that allows shops to stay open on the Sabbath. But Sunday traditions are strong in the European nation, and the change provoked strong resistance from religious and secular groups." - Alessandro Speciale, "*Vatican Works To Stop Sunday Shopping In Italy.*" Huffington Post, December 20, 2012

This is real friend. This should wake you up to the reality that prophecy is quickly being fulfilled as the Bible has predicted. Even the Jewish nation of Israel who officially keep Sabbath from sunset Friday to sunset Saturday have succumbed to the worldwide pressure of the Sunday "sabbath."

"Israel Adopts Sundays - Off," by Shalom Bear February 23, 2013, JewishNewsPress.com: "The first vote on new legislation in the 19th Knesset was initiated as a joint effort between Yesh Atid's Rabbi Dov Lipman, Jewish Home's Naftali Bennett, and surprisingly, Prime Minister Benjamin Netanyahu. Easily passing the vote, the Knesset decided that Sundays would now be an official day off from work... But, as proponents of the Sunday-Off plan repeatedly told us, it will make us just like all other nations." - www.jewishpress.com/news/israel-adopts-sundays-off/2013/02/23/

What does Jesus say about rejecting His commandments in order to follow the tradition of man, such as the Sunday "sabbath movement"?

Mark 7:6-9
6 "He answered and said unto them, Well hath Esaias prophesied of you hypocrites, as it is written, This people honoureth me with their lips, but their heart is far from me.
7 Howbeit in vain do they worship me, teaching for doctrines the commandments of men.
8 For laying aside the commandment of God, ye hold the tradition of men, as the washing of pots and cups: and many other such like things ye do.
9 And he said unto them, **Full well ye reject the commandment of God, that ye may keep your own tradition.**"

The Sunday "sabbath" is a counterfeit made by Papal Rome and has become a tradition of millions around the world from various Christian churches and denominations. Even though the majority of the world has rejected the true seventh-day Sabbath, what are you going to do? Follow God or follow after tradition? The choice is clearly up to you.

What does Jesus teach us about following the "majority"?

Matthew 7:13, 14
13 "Enter ye in at the strait gate: for wide is the gate, and broad is the way, that leadeth to destruction, and many there be which go in thereat:
14 Because strait is the gate, and narrow is the way, which leadeth unto life, and few there be that find it."

Blindly following the lies promoted by the majority will lead to destruction. But if people would just open their eyes, study, and apply God's Word for themselves they would be able to walk the narrow way that leads to eternal life through Jesus Christ. If you are looking for comfort in numbers, you will never find it. True comfort can only be found in knowing that you are following truth based on God's Word, not man-made traditions and philosophies.

Are you a Protestant?

The reality today is that many Christian Protestants don't even know the history of the Protestant Reformation. Many do not even know what the word "Protestant" means. Some think it is a specific denomination. It is not. Protestantism came out of centuries of blood, sweat, tears, and prayers by the grace and power of God during the time of the Papal Roman Empire. Papal Rome, who ruled from 538 to 1798 AD, had systematically suppressed God's truth and His Holy Bible. They destroyed both the books as well as the people that revealed the truth. Those who followed God's Word and rejected the false teachings of Papal Rome were killed by the millions. In those dark years God raised up voices to protest against the errors and unbiblical doctrines of Papal Rome. Voices such as the Waldenses, John Wycliffe, Martin Luther, John Huss, Huldrych Zwingli, William Tyndale, John and Charles Wesley, and many others spoke up loudly against Papal Rome. They brought about a world-wide reformation that shed light on God's Bible truths. Many of these Protestant reformers were persecuted and some killed for the sake of TRUTH! For example, William Tyndale was strangled and burned to death for translating the New Testament from Greek to English and parts of the Old Testament from Hebrew to English. He was martyred while working on the translation of the Old Testament before its completion.

Over the years many church denominations were established from the Bible doctrines of the Protestant reformers. Many lived up to the light that they knew at the time. But as the light of truth continued to shine out of the darkness, some lived up to the light while others did not continue to progress. For example, the Methodists based on the teachings of John and Charles Wesley believed in righteousness by faith in the atoning blood of Jesus "and the renewing power of the Holy Spirit upon the heart, bringing forth fruit in a life conformed to the example of Christ." - Ellen White, Great Controversy p. 256. For this truth, they were ridiculed by the ungodly as being "Methodist." Though they brought to light this great truth, they and their followers did not baptize by immersion, they sprinkled with water. They did not have clear understanding of the truth of water baptism by immersion. When a group of Christians learned that they needed to be baptized by immersion, they wanted to follow it. Many of these Christians became known as Baptists because they believed in the Bible truth of baptism by immersion. As God's light of truth progressed after Papal Rome fell in 1798, He expected His people to walk in the light of truth.

As the Protestant movement grew this caused extreme hatred within Papal Rome towards Martin Luther and the Protestants. As a result of Luther's ministry in his home country of Germany, many who used to be Catholic joined the Protestant reformation movement. This is the main reason why the Jesuit order of the papacy was created, to stop the Protestant reformation by any means necessary. Since the time of Martin Luther the Jesuits have been at work. Years after the height of the Protestant reformation in Germany, they successfully overthrew Protestantism in Germany.

Today the papacy, including the Jesuits, have been successful in deceiving millions of Protestant Christians to abandon their Bible beliefs and join the philosophies and doctrines of Papal Rome. Over the past several years, especially in the 2000's, many Protestant churches stopped referring to themselves as "Protestant." They adopted a more acceptable term known as "Evangelicals" instead. Sometimes you may see both terms together, "Evangelical Protestants."

Vatican's Ecumenical Movement

From 1962 to 1965 Papal Rome held a council with church officials that met periodically during the three years known as The Second Vatican Ecumenical Council, also known as Vatican II. The purpose of this council was how to address "relations between the Catholic Church and the modern world." - Wikipedia (en.wikipedia.org/wiki/Second_Vatican_Council). The main purpose of the council was to plan and create strategic methods on how to reach out to other religions and beliefs around the world. They wanted other religions to unite with them in purpose.

At the opening of the first session in 1962 Pope Paul XXIII said, "What is needed at the present time is a new enthusiasm, a new joy and serenity of mind in the unreserved acceptance by all of the entire Christian faith, without forfeiting that accuracy and precision in its presentation which characterized the proceedings of the Council of Trent and the First Vatican Council." - Ibid In the second session in 1963, Pope Paul VI stressed that the council needs to "restore unity among all Christians, including seeking pardon for Catholic contributions to separation; and to start a dialogue with the contemporary world." - Ibid. The implementation of the approved strategies from Vatican II gave rise to the modern ecumenical movement between Protestants, Catholics, and other religions. The word "ecumenical" means "universal, pertaining to the whole Christian church" worldwide. - Dictionary.com

The main purpose of the Ecumenical Movement led by the papacy is to unite the Christian churches and other religions together on issues of mutual concern. They are to put away all belief and doctrinal differences and unify on things that they care about together. They are to be united as one big world-wide family. On the surface that appears to be a notable cause, but understanding prophecy and history, underneath the surface of their agenda is the plan of Satan to join the world together for Papal supremacy and to push the Sunday "sabbath," the mark of the papacy. That's the bottom line. The papacy wants its dominance back and this time it wants the whole world.

Is the "protest" over between the Protestants and Papal Rome?

Millions of Christian individuals, denominations, groups, Protestants, and non-Christian religions and beliefs have been swept away in the tidal wave of the papacy's modern day charisma and the excitement of the Ecumenical Movement. Thousands of groups and religions have officially become part of the papacy's ecumenical movement to address issues of climate change, poverty, slavery, and the Sunday "sabbath."

"In 1999 after intense ecumenical meetings between the Lutheran World Federation and the Catholic's Pontifical Council for Promoting Christian Unity there was an agreement to settle their differences based on the nature of justification. They believed that this was at the heart of Martin Luther's protest. They voted and signed a document known as the Joint Declaration on the Doctrine of Justification (JDDJ) which declares that both churches now share "a common understanding of our justification." - Wikipedia

"On July 18, 2006, members of the World Methodist Council, meeting in Seoul, South Korea, voted unanimously to adopt the document." - Ibid

America at one time was known as a "Protestant" nation. But today it has lost that status and joined with the papacy's ecumenical agenda. Even many former Protestant and Evangelical churches and ministries have joined the papacy's ecumenical movement. For example, in January 2014, a charismatic Protestant minister from the Communion of Evangelical Episcopal Churches, Tony Palmer, spoke to 3,000 evangelicals at the Kenneth Copeland's international leaders' conference in Fort Worth, Texas. Tony Palmer, who was a close friend to Pope Francis and a prominent advocate of the papacy's ecumenical movement, passionately spoke to the spellbound crowd about unifying with Papal Rome and other Christians around the world. He told the group of his close relationship with Francis. He told them how he recorded a personal message from Francis on his cell phone to be shown at the conference. Before he showed the video, Palmer spoke about the historic declaration of the 1999 agreement between the Catholic and Lutheran Churches. He said that the Methodist Church also signed an agreement with Papal Rome and that the evangelical Protestants need to sign on. Then he declared, "Brothers and sisters Luther's protest is over. Is yours?... The protest has been over for fifteen years. If there is no more protest how can there be a Protestant church... Maybe now we are all Catholics again but we are reformed... We preach the same gospel now. The protest is over. The protest is over." - YouTube. Then after his presentation he showed the video of Francis speaking about unity and love. After the video was over the crowd got very excited and enthusiastic. Kenneth Copeland whose TV ministry is seen by millions around the world led out in the excitement and accepted Francis' charge.

A few months after the conference in July 2014, Palmer arranged for a delegation of evangelical Protestant ministers led by Kenneth Copeland and James and Betty Robison to Vatican to meet with Pope Francis in a private ecumenical meeting. It is not a coincidence that Copeland, the Robisons, and other TV ministries that joined them have a combined reach of 700 million people worldwide. They presented to the pope an ecumenical document to "unify" them. Only a few days after this papal visit, Tony Palmer was killed in a motorcycle accident. James Robison believed that the meeting with Francis was a miracle from God. Do you think it was a miracle from God or the dragon, Satan, himself? **This united "power" is that image of the beast that will gain more political power in the United States.** Deception does not make itself obvious, if so it would cease from being deception. Remember, Tony Palmer declared, "We are all Catholics again but we are reformed." Is that you? Have you reformed to this deception? You should have enough knowledge from this study to see prophetically and spiritually the deceptive moves of the Devil in these last days.

The ecumenical movement is growing bigger and bigger with many associations and organizations. Remember, it is the United States of America that makes an image of the beast. They are also deeply involved as a government in the ecumenical movement internationally. In 1998, it created the United States Commission on International Religious Freedom (USCIRF) that monitors the universal right to freedom of religion or belief abroad and makes policy recommendations to the Secretary of State, Congress, and the president. It is comprised of nine commissioners who are appointed by the U.S. president and majority and minority leaders of both the House and the Senate. - Uscirf.gov. This is an extremely influential group to Congress and the U.S. president on religious issues facing the world. "USCIRF initiated an effort in 2014 to network parliamentarians from across the globe who support freedom of religion or belief for all." - Ibid. A parliamentarian is "a person who is an expert in the formal rules and procedures of deliberative assemblies and other formal organizations." - Dictionary.com. "Thirty parliamentarians who represented different regions, political parties and religions, signed an unprecedented joint statement committing themselves to advance religious freedom for all." - Uscirf.gov. The stage and the infrastructure to implement a national and international Sunday "sabbath" law is set. Remember, Papal Rome believes that religious freedom is through the Sunday Eucharist under the papacy. In 2016 President Barack Obama appointed Thomas J. Reese, S.J., a Jesuit priest, as the chair over the USCIRF. A Jesuit priest to protect religious freedom? Do you think that this was by coincidence? Of course not. Jesuits have risen to many influential and prominent positions worldwide to wipe out Protestantism and raise Papal Rome to world domination.

Pope Francis' ecumenical program has been unprecedented and historic. He has managed to meet and form ecumenical relationship with leaders of most major religions, Christian and non-Christian around the world. He has even formed friendly and open relations with top Muslim leaders. This would have been unthinkable just a few years ago. The papacy is cleverly leading the conversation on many issues that unify the world and form ecumenical ties. The papacy has an extremely high status on the world stage as they position themselves to be advocates of peace. For example, The Catholic

Herald reported that "Former Israeli President Shimon Peres has said that Pope Francis is more powerful than the United Nation when it comes to advocating peace… Peres said that the United Nations and its peacekeepers 'do not have the force or the effectiveness of any one of the Pope's homilies, which can draw half a million people just in St Peter's Square alone.' " - Catholic News Service, Catholic Herald, September 4, 2014, *"Shimon Peres: Francis is a more powerful peace advocate than UN."* Peres requested that Francis lead out in a parallel United Nations called the "United Religions" to counter religious extremism. He believes that Francis is an "unquestionable moral authority." - Ibid

This should really have you on your knees right now. Many leaders around the world have the same positive thoughts as Peres about Pope Francis and the papacy as a whole. Are you praying, now? Do you realize that you are living at the end of time? Are you ready? Jesus, please help us all who have submitted to your truth to be ready.

Papal Rome's Wine of Babylon = False Doctrines

Papal Rome has not changed their mission, it's still the same. It is still pushing the same unbiblical doctrines that it pushed for hundreds of years. It is an apostate church that adopted the pagan practices of the Roman Empire. In addition to the Sunday false sabbath, it instituted other man-made doctrines that kept people in darkness. It sold certificates of indulgences that allowed a person to buy "forgiveness" even before he or she sinned. It is a sin "gift card" that credits automatic forgiveness when a person sins. This apostate church also teaches that there is a place known as purgatory, a place of limbo between heaven and hell. The doctrine of purgatory allows a living person to pay money to the Catholic church to buy their dead love one's way from purgatory to heaven. If they don't pay enough or at all they may go to hell! Papal Rome teaches that a person can attain salvation through acts of penance, pilgrimages, rosaries, hail marys, masses, etc. Other false doctrine include spiritualism and idol worship. Many of the idols were pagan gods worshiped by the heathens and when they became Christians they continued to worship the same idols, they just changed the names. For example, the statue of Jupiter became St. Peter. Today, they continually serve and make others drink these false doctrines of Babylon. The false doctrines of Papal Rome have been their teachings for centuries even until modern times. They have not changed. They want to still keep people in darkness, but you don't have to be in darkness.

CHAPTER 18
COME OUT OF HER, MY PEOPLE!

If you have read and studied the entire contents of this book you should have an understanding of God's true Biblical seventh-day Sabbath, the beast, its image, the lamb-like beast, and the mark of the beast crisis. Let's go back to the third message of Revelation chapter 14 to complete this study.

What will happen to those who worship the beast and his image and accept the mark of the beast?

Second part of the third angel's message:

Revelation 14:10, 11

10 "The same shall drink of the wine of the wrath of God, which is poured out without mixture into the cup of his indignation; and he shall be tormented with fire and brimstone in the presence of the holy angels, and in the presence of the Lamb:

11 And the smoke of their torment ascendeth up for ever and ever: and they have no rest day nor night, who worship the beast and his image, and whosoever receiveth the mark of his name."

In summary, those who receive the mark of the beast are those who submit to the enforcement of the Sunday "sabbath" law. They will: 1) Receive the wrath of God; 2) Be tormented with fire and brimstone; and 3) Have NO REST. This is serious business. Why? All those who receive the mark of the beast, who were at one time drinking the wine of Babylon, will in the end drink the wine of the wrath of God that will be mixed with no mercy.

What is the "wrath of God" at the end of time?

Revelation 15:1 - "And I saw another sign in heaven, great and marvellous, seven angels having the seven last plagues; for in them is filled up the **wrath of God**."

The seven last plagues as described in Revelation chapter 16 is the "wrath of God." Those who receive the mark of the beast will drink this cup that will be poured out on all who have rebelled against God's call to repentance and truth in the last days. It will be poured without the mixture of grace and mercy. It will be FULL STRENGTH! In Revelation chapter 16, the "**cup of his indignation**" filled with the wrath of God will be poured into seven vials or cups that will be poured out unto the earth one by one - the seven last plagues. **Revelation 16:1** says, "And I heard a great voice out of the temple saying to the seven angels, Go your ways, and pour out the vials [cups] of the wrath of God upon the earth."

What is the meaning of "tormented with fire and brimstone"?

Fire and brimstone is a description of "hell" when God will execute His judgment on the wicked, those who choose to hold on to sin and reject God's plan of salvation and mercy. Hell is not burning in a pit deep under the earth with the Devil in charge of it. That is fiction. When God rains hell fire and brimstone from heaven the wicked will not burn throughout the ceaseless ages of eternity. The Bible does not teach that the wicked will receive eternal life in hell. Only those faithful to Jesus will receive eternal life in the Heavenly kingdom. The wicked will perish. "The smoke of the torment" of the wicked will eventually dissipate and be gone forever. The book of Malachi teaches that hell fire will not burn forever, but it will burn all the wicked until their punishment is complete. **Malachi 4:1, 3** says, [1]"For, behold, the day cometh, that shall burn as an oven; and all the proud, yea, and all that do wickedly, shall be stubble: and the day that cometh shall **burn them up**, saith the LORD of hosts, that it shall leave them neither root nor branch. [3]And ye shall tread down the wicked; for they shall be ashes under the soles of your feet in the day that I shall do *this,* saith the LORD of hosts." To add to that **2 Peter 3:10** says, "But the day of the Lord will come as a thief in the night; in the which the heavens shall pass away with a great noise, and the elements shall melt with fervent heat, the earth also and the works that are therein shall **be burned up**." God's hell fire is "eternal fire" with everlasting results, those who are burned up by it will never rise again. This is actually what Jude teaches in **Jude 1:7**, "Even as Sodom and Gomorrah, and the cities about them in like manner, giving themselves over to fornication, and going after strange flesh, are set forth for an example, suffering the vengeance of **eternal fire**." Sodom and Gomorrah are not still burning today. The eternal fire has eternal results. Eternal fire cannot be put out by water hoses or extinguishers, it only burns out after it has completed its task of burning up Satan, his demons, and the wicked until they are ALL ashes.

What is the meaning of "have no rest day nor night"?

The end of Revelation 14:11 shows that all those who submit to the false Sunday "sabbath" when it is enforced will have "no rest day nor night," meaning that they will have no peace of mind. They will be in a continual state of stress and worry. There is never true peace and rest in living a lie. Why? **Isaiah 48:22** says, "*There is* no peace, saith the LORD, unto the wicked." **Romans 3:16, 17** continues, [16]"Destruction and misery *are* in their ways: [17]And the way of peace have they not known." In contrast, those truly abiding in Christ in the last days will have peace even in the midst of the great time of trouble. **Isaiah 26:3** says, "Thou wilt keep *him* in perfect peace, *whose* mind *is* stayed *on thee:* because he trusteth in thee." Plus, Jesus promises true peace for the faithful even until the end of time. He says in **John 14:27**, "Peace I leave with you, my peace I give unto you: not as the world giveth, give I unto you. Let not your heart be troubled, neither let it be afraid."

Urgent Loud Cry Message

Remember, in Revelation 14:8 God gives a solemn and urgent warning to the world that "Babylon is fallen, is fallen, that great city, because she made all nations drink of the wine of the wrath of her fornication." Babylon, a system of confusion and false doctrine which includes the papacy, all apostate Christian churches, all non-Christian false religions, and pop culture, through deception and force has made all people drink the Babylonian wine of false doctrine that leads to destruction. God out of His great love for His people ALWAYS gives warning before destruction giving everyone an opportunity to choose everlasting life or everlasting death. Time on earth is coming to an end. Jesus will fulfill His promise. He will come again very soon.

God has very sincere people who are still in Babylon who honestly don't know His truth about the seventh-day Sabbath and the mark of the beast crisis. God has sincere people in many denominations, including the Catholic church, who are living up to the light that they know. During the mark of the beast crisis, God will make known to ALL the world His truth about the seventh-day Sabbath and its counterfeit. God is fair. **1 Timothy 2:4** says that God "will have all men to be saved, and to come unto the knowledge of the truth." **John 4:23, 24** says, [23]"But the hour cometh, and now is, when the true worshippers shall worship the Father in spirit and in truth: for the Father seeketh such to worship him. [24]God is a Spirit: and they that worship him must worship him in spirit and in truth." Now is the time! Those who want to follow the true Jesus Christ of the Bible MUST worship Him in spirit and in truth. The counterfeit Sunday "sabbath" is a lie.

During the mark of the beast crisis, what urgent "loud cry" message does

God give to his people who are still in Babylon?

Revelation 18:1-4

1 "And after these things I saw another angel come down from heaven, having great power; and the earth was lightened with his glory.

2 And he cried mightily with a strong voice, saying, Babylon the great is fallen, is fallen, and is become the habitation of devils, and the hold of every foul spirit, and a cage of every unclean and hateful bird.

3 For all nations have drunk of the wine of the wrath of her fornication, and the kings of the earth have committed fornication with her, and the merchants of the earth are waxed rich through the abundance of her delicacies.

4 And I heard another voice from heaven, saying, **Come out of her, my people**, that ye be not partakers of her sins, and that ye receive not of her plagues."

Come out of Babylon, MY PEOPLE!

Revelation 18:1-4 is a repeat of the second angel's message of Revelation 14:8 during the time of the mark of the beast crisis, but with greater emphasis than before. This message has great authority and has "lightened" the whole earth with truth. Satan's lies are totally exposed. This message "cries mightily with a strong voice" showing the urgency of this end time message that Babylon has not only "fallen" but that it has become the "habitation" or home of the Devil and his demons. Revelation 18:2 says that Babylon is the "hold of every foul spirit." The word "hold" is referring to a "prison." Babylon's lies keep its victims in bondage. It is a prison full of every sin imaginable.

This "hold" or "prison" is also referred to as a "cage" that is full of "every unclean and hateful bird." These birds are like the ones in Jesus' parable in **Luke 8:5** which says, "A sower went out to sow his seed: and as he sowed, some fell by the way side; and it was trodden down, and the fowls of the air devoured it." Jesus explains in **Luke 8:11, 12**, [11]"Now the parable is this: The seed is the word of God. [12]Those by the way side are they that hear; then cometh the devil, and taketh away the word out of their hearts, lest they should believe and be saved." The unclean and hateful birds in Babylon hate the truth and God's Word. Like the Devil, they take away the truth from the hearts of the people. Many unconverted pastors and leaders are like these hateful birds, when the seeds of God's truth about the seventh-Sabbath are sown among their churches they steal away these seeds of truth from their members by making excuses or misrepresenting God's Word. Beware!

Babylon is full of them.

Revelation 18:3 reveals that all people have been drinking Babylon's lies and sin, even the kings, leaders, and presidents of various nation. Many businesses have become very wealthy because of Babylon.

In verse 4, despite all the moral filth, devils, lies and deceptions that are in Babylon, God out of great compassion for all people gives His last urgent plea to those in Babylon during the mark of the beast crisis. He says, "Come out of her [Babylon], my people". God does **not** say, "It is okay to stay or hang around Babylon." He urgently cries, "GET OUT!" When He was about to destroy Sodom and Gomorrah, what message did He tell Lot and his family to do? "GET OUT!" (see Genesis 19:12-15). All who stayed in Sodom were destroyed. All who stay in Babylon will receive the mark of the beast and will be destroyed because they choose to reject or ignore the warning. No one can blame God if they are lost. "My people" that God is referring to are those who are sincerely seeking truth and living up to the Biblical light that they know. When the seventh-day Sabbath truth comes their way they do not hesitate to obey God. In humble gratitude to God they will repent and get out!

Has "Babylon" been clearly identified from the Bible? Are you in Babylon? If you are, what are you going to do? Don't hesitate, get out and run to the "Mountain of Truth." All those who come out of Babylon will be obedient to God's truth. Out of love for God, they will keep all His commandments including the seventh-day Sabbath. They will be sealed with the seal of the living God before the seven last plagues are poured out on the earth as described in Revelation chapter 16. God will have a people who will be saved in the end of time covered with the blood of Jesus, worshiping God in spirit and in truth. Will that be you? Are you going to honor God or man, keep the commandments of God or man, worship God or man? The choice is yours. Choose you this day, who you are going to serve (Joshua 24:15).

God says in **Ezekiel 33:11**, "*As* I live, saith the Lord GOD, I have no pleasure in the death of the wicked; but that the wicked turn from his way and live: turn ye, turn ye from your evil ways; for why will ye die, O house of Israel?" There will be NO EXCUSE in the end. God has given us plenty of time to make the right decision. Those in Babylon do not have to be partakers of her sin and punishment. That is why God is giving an urgent appeal to come out.

CHAPTER 19
PHARMAKEIA

Revelation chapter 18 gives a description of the fall of Babylon and in verse 23 it gives us the reason why all nations were deceived. This may be shocking for many people. Let's read what the Bible says.

Why were all nations deceived by Babylon and destroyed with Babylon?

Revelation 18:23 - "And the light of a candle shall shine no more at all in thee; and the voice of the bridegroom and of the bride shall be heard no more at all in thee: for thy merchants were the great men of the earth; **for by thy sorceries** were all nations deceived."

By the "sorceries" of Babylon all nations were deceived. The Greek word for "sorceries" in verse 23 is "pharmakeia" [far-mak-i'-ah]. According to the Thayer Greek Dictionary "pharmakeia" is "the use or administering of drugs; poisoning; and sorcery, magical arts, often found in connection with idolatry and fostered by it." If you put the original Greek word "pharmakeia" in place of the English word "sorceries" the end of verse 23 would say, "For by thy **pharmakeia** were ALL nations deceived"! "Pharmakeia" is where we get our English word "pharmacy"! Pharmacy is a well organized and professionalized system that administers poisonous drugs. The Bible reveals that Babylon will deceive all nations by the use of pharmacy that is in connection to "magical arts" and idolatry. "Magical arts" has its deep roots in witchcraft and the occultic world. We don't have to do a deep Bible study to know that Satan is directly behind the magical arts and God's people should have nothing to do with it. In general those involved in sorcery, witchcraft, and magic are known to use "magic" potions to "heal", deceive, poison, or kill someone.

Pharmacy mainly uses a mixture of toxic chemicals, metals, and/or synthetic elements to produce "pharmaceuticals" that are designed to manipulate the biochemistry or metabolic functions of the body in an attempt to get a "desired" affect in the treatment of a disease or sickness. In other words, pharmacy mixes up different types of poison, package it, patent it, and claims that it can treat certain types of diseases. The main problem with that system is that poison is poison. Pharmaceutical drugs are poisonous. When poison is put into the body it has negative effects on the entire body system from head to toe. These are not just "side effects" or "unintended" sicknesses or diseases that a person suffers as a result of using a drug. These are "direct effects" because the reality is that drugs have direct effects on the entire body system including the brain.

When you go back to Revelation 18:23, Jesus uses the Greek word "pharmakeia" to reveal to us the main thing that will be used to deceive ALL people in the last days is a well organized system of administering poisonous drugs to billions of people that are not only toxic to the organs of body, but have direct negative effects on the brain. Many of these drugs used for a variety of reasons are known to cause problems with memory, mood, and contribute to negative personality changes.

Who is the main one behind the system of pharmacy and the administering of poisonous drugs that Babylon uses to deceive all nations?

A logo or symbol reveals the values and the purpose of a business, organization, or professional occupation. They use a logo or symbol as an identifying "mark" to the world. In other words, that logo makes a direct link to a business or occupation. When a person thinks of the "swoosh" they immediately think of the Nike corporation. The symbols and logos of modern medicine clearly reveal who is behind the scenes orchestrating the whole system of the administering of poisonous drugs that manipulate the bodies and minds of billions of people around the world. Let's just look at three recognizable symbols and unmask the truth!

Figure A: Bowl of Hygieia

The symbol in Figure A is the international symbol for pharmacy known as the "Bowl of Hygieia." Who is Hygieia? Hygieia comes from Greek mythology. Mythology is the study of myths, or lies and pagan false gods. In other words, though it is not true, millions worship it as if it is true. Who is the father of lies? Satan. According to Greek pagan worship, Hygieia is the goddess of health and hygiene, the daughter of Aesculapius. He is the god of medicine, healing, and physicians.

Ettie Rosenberg, a doctor in pharmacology and attorney describes the meaning of the Bowl of Hygieia. She says, "The 'Bowl of Hygieia' symbol is the most widely recognized international symbol of pharmacy. In Greek mythology, Hygieia was the daughter and assistant of Aesculapius, the God of Medicine and Healing. Hygieia's classical symbol was a bowl containing a medicinal potion with the serpent of Wisdom (or guardianship) partaking it. This is the same serpent of Wisdom, which appears on the caduceus, the staff of Aesculapius, which is the symbol of medicine." - Ettie Rosenberg, Pharm.D., Esq.

Top pharmacists are given brass or "golden" bowls of Hygieia as awards for

their accomplishments. Figure B is a picture of the statue of Hygieia. Notice the serpent drinking the magic potion from the "bowl of wisdom". In **Genesis 3:1-14**, Satan, known as the serpent, used a serpent to deceive Eve. Verse 1 reveals that this serpent was "more subtil" meaning that it was thin or very light, not dense or gross, but smooth and refined in order to accomplish its deceptive purpose.

In verse 6, Eve believed the serpent's subtil lies. Thinking that she could become wise, Eve disobeyed God by eating from the tree that God said not to eat from. In verse 13 after

Figure B: "Hygieia"

eating the fruit from the forbidden tree, Eve acknowledged that the serpent deceived her. When a person is deceived, are they aware of it? According to Webster's dictionary to deceive means "to cause to believe what is false." So when people are deceived, they really believe the lie. Notice Satan used the serpent to deceive Eve so she would believe the lie. This serpent drinking from the "bowl of wisdom" is from Satan. **It represents the deceptive character of Satan that is still deceiving people today.** Should God's people have anything to do with this deception?

Figure C is known as the staff of Aesculapius. His rod represents the healing

aspects of the art of medicine. Many Christians think that this symbol is the same as the serpent of brass that Moses put on a pole, but it is not. Let's read the story in the Bible and see the subtle distinction between the two for yourself. **Numbers 21:6-9** says, [6] "And the LORD sent fiery serpents among the people, and they bit the people; and much people of Israel died. [7] Therefore the people came to Moses, and said, We have sinned, for we have spoken against the LORD, and against thee; pray unto the LORD, that he take away the serpents

Figure C: Rod of Aesculapius

from us. And Moses prayed for the people. [8]And the LORD said unto Moses, Make thee a fiery serpent, and set it upon a pole: and it shall come to pass, that every one that is bitten, when he looketh upon it, shall live. [9]And Moses made a serpent of brass, and put it upon a pole, and it came to pass, that if a serpent had bitten any man, when he beheld the serpent of brass, he lived."

A major difference between the two symbols is that one serpent is poisonous and the other serpent is not. The serpent on the rod of Aesculapius is not poisonous and the serpent on the pole that Moses had was very poisonous. In fact, the Bible says that they were fiery serpents. According to Strong's Hebrew Dictionary, fiery means "*burning,* that is, (figuratively) *poisonous* (serpent)." In fact, the fiery sting of the serpent was so great that death was sure to follow. This is important because of what the pole with the brazen serpent symbolized. The people were being bitten by the fiery serpents because they had sinned. Look at verse 7 again in detail. The people said that they had sinned and they asked Moses to take away the serpents from them. They did not want to be bitten by their fiery sting and die. God then in verse 8 makes a provision for them to be saved. God told Moses to make a fiery serpent and set it on a pole that "every one that is bitten, when he looks upon it shall live." Even though they had been bitten if they truly believed and were obedient to His command and looked at the brazen serpent they would live. The fiery serpent was sure to cause death without this provision that was made. This is <u>very</u> important and explained by Jesus Himself in John chapter 3. **John 3:14-16** says [14]"And as Moses lifted up the serpent in the wilderness, even so must the Son of man be lifted up: [15]That whosoever believeth in him should *not perish,* but have *eternal life.* [16]For God so loved the world, that he gave his only begotten Son, that whosoever believeth in him should *not perish,* but have *everlasting life.*" The fiery serpent on the pole and its venomous bite represented sin and death as a result of disobedience to God. God out of His love for us made a provision for man to be saved from eternal death. Jesus Christ was lifted up on the cross. In so doing, He took the penalty of our sin. He took the fiery sting of sin so we do not have to perish. **2 Corinthians 5:21** says, "For he hath made him to be sin for us, who knew no sin; that we might be made the righteousness of God in him."

If Jesus did not take the fiery sting of sin away from us we would be doomed to eternal death but through Jesus Christ we have hope. **Romans 3:23** says, "For all have sinned, and come short of the glory of God." **Romans 6:23** says, "For the wages of sin is death; but the gift of God is eternal life through Jesus Christ our Lord." The fact that the serpent was poisonous and would surely cause death shows us clearly why we need Jesus. He alone can save us from the deadly poison of sin.

The serpent on the rod of Aesculapius on the other hand was not poisonous. The nonvenomous serpent on the rod of Aesculapius is a counterfeit to Moses' bronze serpent on the pole. This counterfeit symbol gives a false message that the serpent is wise and harmless. It also conveys that sin is NOT poisonous and deadly. Satan is implying that if sin is not poisonous, we do not need a Saviour to save us from its sure results of death.

Remember what Satan told Eve in the Garden of Eden, "Ye shall NOT surely die." In other words, the Deceiver is implying that even if you disobey God and partake in sin that it will not kill you. This is a lie. Sin is poisonous and very deadly and we ALL need to be saved from it. This is why we all need Jesus.

When we recognize the importance of what Jesus did for us it will draw us nearer to Him. In **John 12:32, 33** Jesus says, [32]"And I, if I be lifted up from the earth, will draw all men unto me. [33]This he said, signifying what death he should die." Jesus took the fiery sting of sin for us by His death on the cross. He died so we do not have to suffer eternal death. This should inspire us to love Him for what He has done and to serve Him in sincerity and in truth. Jesus saves us from our sin and our response of love to Him is to obey Him. Remember, Jesus says, "If you love me, keep my commandments." - **John 14:15**

Moses' bronze serpent on the pole was a perfect illustration of sin, its deadly results, and what our Saviour has done for us. Years later, some people worshiped this symbol rather than the Saviour and what it represented. God never intended that the people worship the symbol of the bronze serpent on the pole. They thought the power was in the serpent on the pole and not in God. The Bible records that God commanded king Hezekiah to brake the bronze serpent in pieces to show that this symbol was not to be worshiped. It was powerless. The power of the symbol was in the belief and obedience to the provision that God has made for our salvation. In **2 Kings 18:4** it says that Hezekiah "removed the high places, and brake the images, and cut down the groves, and **brake in pieces the brasen serpent that Moses had made**: for unto those days the children of Israel did burn incense to it: and he called it Nehushtan."

Remember, the serpent on the rod of Aesculapius is the same serpent that is drinking from the Bowl of Hygieia. The message that the serpent of this Satanic symbol is also giving is that it is okay to take the poisonous "magic potent" from the bowl. These symbols that are used to represent the professions of pharmacy and medicine are giving a deceptive message from Satan that taking poisonous drugs are wise and has the power to heal and not kill. This is a lie! Those who submit to this poisonous counterfeit system will be swept away in the mark of the beast crisis.

Figure D is a statue of Aesculapius with his rod wrapped with the "Snake of Wisdom". This "Snake of Wisdom" is seen throughout the symbolism of the modern medical profession. It is in the symbol of the American Medical Association, an association that set the standards for physicians and the medical profession in America. It is found in the middle of the logo of the World Health Organization. It is also found on the logos of medical schools, doctor offices, and many other medical organizations.

Figure D:
Statue of Aesculapius

The next symbol in figure E really sums up who is really behind the poisonous drugging system of Babylon. Figure E is another symbol recognized throughout the medical field, it is known as the "caduceus." A caduceus has two serpents mating around a rod, topped by a pair of wings. The caduceus,

also known as a magic wand, belongs to the Greek god Hermes or the Roman god Mercury. These gods are supposed to be the messengers of gods, inventors of magic, communicators to the "dead" and one who protects business and thieves (drblayney.com/Asclepius.html). Many in witchcraft and sorcery still use the caduceus for magic and to cast spells. Also the caduceus in sorcery is known to "restrain and control" its victims.

Figure E: Caduceus

In Greek mythology and the occultic world the caduceus had nothing to do with medicine, healing or health. So why has modern medicine adopted the caduceus as their symbol of medicine? Remember its original function and meaning. Who holds the caduceus? The false god of Mercury holds it. What is his claim? Inventor of magic, conductor of the dead, protector of merchants, thieves, and to restrain and control is his claim! Could it be that modern medicine has adopted the caduceus as their symbol of medicine and physicians to PROTECT the merchants of the earth that make billions of dollars poisoning people and to protect the corporate thieves and to control and restrain masses of people? This may shock you. Even though the caduceus had nothing to do with healing or medicine, an officer in the U.S. ARMY Medical Corps in 1902 insisted to adopt the caduceus as their symbol. Since then others in the medical profession began to adopt the caduceus as a symbol of medicine or physicians.

Let's lift the veil of what the caduceus really means. In the occultic world, Satan depicts himself as a goat known as Baphomet with two wings and a caduceus between his crossed legs! Yes, Baphomet has a caduceus between his legs. Look at the pictures in Figure F and compare. Here is the direct link between the poisonous practices of modern medicine through pharmakeia and Satan. Satan is behind this drugging system. A caduceus is actually an abbreviated version of Baphomet, Satan himself.

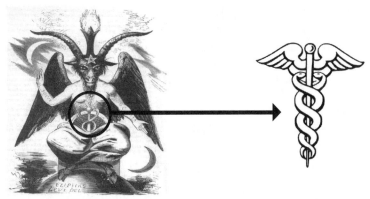

Figure F: Baphomet

Caduceus = Baphomet = Satan

Do you think Jesus is a part of this system? NO. Should true Christians be a part of this drugging system? No. This systematic poisoning is of Babylon and God's people need to get out. We need to learn natures way of healing that God approves of through lifestyle and plant-based eating and herbs.

<u>Did you know that the "father" of pharmacology was an occultist? He was a worshiper of Satan!</u> Born as Philippus Aureolus Theophrastus Bombastus von Hohenheim in 1493, he called himself Paracelsus. He was well known as a Swiss German physician, botanist, alchemist, astrologer, and general occultist. He founded the field of toxicology better known as pharmacy. For hundreds of years physicians used natural herbs and food for healing. Paracelsus defied this notion. From his studies on chemistry and metallurgy with the mix of occultic worship and astrology, he theorized that metals such as mercury, lead, tin, copper, and gold could "purify" the body. He believed that the stars and planets were the main cause of human illness and disease. He believed that ALL diseases should be treated with metals which are poisonous to the body. This was a very radical practice during his time. He treated many diseases with mercury better known as quicksilver. Many physicians who bought into Paracelsus method and used quicksilver (mercury), also known as Quack Salber, were known as "quacks". This was a very rebellious way of treating the body at the time (Jethro Kloss, *Back to Eden*, 2nd ed., pp. 52, 53). Many died as a result of Paracelsus way of treatment. At 50 or 51 years old the story is told that Paracelsus was thrown out the window by other physicians at the time who believed him to be very dangerous in 1541. It is amazing today that Paracelsus is known as the father of modern pharmacy! Where did he get his inspiration? Baphomet, Satan!

<u>Modern Medicine – Poisonous Drugs</u>
This system of Paracelsus is the foundation in which modern medicine is built. It has killed and poisoned millions of people. Pharmaceutical drugs never cure disease – they only try to manage it by inhibiting or manipulating a function in the body that is supposed to happen naturally.

- In a June 2010 report in the *Journal of General Internal Medicine*, authors said that in looking over records that spanned from 1976 to 2006 they found that out of 62 million death certificates, **<u>25 million deaths</u>** were coded as having *occurred in a hospital setting due to medication errors.*

- The total number of deaths due to the American modern medical system of drugging, unnecessary surgeries, infections, medical errors, etc., is nearly **800,000 people per year!** This is more than people who die from heart disease with over 600,000 deaths per year and cancer with over 500,000 deaths per year. - articles.mercola.com/sites/articles/archive/2003/11/26/death-by-medicine-part-one.aspx

This system of administering poisonous drugs worldwide is a trillion dollar industry and the medical merchants of the earth profit greatly from it. They love the money it produces and ignore the many lives it destroys. Millions worship the system as an idol. For example, Novo Nordisk, a billion dollar plus company, is well known for its diabetic drugs. They tell you straight out who they serve and where they get their inspiration from through their company logo. Based on Novo Nordisk's website their logo is the Apis bull (see Figure G). They say, "The Novo Nordisk logo identifies our company instantly and represents the sum of all our values in one symbol.

The Apis bull has been Novo's logo since the year after the foundation of Novo Terapeutisk Laboratorium in 1925. The choice of the logo follows

Figure G: Apis bull
Novo Nordisk's logo

a European chemist tradition of identifying pharmacies through an animal symbol. The logo is a stylized reproduction of an Egyptian statuette dating from circa 664–323 BC. It is richly ornamented with symbols representing among other things, the eternal dualities of life, day and night, life and death. The Apis bull was worshiped as the incarnation of Ptah, creator of the universe, city god of Memphis and the patron deity of craftsmen." - www.novonordisk.com/about-novo-nordisk/ novo-nordisk-in-brief/our_logo.html. This is idolatry and false worship! Novo Nordisk are bold in their pagan beliefs. They are inspired by Satan. The Apis bull can be compared to the golden calf that the children of Israel worshiped out of rebellion after God freed them from Egyptian bondage. God was not pleased when He saw His people worshiping the golden calf and He is not please when millions are "dancing" around Novo Nordisk's Apis bull!

Can poisonous drugs cure diseases?
Poisonous drugs are NOT a cure for disease. Many who prescribe and administer pharmaceutical drugs will admit it. If drugs cured disease, why are many who are being treated for diseases prescribed to take drugs until the day they die. This does not sound like a cure but a money making hoax.

"People need to be taught that drugs do not cure disease. It is true that they sometimes afford present relief, and the patient appears to recover as the result of their use; this is because nature has sufficient vital force to expel the poison and to correct the conditions that caused the disease. Health is recovered in spite of the drug. But in most cases the drug only changes the form and location of the disease. Often the effect of the poison seems to be overcome for a time, but the results remain in the system, and work great harm at some later period. By the use of poisonous drugs, many bring upon themselves lifelong illness, and many lives are lost that might be saved by the use of natural methods of healing." - Ellen White, Counsels on Health, p. 89

"Drugs never cure disease. They merely hush the voice of nature's protest, and pull down the danger signals she erects along the pathway of transgression. Any poison taken into the system has to be reckoned with later even though it palliates present symptoms. Pain may disappear, but the patient is left in worse condition, though unconscious of it at the time." -

Daniel H. Kress, M.D.

"The person who takes medicine must recover twice, once from the disease and once from the medicine." - William Osler, M.D.

You have common sense. Be honest with yourself, how can poison heal anything when it is poison! It would not be poison if it did not do damage to the body. Long term uses of these drugs can contribute to many cancers and other diseases because they are doing untold harm to cells in the body.

How do the merchants of the earth keep this BIG profit machine going?

Private and public health insurance keeps this poisoning machine moving. The government is trying to force many people into this system through universal health insurance often referred to as Obamacare. If you don't have health insurance you can be penalized. This is a precursor of the enforcement of the counterfeit Sunday "sabbath" here in the United States and around the world. Babylon is trying to force ALL to pay into this system of poisoning! Without this system of insurance the average person could not afford to be a part of it. Universal health care has paved the way for the universal mark of the beast crisis.

What will those who are a part of pharmakeia and are suffering from the torment of Satan during the sixth plague not do?

Revelation 9:20, 21
20 "And the rest of the men which were not killed by these plagues yet repented not of the works of their hands, that they should not worship devils, and idols of gold, and silver, and brass, and stone, and of wood: which neither can see, nor hear, nor walk:
21 Neither repented they of their murders, nor of their **sorceries [pharmakeia]**, nor of their fornication, nor of their thefts."

Greek word for "sorceries" in verse 21 is pharmakeia. The wicked who got rich from the system of poisoning will not repent even while suffering from the six plague.

What message does the Bible give for those in pharmakeia – the poison of Babylon?

Galatians 5:19-21
19 "Now the works of the flesh are manifest, which are these; Adultery, fornication, uncleanness, lasciviousness,

20 Idolatry, **witchcraft [pharmakeia]**, hatred, variance, emulations, wrath, strife, seditions, heresies,
21 Envyings, murders, drunkenness, revellings, and such like: of the which I tell you before, as I have also told you in time past, that they which do such things shall not inherit the kingdom of God."

The Greek word for "witchcraft" in verse 20 is pharmakeia. Those who are in this poisoning drugging business who do not repent will not inherit the kingdom of God. This is confirmed in the book of Revelation.

Revelation 21:7, 8

7 "He that overcometh shall inherit all things; and I will be his God, and he shall be my son.
8 But the fearful, and unbelieving, and the abominable, and murderers, and whoremongers, and **sorcerers [pharmakeus =druggist/poisoner]**, and idolaters, and all liars, shall have their part in the lake which burneth with fire and brimstone: which is the second death."

The Greek word for sorcerers in verse 8 is "pharmakeus" defined as a druggist or poisoner. This is repeated in the last chapter of the Bible.

Revelation 22:14, 15

14 "Blessed are they that do his commandments, that they may have right to the tree of life, and may enter in through the gates into the city.
15 For without are dogs, and **sorcerers [pharmakeus = druggist]**, and whoremongers, and murderers, and idolaters, and whosoever loveth and maketh a lie."

Pharmakeia is a part of Babylon. This is what the Bible predicts that Babylon would use to deceive all nations. You don't have to be deceived. There is no way to be a part of God's true people at the end of time and be connected with this system of administering poisonous drugs that manipulate and confuse the mind. This comes from Satan himself. You have seen the evidence. Babylon is fallen, get out before it is too late. It is a broken and poisonous system, "GET OUT" is God's earnest plea.

So why are ALL in Babylon attracted to this system of drugging?

As a result of Babylon's self-indulgent lifestyle many get sick because they continually violate the laws of the body. Many believe that they can manage or even cure their disease with poisonous drugs without major changes to their self-indulgent lifestyle. This is all a deception.

God's Plan - ANEW STARTT

To counteract Satan's system of drugging, God has a lifestyle health plan that will naturally heal the body and give clarity to the mind. It is not based on self-indulgence, but self-control. Jesus contrasts His plan to Satan's plan in **John 10:10.** Jesus says, "The thief cometh not, but for to steal, and to kill, and to destroy: I am come that they might have life, and that they might have it more abundantly." The only way we can have this more abundant life is that we live in Christ by keeping both His moral law of the Ten Commandments and His health laws. In **Exodus 15:26** God gives us a health promise. He says, "If thou wilt **diligently** hearken to the voice of the LORD thy God, and wilt do that which is right in his sight, and wilt give ear to his commandments, and keep all his statutes, I will put none of these diseases upon thee, which I have brought upon the Egyptians: for I am the LORD that healeth thee." Research has revealed that millions of people today suffer from the same diseases of the Egyptians such as heart disease, cancer, diabetes, strokes, and obesity. True healing is possible by eating foods and following a healthy lifestyle that is in harmony with God and the law of the body. Pharmakeia's drugs violate the law of the body. Every cell of the body requires, air, water, nutrition, waste elimination, and freedom from poison. The healthy lifestyle plan that gives us this plus more is the "Ten Commandments of Health" known by the acronym **ANEW STARTT**: *A* - **Attitude**, have the right everyday; *N* - **Nutrition**, eat God's original plant based diet found in Genesis 1:29 and 3:18; fruits, nut, grains, seeds, and veggies; *E* - **Exercise**, 30 minutes 5 days per week; *W* - **Water**, drink 8 cups plus per day; *S* - **Sunshine**, 30 minutes getting vitamin D; *T* - **Temperance**, avoid poisons and harmful habits; *A* - **Air**, fresh everyday; *R* - **Rest**, 8 hours per night, plus Sabbath rest; *T* - **Trust in God**, prayer and daily Bible study; *T* - **Tell Somebody**, share this truth with others. For more information on ANEW STARTT go to PathwaytoPeace.net.

1 Corinthians 6:20 says, "For ye are bought with a price: therefore glorify God in your body, and in your spirit, which are God's." God owns our bodies and everything that goes in our mouths and ALL that we do should glorify Him. "Whether therefore ye <u>eat</u>, or <u>drink</u>, or whatsoever ye do, <u>do all</u> to the glory of God." - **1 Corinthians 10:31**

CHAPTER 20
PATIENT, OBEDIENT, & FAITHFUL

The conclusion of the third angel's message found in Revelation 14:12, 13 reveals a faithful people of God who refuse the mark of the beast, they refuse to worship the beast and his image. They stand firm to truth and worship the God of Heaven rather than the commandments and traditions of man.

How are God's people able to stand firm to truth during the mark of the beast crisis?

Revelation 14:12 - "Here is the **patience of the saints**: here *are* they that **keep the commandments of God**, and the **faith of Jesus**."

In Revelation 14:12, after God gives the urgent message of Babylon, the beast, its image, and the mark of the beast, He reminds us that He will have a faithful people who will go through the mark of the beast crisis. During the crisis it will appear that the whole world is under Satan's banner. Like the fall of literal Babylon, Satan's "Babylon" will completely fall at the end of time as prophesied. Right before the fall of literal Babylon King Belshazzar had a grand party according to Daniel chapter 5. During the peak of the party an armless hand mysteriously wrote cryptic words on the wall at the party. The music ceased and the party stopped. No one was able to read the writing on the wall. By suggestion, Daniel was called to interpret the cryptic message. Daniel told Belshazzar that the message was from God. This message revealed that Babylon would fall that night to the Medes and Persians. It happened as the prophecy foretold.

You can imagine Satan and his demons celebrating about what they were able to accomplish during the mark of the beast crisis and Satan saying in his hellish laugh, "The whole world is wondering after the beast! Who is like unto the beast, who is able to conquer us! Nobody, nobody, nobody!" But the celebration will be interrupted with the words of Revelation to remind Satan that he does not have everybody, "Here is the **patience of the saints**: here *are* they that **keep the commandments of God**, and the **faith of Jesus**." These are they who have not received the mark of the beast, but have the mark of God. Satan's Babylonian kingdom is doomed, it will come to an end. Jesus will soon set up His everlasting kingdom!

There are four main characteristics in Revelation 14:12 that Jesus reveals we must have to make it through the mark of the beast crisis:

1. PATIENCE
2. OBEDIENCE TO ALL GOD'S COMMANDMENTS
3. HAVE THE FAITH OF JESUS
4. SAINT

PATIENCE

What is patience?

The Greek word for "patience" in Revelation 14:12 means "cheerful (or hopeful) *endurance, constancy:* - enduring, patience, patient continuance (waiting)." - Strong's Greek Dictionary

"Cheerful or hopeful endurance" is the kind of patience that God's people must have. How is this developed?

There are three key things that develop patience:
1) Study, understand, and apply God's Word in your life
2) Tribulations
3) Temperance (Self-control)
Let's look at each one.

1) Study, understand, and apply God's Word in your life
Luke 8:15 - "But that on the good ground are they, which in an honest and good heart, **having heard the word**, keep *it,* and bring forth **fruit with patience**."

Romans 15:4 - "For whatsoever things were written aforetime were written for our learning, that we through **patience** and comfort of the scriptures might have hope."

2) Tribulations
James 1:3, 4
3 "Knowing this, that the **trying of your faith worketh patience**.
4 But let patience have her perfect work, that ye may be perfect and entire, wanting nothing."

Romans 5:1-4
1 "Therefore being justified by faith, we have peace with God through our

Lord Jesus Christ:
2 By whom also we have access by faith into this grace wherein we stand, and rejoice in hope of the glory of God.
3 And not only so, but we glory in tribulations also: knowing that **tribulation worketh patience;**
4 And patience, experience; and experience, hope:"

1 Peter 1:6, 7
6 "Wherein ye greatly rejoice, though now for a season, if need be, ye are in heaviness through manifold temptations:
7 That the **trial of your faith**, being much more precious than of gold that perisheth, though it be tried with fire, might be found unto praise and honour and glory at the appearing of Jesus Christ."

James 5:11 says, "Behold, we count them happy which endure. Ye have heard of the patience of Job, and have seen the end of the Lord; that the Lord is very pitiful, and of tender mercy." When Job's faith was tested, he proclaimed in **Job 23:10**, "But he knoweth the way that I take: when he hath tried me, I shall come forth as gold."

God's people MUST go through tribulations in order to develop a patience that will cheerfully endure until the end. This is a witness that can inspire others to have faith in God and develop the same patience. Tribulations reveal real faith from a counterfeit faith. **Revelation 12:17** says, "And the dragon was wroth with the woman, and went to make war with the remnant of her seed, which keep the commandments of God, and have the testimony of Jesus Christ." This will be at its greatest intensity during the mark of the beast crisis as a major trial of your faith. This will be ALL out WAR against God's people! Those who keep ALL of the commandments of God will experience the wrath of Satan, but you do not have to fear, God will give you the strength to endure. In the midst of the battle God's people must stand up for TRUTH. God's people will be a constant reminder to those who are in apostasy that they have compromised truth. This will incite the most bitter hatred and intense persecution against the people of God - like a dragon.

Jesus did not promise His true followers a life of ease, but He does promise, "lo, I am with you alway, even unto the end of the world. Amen." - **Matthew 28:20**. Jesus was in the midst the fiery furnace with the three Hebrew young men when they refused to worship the image of the king of Babylon in Daniel chapter 3. He will also be in the midst of the trials and tribulations for those who refuse to worship the beast and its image. Like the faithful who were persecuted in the past they will declare, [8]"We are troubled on every side, yet not distressed; we are perplexed, but not in despair; [9]Persecuted, but not forsaken; cast down, but not destroyed." - **2 Corinthians 4:8, 9.** Their patience in the midst of persecution will shine even brighter and bring others to know the truth.

Jesus says, "If they have persecuted me, they will also persecute you." - **John 15:20.** **2 Timothy 3:12** says, "Yea, and **ALL** that will live godly in Christ Jesus shall suffer persecution." Jesus says, "They shall put you out of the synagogues: yea, the time cometh, that whosoever killeth you will think that he doeth God service." - **John 16:2.** Through the centuries all of God's faithful have gone through persecution and tribulations, but it will be at its peak during the mark of the beast crisis. If you are faithful to Jesus, you will be mocked, scoffed, and rejected. Some will be put into prison, tortured, or even killed for the sake of Bible truth. During these times of tribulation your patience will be tried with fire, but if you endure, continue to abide in Christ, you will be saved. You will learn to rejoice even in the midst of trials and tribulations. You will repeat the words of **1 Peter 4:12, 13,** [12]"Beloved, think it not strange concerning the fiery trial which is to try you, as though some strange thing happened unto you: [13]But rejoice, inasmuch as ye are partakers of Christ's sufferings; that, when his glory shall be revealed, ye may be glad also with exceeding joy." You will remember the words of Christ in **John 16:33** as you are being falsely accused and ridiculed, "These things I have spoken unto you, that in me ye might have peace. In the world ye shall have tribulation: but be of good cheer; I have overcome the world." To "be of good cheer" means to have courage and boldness. Jesus tells us in **Matthew 10:17-22,** [17] "But beware of men: for they will deliver you up to the councils, and they will scourge you in their synagogues; [18]And ye shall be brought before governors and kings for my sake, for a testimony against them and the Gentiles. [19]But when they deliver you up, take no thought how or what ye shall speak: for it shall be given you in that same hour what ye shall speak. [20]For it is not ye that speak, but the Spirit of your Father which speaketh in you. [21]And the brother shall deliver up the brother to death, and the father the child: and the children shall rise up against *their* parents, and cause them to be put to death. [22]And ye shall be hated of all *men* for my name's sake: but he that endureth to the end shall be saved." To endure is to remain in God's truth no matter what happens to you or someone you love through trials and tribulations.

3) Temperance "Self – Control"
2 Peter 1:4-8

4 "Whereby are given unto us exceeding great and precious promises: that by these ye might be partakers of the divine nature, having escaped the corruption that is in the world through lust.
5 And beside this, giving all diligence, add to your faith virtue; and to virtue knowledge;
6 And to knowledge **temperance; and to temperance patience**; and to patience godliness;
7 And to godliness brotherly kindness; and to brotherly kindness charity.
8 For if these things be in you, and abound, they make you that ye shall neither be barren nor unfruitful in the knowledge of our Lord Jesus Christ."

The Greek meaning for "temperance" is "self control." - Strong's Greek Dictionary. In order to develop patience, according to 2 Peter 1:6, you first must develop temperance, self-control. Paul explains it best in **1 Corinthians 9:27**, "But I keep under my body, and bring *it* into subjection: lest that by any means, when I have preached to others, I myself should be a castaway." In other words, instead of your natural fleshy desires controlling you, you through the power of Jesus must control it. For example, hunger is a natural desire that we all have. It is not a sin to be hungry nor is it a sin to eat, but should you allow hunger to control what you eat? Can you eat just anything because you are hungry? Of course not. Your decisions must have control over what you eat. Are you eating healthy food that will build the blood, nourish, and strengthen the body or are you going to eat food that will harm and eventually kill the body? Remember, "Whether therefore ye eat, or drink, or whatsoever ye do, do all to the glory of God. - **1 Corinthians 10:31**. It is literally impossible to develop patience without temperance. If you have not learned how to have temperance ask God to help you live a temperate life in which He has full control.

OBEDIENCE TO ALL OF GOD'S COMMANDMENTS

The second characteristic we must have to make it through the mark of the beast crisis is that we MUST be obedient to ALL of God's commandments, including the seventh-day Sabbath. It does not matter what others profess, say, or do, we must stay loyal and obedient to what God reveals in His Word. **Deuteronomy 13:1-4** says, [1]"If there arise among you a prophet, or a dreamer of dreams, and giveth thee a sign or a wonder, [2]And the sign or the wonder come to pass, whereof he spake unto thee, saying, Let us go after other gods, which thou hast not known, and let us serve them; [3]Thou shalt not hearken unto the words of that prophet, or that dreamer of dreams: for the LORD your God proveth you, to know whether ye love the LORD your God with all your heart and with all your soul. ⁴Ye shall walk after the LORD your God, and fear him, and keep his commandments, and obey his voice, and ye shall serve him, and cleave unto him."

Remember the words of Jesus:
John 14:15 - "If ye love me, keep my commandments."

John 14:21 - "He that hath my commandments, and keepeth them, he it is that loveth me: and he that loveth me shall be loved of my Father, and I will love him, and will manifest myself to him."

John 14:23, 24
23 "Jesus answered and said unto him, If a man love me, he will keep my words: and my Father will love him, and we will come unto him, and make our abode with him.
24 "He that loveth me not keepeth not my sayings: and the word which ye hear is not mine, but the Father's which sent me."

FAITH OF JESUS
The third characteristic we must have to make it through the mark of the beast crisis is the faith of Jesus.

It is the faith of Jesus alone that makes us righteous. **Hebrews 11:1** says, "Now faith is the substance of things hoped for, the evidence of things not seen." The word *faith* has the same meaning as belief or trust. Hope is the expectation that God will fulfill His promises and you believe it by faith. Faith is something you can't see, but you believe in the evidence that has been revealed through Creation, God's Word, and the great blessings in your life. Your belief produces action and obedience to God's Word.

When you are going through the mark of the beast crisis you cannot depend on your emotions to make it through, you must wholly depend on God and His Word. **Jeremiah 17:9** says, "The heart *is* deceitful above all *things,* and desperately wicked: who can know it?" You can't trust yourself! **Proverbs 28:26** says, "He that trusteth in his own heart is a fool: but whoso walketh wisely, he shall be delivered." You can't even put your trust in people. **Psalm 146:3** says, "Put not your trust in princes, *nor* in the son of man, in whom *there is* no help." To add to that **Jeremiah 17:5** says, "Thus saith the LORD;

Cursed *be* the man that trusteth in man, and maketh flesh his arm, and whose heart departeth from the LORD."

You MUST have ALL your faith in Jesus to make it through. **Proverbs 3:5** says, "Trust in the LORD with all thine heart; and lean not unto thine own understanding." **Psalm 37:5** says, "Commit thy way unto the LORD; trust also in him; and he shall bring *it* to pass." **Psalm 125:1** says, "They that trust in the LORD *shall be* as mount Zion, *which* cannot be removed, *but* abideth for ever." And **Jeremiah 17:7** says, "Blessed *is* the man that trusteth in the LORD, and whose hope the LORD is."

SAINTS

The fourth characteristic we must have to make it through the mark of the beast crisis is that we must be true saints of God. A true saint of God is not a hypocrite or pretender, but the real deal.

The word "saint" in the Greek means "sacred" (**physically** *pure*, **morally** *blameless* or *religious*, ceremonially **consecrated**). – Strong's Greek Dictionary

Saints are not conformed to the sinful world's way of eating, drinking, dressing, and behaving. They are transformed through the Word and thinking of Jesus Christ. Their diet promotes healthy living. They are not enslaved to the fashions of the world. Their dress is neat, wholesome and pure. They dress modestly. They do not wear tight or revealing clothes that do not cover their private parts. They avoid anything that promotes the lower passions and the lust of the flesh. Their character is morally blameless and consecrated to God through the holiness of Jesus Christ. They are totally unspotted by the sinful world. Through the power of God, they have learned to live in the world but not be a partaker of the sinful things of the world. They do not waste God's time in the mindless and idle hours of amusements, movies, and entertainments of the world. Their music is uplifting to God and directs their attention to Him.

What does the Bible say about the character of a true saint of God?

James 1:27 - "Pure religion and undefiled before God and the Father is this, To visit the fatherless and widows in their affliction, *and* to keep himself unspotted from the world."

Titus 2:11, 12
11 "For the grace of God that bringeth salvation hath appeared to all men,
12 Teaching us that, denying ungodliness and worldly lusts, we should live
soberly, righteously, and godly, in this present world."

1 Peter 1:14-16
14 "As obedient children, not fashioning yourselves according to the former
lusts in your ignorance:
15 But as he which hath called you is holy, so be ye holy in all manner of
conversation;
16 Because it is written, Be ye holy; for I am holy."

2 Peter 1:4 - "Whereby are given unto us exceeding great and precious
promises: that by these ye might be partakers of the divine nature, having
escaped the corruption that is in the world through lust."

2 Corinthians 7:1 - "Having therefore these promises, dearly beloved, let us
cleanse ourselves from all filthiness of the flesh and spirit, perfecting holiness
in the fear of God."

Ephesians 1:4 - "According as he hath chosen us in him before the
foundation of the world, that we should be holy and without blame before
him in love."

Those are some very powerful promises for the true saints of God. We are
to constantly look to Jesus in order to stay holy in Jesus. We cannot afford
for one moment to take our eyes off Jesus. The worldliness, violence, and
entertainment on the cable TV, satellite dish, and Internet will NOT prepare
you for the final crisis. Hollywood, NBA, NFL, PGA, MLB, WWE, NHL,
video games, and all things similar will prepare you to receive the mark of
the beast. So if those are things you are still attached to, you must ask God
for help and detach yourself from ALL things that conform you to the ways
of the world. Studying, understanding, and applying God's Word in your life
will be the only thing that will prepare you for the mark of the beast crisis.
It will be impossible to make it through without being a true saint of God.
True saints have total victory OVER sin! Saints are patient, obedient, and
faithful.

**At the end of the three angels' message, what precious promise does God
give those who may be killed as a result of standing for truth during the**

mark of the beast crisis?

Revelation 14:13 - "And I heard a voice from heaven saying unto me, Write, Blessed *are* the dead which die in the Lord from henceforth: Yea, saith the Spirit, that they may rest from their labours; and their works do follow them."

Those who die for upholding the banner of truth during the mark of the beast crisis will rest, but the result of their labor will grow fruit for the kingdom of God. Their death is more seed for the gospel. Jesus remembers their labors. A martyr's death inspires others with more boldness and endurance until the end of time.

During the mark of the beast crisis why are some of God's saints beheaded and killed?

Revelation 20:4 - "And I saw thrones, and they sat upon them, and judgment was given unto them: and *I saw* the souls of them that were beheaded for the witness of Jesus, and for the word of God, and which had not worshipped the beast, neither his image, neither had received *his* mark upon their foreheads, or in their hands; and they lived and reigned with Christ a thousand years."

Some of God's saints will be beheaded for witnessing about Jesus and standing firm for God's Bible truth. They know and keep the true Sabbath, and refuse to worship the beast and his image, not receiving the mark of the beast. As a result, some are killed. But as Revelation 20:4 reveals, they will rise again when Jesus comes again and be seen in Heaven!

The mark of the beast crisis is real, but no one needs to be caught unaware. The Bible has revealed the truth about the true seventh-day Sabbath, the beast, the image of the beast, the lamb-like beast, and the mark of the beast. Jesus is appealing to every reader to study and obey His Word. There is only safety in following God's Word in these last days. Out of love Jesus has exposed the crisis before us so we can be ready. Remember God's promise that He will be with us when we go through the great tribulation. If we patiently endure, keep God's commandments, have the faith of Jesus, and are saints, we will come out of GREAT TRIBULATION and stand before the throne of God (Revelation 7:14, 15).

CHAPTER 21
WHY GOD CREATED TIME

One of the greatest evidences that God is real is TIME. Have you ever thought about where time came from? Humans are NOT the inventors of time. Did you know that God is the Creator of time? Have you ever thought about why God created time even before humans sinned? What is the purpose of time from the beginning when He created humans to live forever?

Remember, in Genesis God created this world in six literal 24 hour days and on the seventh day He rested, blessed, and made it holy as a blessing for all humanity. From the beginning, even before sin entered this world, God created the seventh-day Sabbath as a special time that completes a seven day week cycle. The seventh-day Sabbath is the only day in God's Creation that God commanded us to remember.

What is the purpose of time without an anticipated appointment? The seventh-day Sabbath is the only specific anticipated appointment that God has given throughout His Creation. If you come at a different time other than the specified time set for the appointment, you will miss it. The creation of time is centered on this divine appointment of the seventh-day Sabbath. Without time, the seventh-day Sabbath could not exist. During the other six days of the week, God wants us to look forward with great anticipation to the Sabbath. Time points to a weekly Sabbath. **The seventh-day Sabbath is a special time that unifies us to God.** If God did not want to have a special time to unify His people, coming together for this sanctified time to worship, there would be no reason to have time. Think about it. Time was not created for the sole purpose of just counting days and years gone by. What would be the purpose of time especially in the context of eternity? In the new Heaven and Earth you would have no reason to keep track of your age. Can you imagine someone asking you in the new Heaven and Earth, "How old are you?" Your reply, "I'm one million, four hundred thousand, nine hundred and sixty-two years old." The only reason we track our ages now before eternity is because of the anticipation of growing old and death. But even before sin and death, God created time for the divine appointment of His people coming together on the Sabbath day.

Even in the new Heaven and new Earth, throughout the ceaseless time of eternity, God will still have a seven-day weekly cycle. At the end of each week we will ALL unify to meet on the seventh-day Sabbath to worship our Creator. **Isaiah 66:22, 23** says, [22]"For as the new heavens and the new earth, which I will make, shall remain before me, saith the LORD, so shall your seed and your name remain. [23]And it shall come to pass, *that* from one new moon to another, and from one sabbath to another, shall all flesh come to worship before me, saith the LORD."

The creation of time which points to the Sabbath is proof of the existence of God and His power. Let's take time and study TIME that God created at the beginning of the world that proves His existence and power.

When did God create time?

Genesis 1:1, 2
1 "In the beginning God created the heaven and the earth.
2 And the earth was without **form [desolation-no shape]**, and **void [empty]**; and **darkness** *was* upon the face of the deep. And the Spirit of God moved upon the face of the waters."

Darkness is the absence of light. It cannot be measured. It has no speed.

Genesis 1:3 - "And God said, Let there be light: and there was light."

God made visible light. Notice, on the first day of creation God did not make the sun. God's word illuminated a dark world by suspending light in space without the aid of a sun. Visible light is electromagnetic waves with illuminating energy that penetrates darkness and illuminates our space allowing us to see our surroundings and its objects. Visible light is measured by its illuminating speed as it cuts through darkness. Light can travel 186,282 miles per second! That's approximately 671 million miles per hour. When a light wave travels from the sun to light the earth it takes at least 8 minutes and 17 seconds to get here.

Light was created first because it defines time. Without the visible light time could not be established, time as we know it could not exist. How is this proven?

Genesis 1:4, 5
4 "And God saw the light, that *it was* good: and God **divided** the light from the darkness."

5 And God called the **light Day**, and the **darkness he called Night**. And the evening and the morning were the first day."

This is the introduction of time to the earth. Light = day. Darkness = night. "Evening" is defined as dusk or sunset at the beginning of darkness. Time was created on the first day of Creation.

Again, the first day is defined by the separation of light and darkness. Do you remember when an official day begins? Think about this. When God created the earth on the first day, what was first the light or darkness? Darkness, of course. The light divided the darkness. The first day began in the dark until God penetrated it with light.

In **Genesis 1:5** it says, "And God called the light Day, and the darkness he called Night. And the evening and the morning were the first day." At the end of each day of Creation, God said that the evening and the morning was the day. You see this same pattern at the end of each day of the Creation week in Genesis 1:8, 13, 19, 23, and 31. So the day began at evening or sunset and continued throughout the next morning until the next evening when the next day would begin. Each day was a complete 24 hour day.

24 Hours is Universal

All over the world the measurement of time is the same. Why? God designed it that way to point to His special seventh-day Sabbath and as a **sign** of His awesome power, glory, and promises.

Sun and Moon: The Big Clock in the Heavens

According to Genesis 1:14-19 the sun, moon, and stars were created on the fourth day of Creation. Before the sun was created it is obvious that light was suspended in space to light the world. On the fourth day God gathered the visible light and put it in a round star we call the sun in the midst of space. This round earth orbits around the sun as it rotates on its axis. Also, on the fourth day, God made the moon to revolve around the earth to reflect the light of the sun at night. He also gathered the light and put it in distant stars millions of light years away from our planet that can only be seen at night.

Why did God make the sun and the moon?

Genesis 1:14 - "And God said, Let there be lights in the firmament of the heaven to divide the day from the night; and let them be for **signs**, and for seasons, and for days, and years."

FIVE MAIN Purposes for the sun and moon
1. Divide day from night
2. Seasons (determined by the position of the earth and tilt of the axis as it orbits around the sun – spring, summer, fall and winter.)
3. Days (24 hours, evening [sunset] to evening – one complete literal day.)
4. Years (one complete rotation around the sun)
(Notice: The sun and the moon are the earth's physical clock that tracked time before sin.)
5. Signs

Why is one of the main purposes for the sun and moon used as "signs"?

Remember, "sign" in Hebrew means:
1) Monument
2) Evidence-Proof
3) Distinguishing Mark.

In other words, the sun and the moon are monuments, proof, and God's special distinguishing mark of His Creation, power, glory, and promises. The sun and the moon are God's time clock to count the days (24 hours), months (12), seasons (spring, summer, fall, and winter), and years as a monument or sign of His power, authority, Creation, and promises. It is also the mark of His authority over the creation of time and its management. **Psalms 19:1-3** says, [1] "The heavens declare the glory of God; and the firmament sheweth his handywork. [2]Day unto day uttereth speech, and night unto night sheweth knowledge. [3]There is no speech nor language, where their voice is not heard." "Declare" in Hebrew means "to inscribe." So the heavens inscribes a line in the sky bearing the signature of God as a perpetual monument that speaks loudly to us of the glory, magnificence, and power of our Creator. People all over the world can understand its message for "there is no speech nor language, where their voice is not heard."

CHAPTER 22
360 TO 365 DAYS
"God's Proof to ALL the World"

In this final chapter of this study, God wants to share with the world another clear and distinct sign that He is real, powerful, and all the promises in His Word are true. This sign also has to do with time. Since God is the Creator of time, He has ALL power over time. Remember, the sun and the moon are a part of God's universal clock system to keep track of time. Let's study.

What determines a day? Remember, a complete 24 hour day is from sunset to sunset. As the Earth is revolving around the sun it is spinning on its axis. During daylight about half of the Earth is facing the sun for about 12 hours. At the end of the daylight from our vantage point it appears that the sun is going down as it spins away from the sunlight to face the dark space. One complete 24 hour rotation on the Earth's axis determines a day.

What determines our month? The moon determines our months. God designed the moon to revolve around the Earth in 30 days. The moon goes around the Earth about 30 days and it does this 12 times per year. When the moon has made one complete revolution around a new month begins.

What determines our year? When the Earth makes one complete circle around the sun that represents a year in time. Currently, it takes approximately 365 days for the Earth to make a complete circle around the sun, BUT originally there were only 360 days in a year.

THE CREATOR'S CLOCK

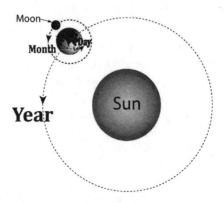

360 Days?

Did you know from the beginning when the sun and moon were created, it only took 360 days for the Earth to make a complete revolution around the sun? Originally, all the world was based on the 360 day calendar year. This is real good, so read carefully and pay close attention.

What is proof that 360 days was used for over 3000 years?

According to the Bible, there were originally exactly 30 days in a month for 12 months for a total of 360 days per year. This can be proven by looking at Noah's account of the worldwide flood recorded in the book of Genesis. Genesis 7:11, 24 says, [11]"In the six hundredth year of Noah's life, **in the second month, the seventeenth day of the month**, the same day were all the fountains of the great deep broken up, and the windows of heaven were opened. [24]And the waters prevailed upon the earth an **hundred and fifty days**." The flood started on the second month and seventeenth day. The Earth was completely covered with water for 150 days. When did the floodwaters recede? Let's read Genesis 8:3, 4. It says, [3]"And the waters returned from off the Earth continually: and after the **end of the hundred and fifty days the waters were abated.** [4]And the ark rested in the **seventh month,** on the **seventeenth day** of the month, upon the mountains of Ararat." The water receded on the seventh month and seventeenth day, five months later. To figure out how many days were in each month during the time the floodwaters covered the Earth, divide 5 months into 150 days which equals to 30 days per month (150/5 = 30). 1 Chronicles 27:1, 15 shows us clearly that "all the months of the year" were 12. There are ancient records that Egyptians, Babylonians, Chinese, Indians, Mayans, and the Jewish cultures used the 360 day calendars. Then a major change took place that effects us even today. However, this change did not interfere with God's seven day weekly cycle.

Perfect harmony Sun and Moon = 360 Days

At the beginning of time, the revolution of the moon around the Earth and the 360 days of the Earth's revolution around the sun were in perfect harmony. Every 30 days was a month, a complete revolution of the moon around the Earth. It did that perfectly 12 times per year (12 x 30 days = 360 days). This harmonized perfectly with the exact amount of time it took for the Earth to revolve around the sun. The sun and moon were synchronized in perfect harmony like a big clock in the sky as the Earth rotated on its axis.

Circle = 360 degrees

In math a circle is divided into 360 degrees. All circles, whether they are big or small, have 360 degrees. The 360 degrees of a circle is based on the 360 days that it took for the Earth to circle around the sun. Each degree corresponded to a day around the sun. The Bible says that the Earth is a round ball shaped circle. **Isaiah 40:21, 22** says, [21]"Have ye not known? have ye not heard? hath it not been told you from the beginning? have ye not understood from the foundations of the earth? [22]*It is* he that sitteth upon the circle of the earth, and the inhabitants thereof *are* as grasshoppers; that stretcheth out the heavens as a curtain, and spreadeth them out as a tent to dwell in." **The circle of the Earth was clearly known in Bible days and taught from generation to generation.**

This Earth spins on its axis one complete rotation in 24 hours. As it spins, it is also revolving around the sun. It took 360 days for the Earth to completely revolve around the sun to determine a year. It took 30 days for the moon to revolve around the Earth to determine a month. It took 12 months of 30 days each for the Earth to revolve around the sun as the moon revolves around the Earth for a total of 360 days a year. **Man did not make this process, they simply WATCHED this natural occurring phenomenon as time was displayed.** All around the world it WAS the same. This was very simple and easily understood. There was perfect harmony between the Earth and the moon going around the sun like clockwork. The year was synchronized at 360 days by the hands of the Creator. Just like beautiful music, this melody of time was understood by people around the world regardless of their different languages.

When time stood still

Since you know what determines time, let's look at a time when time stood still. In order for time to stand still the "big clock" in the heavens would have to stop. The Earth's revolution around the sun, the moon's revolution around the Earth, and the Earth spinning on its axis must ALL stop at the same time for the same length of time in order for time to stand still. This is totally impossible for us to do. Remember, since God is the Creator of time, ONLY He has the power to stop time.

Is there an example in the Bible in which God stopped time completely?

Yes, you find the story in the book of Joshua during the time the Israelites were at war with the Amorites. Joshua, the commander of the Israelites, asked God to stop time so that they could have more day light in order to defeat the Amorites.

Joshua 10:12-14

12 "Then spake Joshua to the LORD in the day when the LORD delivered up the Amorites before the children of Israel, and he said in the sight of Israel, **Sun, stand thou still** upon Gibeon; and thou, **Moon**, in the valley of Ajalon.

13 And the **sun stood still, and the moon stayed**, until the people had avenged themselves upon their enemies. *Is* not this written in the book of Jasher? So the sun stood still in the midst of heaven, and hasted not to go down about a whole day.

14 And there was **no day like that before it or after it**, that the LORD hearkened unto the voice of a man: for the LORD fought for Israel."

Notice, God stopped the revolution of the Earth around the sun, the revolution of the moon around the Earth, and the Earth's rotation! This stopped time! This never happened since. Since God is the author of time, He has ALL authority and power to stop time. This stoppage of time did not interfere with the synchronized harmony of the sun, moon, and the Earth.

From 360 to 365 the sign of God and His power!

We have no power to manipulate or change time. We can only WATCH and observe time made and displayed by God. We may be able to move the hands on a clock, but that does not change real time. Again, there were 30 days in a month determined by the moon, 12 months in a year determined by the Earth's circuit of the sun, and 7 days in a week established by God.

How did we go from 360 days to 365¼ days for the Earth to make a complete revolution around the sun in one year? In other words, how did we go from 360 to 365?

Friends, we do not have to go to the theories of men, the Bible has the answer. Since God is in control, God is the only one who has authority to physically move time, Earth or moon. God explains to us in His Word how and when this change took place to display as proof to the whole world of His power, existence, and great authority.

The change from 360 to 365 days is in the story of Hezekiah, king of Judah. It is found in 2 Kings 20:1-11 and Isaiah 38:1-9. Let's read Isaiah's account.

Isaiah 38:1-9

1 "In those days was Hezekiah sick unto death. And Isaiah the prophet the son of Amoz came unto him, and said unto him, Thus saith the LORD, Set thine house in order: for thou shalt die, and not live.

2 Then Hezekiah turned his face toward the wall, and prayed unto the LORD,

3 And said, Remember now, O LORD, I beseech thee, how I have walked before thee in truth and with a perfect heart, and have done *that which is* good in thy sight. And Hezekiah wept sore.

4 Then came the word of the LORD to Isaiah, saying,

5 Go, and say to Hezekiah, Thus saith the LORD, the God of David thy father, I have heard thy prayer, I have seen thy tears: behold, I will add unto thy days fifteen years.

6 And I will deliver thee and this city out of the hand of the king of Assyria: and I will defend this city.

7 And this *shall be* **a sign** unto thee from the LORD, that the LORD will do this thing that he hath spoken;

8 Behold, I will bring again the shadow of the degrees, which is gone down in the sun dial of Ahaz, **ten degrees backward**. So the **sun returned ten degrees**, by which degrees it was gone down.

9 The writing of Hezekiah king of Judah, when he had been sick, and was recovered of his sickness."

What was the sign that God would heal Hezekiah from his sickness and deliver him from his enemies, the Assyrians?

Isaiah told Hezekiah that the Lord would give him a sign. This sign from the Lord would be clear evidence that would prove "that the LORD will do this thing that he hath spoken." God was going to do something that no man could do, only God. Look at what the Lord said in verse 8, "Behold, I will bring again the **shadow of the degrees, which is gone down in the sun dial of Ahaz, ten degrees backward**. So the **sun returned ten degrees**, by which degrees it was gone down." This was not a small sign, but one of GREAT significance even for us today. **To understand the significance of this you must understand a typical sundial that was used during the time of king Hezekiah.**

Various cultures, such as the Babylonian's, used a sundial to keep track of time. A typical sundial was marked evenly starting with 360 degrees at the top (our 12 o'clock). A stationary needle device cast a shadow on the degree

Typical Sundial

markings of the sundial as the sun tracked across the sky from east to west from sunrise to sunset. In later years the modern world took the same concept and made the clock based on the tracking of the sundial.

On the sundial only half of the time was displayed. At night, there was no need to have a sundial without the sunlight. So the sundial, just like our modern clocks are based upon, only had 12 hours represented.

Like all circles, the sundial had 360 degrees. The 12 hours on the sundial were divided into 360 degrees (see Figure H). Each degree represented a measure of time. To find out how many minutes are in **ten degrees** we will do a little math. From this we will find out exactly how many minutes God

Figure H: 360 Degrees = 720 Minutes

N

12 o'clock

340 350 360 10 20
310 320 330 0 30
300 40
290 50
280 60
W 270   9 o'clock | 3 o'clock   80 E
260 100
250 110
240 120
230 130
220 140
210 200 190 180 170 160 150
6 o'clock

S

reversed the Earth's rotation on in its axis as it revolved around the sun.

<u>Simple Math:</u>
1. First convert the hours to minutes.
    12 hours x 60 minutes/hour = 720 minutes.
2. Then divide minutes by the degrees.
    720 minutes / 360 degrees = 2 minutes each degree
3. Therefore, 10 degrees would be 2 x 10 = <u>**20 minutes**</u>

(**10 degrees = 20 minutes**)

In other words, God moved the rotation of the Earth on its axis back <u>20 minutes as a sign</u> to Hezekiah that He would fulfill His promise. It is also a sign for us that proves that God is powerful, His Word can be trusted, and that He will fulfill the promises in His Word.

<u>When did God move the Earth back 20 minutes?</u>

2 Chronicles 29:1 says, "Hezekiah began to reign *when he was* five and twenty years old, and he reigned nine and twenty years in Jerusalem. And his mother's name *was* Abijah, the daughter of Zechariah." Hezekiah became king of Judah around 715 BC. He was 25 years old when he became king. He reigned for a total of 29 years. 25 + 29 = 54 years old when he died. He was given 15 additional years from the time he was deathly sick. 54 – 15 = 39. Hezekiah was 39 when he was sick. So the time God moved the Earth back 20 minutes (715 – 14 = 701) was between 701 to 700 BC.

<u>Is there any record in the Bible that God moved time forward again to readjust 20 minutes?</u>

NO. Remember in this case God reversed the Earth's rotation back for 20 minutes, but He did not reverse the revolution of the moon around the Earth. When the Earth was reversed the moon continued to revolve around the Earth. When the Earth resumed its rotation after the being set back for 20 minutes the sun and moon were out of sync.

<u>How did this 20 minutes affect the 360 days per year?</u>

When God moved the time back 20 minutes, it made the Earth's rotation 20 minutes late each day! Over the course of a year this seemingly small time added up. It has not caught up. Everyday it is still 20 minutes behind.

1. What does 20 minutes a day for 360 days equal to?
    20 x 360 = 7200 minutes

2. **How many hours are 7200 minutes?** Do the math.
    There are 60 minutes in 1 hour. Simply, 7200 / 60 = 120 hours
3. **How many days are 120 hours?**
    There are 24 hours in 1 day. Simply, 120 / 24 = **5 days**

So when God moved the Earth back 20 minutes it was late for the next 360 days which equaled to 5 extra days to make a complete revolution around the sun. The time it took to make the Earth move back 20 minutes on the sundial is the additional time added to the 5 days. Since then 5 days have been added to the year; **360 + 5 = 365**. This is how the Earth's revolution around the sun went from 360 days to 365 days.

It now takes 365 days for the Earth to make a complete circle around the sun because God moved the Earth back 20 minutes around 700 BC as a sign to Hezekiah that he would heal him and give him victory over his enemy. This is powerful coming directly from the BIBLE! **In other words 360 to 365 is a sign or proof of the power, might, and reality of God.** This movement of the Earth was such a big deal in the time of king Hezekiah, the heathen kings of the Earth were amazed! When God moved the Earth back ten degrees they actually saw the shadow of their sundials go backwards! This event was of GREAT significance around the whole world. News of the sign spread abroad quickly of what happened and why it happened as a sign of the awesome power of God. The king of Babylon sent ambassadors to king Hezekiah "to enquire of the wonder that was done in the land" (**2 Chronicles 32:31**). This was a great time for Hezekiah to witness to the messengers and the heathen king of Babylon about the power of God and the one who has the power to literally move the Earth. Isaiah chapter 39 sadly records that Hezekiah failed in his witness about God and instead showed off his wealth and stuff! **Isaiah 39:3-7** says, [3]"Then came Isaiah the prophet unto king Hezekiah, and said unto him, What said these men? and from whence came they unto thee? And Hezekiah said, They are come from a far country unto me, even from Babylon. [4]Then said he, What have they seen in thine house? And Hezekiah answered, All that is in mine house have they seen: there is nothing among my treasures that I have not shewed them. [5]Then said Isaiah to Hezekiah, Hear the word of the LORD of hosts: [6]Behold, the days come, that all that is in thine house, and that which thy fathers have laid up in store until this day, shall be carried to Babylon: nothing shall be left, saith the LORD. [7]And of thy sons that shall issue from thee, which thou shalt beget, shall they take away; and they shall be eunuchs in the palace of the king of Babylon." Many years later it happened exactly as prophesied because Hezekiah failed to testify about the power and proof of the true God.

This prophecy was literally fulfilled by Daniel. Daniel was taken into captivity by the Babylonians and made a eunuch that served in the kings court. Despite the difficulties of their captivity, God promised the captives that if they would be faithful to Him, He would be faithful to them. Despite the fact that as eunuchs they would be unable to have children to pass on their names, God would give them an everlasting name. **Isaiah 56:4, 5** promises, ⁴"For thus saith the LORD unto the eunuchs that keep my sabbaths, and choose the things that please me, and take hold of my covenant; ⁵Even unto them will I give in mine house and within my walls a place and a name better than of sons and of daughters: I will give them an everlasting name, that shall not be cut off."

Daniel understood that it was his responsibility to witness to the Babylonians of the only true God who is King of kings and Lord of lords and that it was His God who "**changeth the times** and the seasons: he removeth kings, and setteth up kings: he giveth wisdom unto the wise, and knowledge to them that know understanding." - **Daniel 2:21**.

Daniel faithfully declared to Nebuchadnezzar king of Babylon that it is God that controls the time - not just the 20 minutes of time but all the way to the end of time. King Nebuchadnezzar was wondering about what was going to happen to his kingdom. God gave King Nebuchadnezzar a prophetic dream that reveals the rise and fall of kingdoms until the King of kings sets up His everlasting Kingdom. Remember, the kingdoms of Babylon then Media-Persia followed by Greece then Rome, even to now have occurred with precision just as God said they would. **Daniel 2:42-45** says, ⁴²"And as the toes of the feet were part of iron, and part of clay, so the kingdom shall be partly strong, and partly broken. ⁴³And whereas thou sawest iron mixed with miry clay, they shall mingle themselves with the seed of men: but they shall not cleave one to another, even as iron is not mixed with clay. ⁴⁴And in the days of these kings shall the God of heaven set up a kingdom, which shall never be destroyed: and the kingdom shall not be left to other people, but it shall break in pieces and consume all these kingdoms, and it shall stand for ever. ⁴⁵Forasmuch as thou sawest that the stone was cut out of the mountain without hands, and that it brake in pieces the iron, the brass, the clay, the silver, and the gold; the great God hath made known to the king what shall come to pass hereafter: and the dream is certain, and the interpretation thereof sure." God's Word is true. History reveals the accuracy of what was prophesied in Daniel chapter 2 so we can have confidence in the Word of God that all the earthly kingdoms will come to an end and the God of Heaven will establish His kingdom. Jesus Christ, the King of kings, is coming soon do you want to be a part of His kingdom?

Remember, the sun and the moon are like one big time clock in which only God can move the hands on the clock! This caused a major disruption of the world's calendar. Like the tower of Babel when languages were confounded, this change of time was confounding (Genesis 11:1-9). The change in time resulted in a lot of confusion for people around the world. For over 3000 years time had been in harmony. But now the sun and the moon were out of tune with each other. As time went on it was even more out of tune! The seasons were off; it was hot when it was should have been cold, rainy when it was supposed to be dry. Religious and pagan festivals were out of sync with their season; the harvest festivals occurred when it was time to plant.

This change has been confounding for people around the world ever since. Man had to recognize that they could not change time. They could not just move the hands of the Creator's clock and make the adjustments to it; so adjustments have been made to the calendars to stay in sync with the seasons. Some cultures decided to stay with the way the moon revolves around the earth as the way a year is determined. Others decided to go with the way the Earth revolves around the sun and increase the days of the year to 365. The precise adjustments were worked on by many astronomers. During the time of the Roman Empire, Cleopatra told Julius Caesar about an Egyptian astronomer who had a way of reconciling the time. Julius Caesar adopted this method and the Julian Calendar became the standard in 45 BC. It was a 365 day calendar that added a leap year every four years in February. Over time it was observed to be a little longer than the actual time it took for the earth to revolve around the sun. The seemingly insignificant amount of time added up. So in order to stay in sync with the seasonal festivals and holidays, 10 days were removed from the calendar in October 1582 during the reign of Pope Gregory XIII. Today, this calendar is known as the Gregorian calendar and is the most widely used internationally.

Gregorian Calendar
October 1582

Throughout all the discord caused by this change, it is VERY interesting to note that the Sabbath did not change because it was established by the command of God and was not affected by how the moon and earth revolved around the sun. The days of the week remained the same for you to recognize the hand of the Creator (see the calendar p. 219).

Additionally, it is of significance that **without changing the distance** of the earth's orbit around the sun which is about 584,000,000 miles and **without changing the speed** of the earth as it revolves around the sun which is about 67,000 miles per hour; **the time was changed.** Jeremiah 32:27 says, "Behold, I am the LORD, the God of all flesh: is there any thing too hard for me?"

<u>Appeal</u>
Today we are living in the time of this additional five days that proves that God is in control of time and the universe. The Bible reveals what was done and when it was done. The Bible also reveals how Satan through his false church system would try to show his authority by changing time. But Satan can only "think" to change time." Remember what **Daniel 7:25** says, "And he shall speak great words against the most High, and shall wear out the saints of the most High, and **think to change times and laws...**" Satan's change is only a false counterfeit not reality.

God has given us a sign that clearly reveals His power as God and He asks us to give Him a sign that He is the one that we worship. Remember what **Ezekiel 20:12** says, "Moreover also I gave them my sabbaths, to be a sign between me and them, that they might know that I *am* the LORD that sanctify them." Honoring God's holy seventh-day Sabbath is proof that we truly love and believe in God. God has proven that His Word is sure and true. Keeping the seventh-day Sabbath holy is a sign or "mark" of your loyalty to God.

The true seventh-day Sabbath of the Bible has been forgotten by many but God is calling His people today to remember it again. It is a day that He rested, blessed, and sanctified. In Isaiah chapter 58, God tells Isaiah to "cry aloud" and lift up his voice and shew His people their transgression. Isaiah prophesied of a time when God's people would recognize that a "breach" was made in His law that caused people to break His law and that they "would repair the breach." **Isaiah 58:12-14** says [12]"And they that shall be of thee shall build the old waste places: thou shalt raise up the foundations of many generations; and thou shalt be called, The **repairer of the breach**, The **restorer of paths to dwell in**. [13]If thou turn away thy foot from the sabbath, from doing thy pleasure on my holy day; and call the sabbath a delight, the holy of the LORD, honourable; and shalt honour him, not doing thine own ways, nor finding thine own pleasure, nor speaking thine own words: [14]Then shalt thou delight thyself in the LORD; and I will cause thee to ride upon the high places of the Earth, and feed thee with the heritage of Jacob thy father: for the mouth of the LORD hath spoken it." **Will you be a repairer of the breach and a restorer of paths to dwell in?** Or will you rebel against God's truth that is clearly revealed in His Word? If you honor God, He will honor and bless you.

God is calling in these last days for **repairers of the breach** who recognize the "mark" of His authority. Satan has tried to hide the truth of God's Word but God is now calling us out of darkness. He wants us to be ready for His soon coming. The mark of the beast crisis happens just before the seven last plagues are poured out upon those who rebel against God. God does not want His people to receive the plagues that will come upon all those in "Babylon." He is calling His people out of darkness into the light of truth. He is coming soon and He wants YOU to be ready. Do not fear persecution or what man can do, but "Fear God, and give glory to him; for the hour of his judgment is come: and worship him that made heaven, and Earth, and the sea, and the fountains of waters." - **Revelation 14:7.** God controls time and He controls our times. **Psalm 31:14,15** says, [14]"But I trusted in thee, O LORD: I said, Thou art my God. [15]My times are in thy hand: deliver me from the hand of mine enemies, and from them that persecute me." No need to fear man because **Daniel 12:2** says, "And many of them that sleep in the dust of the earth shall awake, some to everlasting life, and some to shame and everlasting contempt." There is a resurrection!

Friend, it is the hope of this entire study that you have seen the clear evidence and proof of God. Don't be like Hezekiah and fail to share all the truth and proof of God to others. Never be ashamed of the Truth. **Share this truth and book to others.** Remember, the seventh-day Sabbath is a sign or a monument (proof) of your loyalty and love toward your Savior and Creator God. God has given you many signs of His power, might, and existence. As a sign or proof of your loyalty to Him, will you keep the seventh-day Sabbath holy and be obedient to all of His commandments out of love for Him? The prophecies of the mark of the beast crisis are sure. Jesus is soon to come, are you ready? Have you made a decision to follow God's truth all the way? Don't delay, make your decision today and be faithful to the Truth daily. Study God's Word daily for yourself in these last days and worship Him in SPIRIT and in TRUTH. Patiently endure until the end with the faith of Jesus. Hold on and teach the Truth no matter the threats or consequences, stay faithful. You will make it through the power of Jesus. See you in Heaven! Amen. OCR

SONGS OF INSPIRATION
"The Creation Song"
Written by: Elene Rodgers   Music Arrangement: Carlene Rodgers

1.   On the first day of Creation, there was nothing to be recognized
No pretty colored flowers and no sun to light the skies
Darkness covered everything, there was nothing in sight
Then God said let there be light and there was light
God said it, then He saw it, and it was good

CHORUS:
The power to create
No man can duplicate
Only God can make a flower or a bee
Only God can make the universe and me
So, My Creator, Create Within Me, A Clean Heart

2.   Day two of the Creation, God made the sky
Parting the waters for air to breathe, for life to survive
Day three He gathered the waters so dry land could appear
Calling the grass, trees, and flowers that we love so dear
God said it, then He saw it, and it was good

3.   On the fourth day of Creation, God made the sun and moon so bright
For signs, and for seasons, for years, day and night
Day five God made the fish that swim and the joyful birds that fly
They brought life to the waters and music to the sky
God said it, then He saw it, and it was good

4.   Day six of the Creation, God made the animals on the land
Then He formed man in His image and for this He used His hands
He made Adam and then his wife and breathed in them the breath of life
There was peace, love, and joy - not strife
God said that all He made was very good

5.   On the seventh day of Creation, God rested
Setting apart a day to remember never forget
To worship Him for all He's done and rest once it's begun
Delightful, Holy, Like no other one
A day He rested, and He blessed it, and sanctified it

To learn song & melody go to
PathwaytoPeace.net
Copyright © 2016

A Re-Creation Song

"Marred No More"

Written by: Elene Rodgers   Music Arrangement: Carlene Rodgers

1 Created in His image, perfectly designed
To reflect the Father's glory, peace and happiness was mine
Till I chose a different path, at first it seemed the way to go
Became marred, instead of joy now full of woe

CHORUS:
Oh, to be used by you again
To be a part of God's perfect plan
Lord, Make me o'er
Marred no More

2 Though I was marred you showed me mercy, and didn't just cast me away
You saw a vessel that could still be used, if remolded like the clay
Now I realize my Creator knows what's best for me
So I yield my will to Him, totally

3 For God so loved the world, that He gave His only Son
If we confess, He forgives and cleanses, the VICTORY is won
No longer a servant of sin, now I have peace within
And can be used to reflect God's glory once again

Jeremiah 18:4 "And the vessel that he made of clay was **marred** in the hand of the potter: so he made it again another vessel, as seemed good to the potter to make it."

To learn song & melody go to

PathwaytoPeace.net

Copyright © 2016

Share to ALL the WORLD!

This book is an **urgent** LOUD CRY message that must reach millions of people around the world. Join us in getting this Bible truth filled book out to the masses. Jesus is soon to come and many are not ready. Individuals, families, groups, and churches can purchase boxes of this book at a great discount. Distribute to family, friends, neighbors, co-workers, and community.

Call 704-695-1441
or go to
PathwaytoPeace.net

PathwaytoPeace.net

Put God's Word In Your Heart
Memorize Scriptures in Song!

Ten Commandments
Beatitudes
Three Angels' Message
in Revelation 14:6-13
Isaiah 58
God's Love Song
in 1 Corinthians 13:1-8
Psalm 91
Psalm 23
Plus more!

Great for family, children, adults, home-schoolers, Bible groups, VBS, church, youth groups, and worship.

For more information on downloads or physical CD copy
go to "Music Projects" at PathwaytoPeace.net